Etched in Sand

Etched in Sand

A True Story of Five Siblings Who Survived an Unspeakable Childhood on Long Island

REGINA CALCATERRA

WILLIAM MORROW

An Imprint of HarperCollinsPublishers

HarperCollins books may be purchased for educational, business, or sales
promotional use. For information please e-mail the Special Markets Department at SPsales@harpercollins.com.

Designed by Diahann Sturge

Library of Congress Cataloging-in-Publication Data has been applied for.

ISBN 978-0-06-221883-4
ISBN 978-0-06-269739-4 (Canadian Edition)

17 18 19 20 21   OV/LSC   10 9 8 7 6 5 4 3 2

To Cherie, Camille, Norman, and Roseanne—
may we always continue laughing and dancing, together.

To the hundreds of thousands of children in the U.S.
who are either abused, in foster care, or homeless.
The journey is long and often dark but you must believe
in your light—you have so much to offer.

Contents

Author's Note

ETCHED IN SAND is the true story of the experiences I shared with my siblings from our childhood to the present day. My siblings consented to the publication of *Etched in Sand* and the use of their proper names in the forthcoming pages. However, some people's names have been changed in order to protect their anonymity, including but not limited to past foster parents and relatives both living and deceased. Specifically worth noting is the name change of the character represented as my biological father, whom I refer to with the pseudonym of Paul Accerbi. For ease of description, my many social workers were consolidated into a few characters and are represented with pseudonyms as well. Also changed is the town that my younger siblings resided in when in Idaho.

Etched in
Sand

Prologue

I HADN'T SEEN New York City this still since 9/11. Lower Manhattan was a ghost town—there were no planes in the sky, no boats on the East River, no buses, no trains rumbling in the subway. This was Wall Street, normally the most bustling street in the world . . . but where I stood at the Wall Street Heliport, I was the only one present.

Because there was no traffic on my drive from Long Island to Manhattan, I was the earliest to arrive for the first official helicopter flyover after Hurricane Sandy. Soon everyone began to emerge from their vehicles: the governor of New York State, Andrew Cuomo; New York's two United States senators, Chuck Schumer and Kirsten Gillibrand; senior gubernatorial cabinet officials; and my colleagues from Nassau and Westchester Counties. We greeted one another in a manner both solemn and cordial, taking note of how a tragedy makes professional interactions seem much more personal. Wearing jeans, windbreakers, and boots, we exchanged details of the storm, our objective intensely clear. It was up to us to try and heal this region after Sandy's destruction.

Within moments three military helicopters broke through the fog as assured as eagles. With the press and security now present, there were a couple dozen of us, all standing quietly as the copters whipped the vinyl of our coats and finally touched down on the pad. I felt a collective awareness among us that not even the roar of the propellers could cut through the heaviness of that morning. It struck me as one of the eeriest moments in my life: The silence was actually louder than the noise.

As the chief deputy executive of Suffolk County, I waited my turn to climb into the helicopter and by chance wound up in a seat that would give me a solid view of Long Island after we surveyed the damage in New York City. We took the military aviator's instructions and placed the headphones over our ears. When the helicopter took off for Breezy Point in Queens, where a fire had ravaged a neighborhood during Sandy, the silence loomed again. Blocks of homes were charred. Families had lost everything. For me to have been managing the storm crises in Suffolk County while hearing the reports of how these Queens residents were trying to escape the area was one thing. Now to witness the damage where homes and lives had been destroyed was a completely surreal moment.

My heart pounded as we neared Suffolk and I prepared to address my county's devastation for this group of elected officials I respected so greatly. "Which town in Suffolk had the most damage?" one of them asked.

I hurried to push the microphone button on the headset as

our aviator had shown us. "Lindenhurst," I answered. The group nodded and gazed back out the window, as though they understood why Lindenhurst holds a special significance to me: It's where I was born. It's also the place where three decades later, I learned my background from family I'd never known existed. My mother left behind scorched earth with the same totality that Mother Nature had swept my island. For years, Suffolk County transported me back to the pain and darkness my four siblings and I endured throughout our fatherless childhoods with a profoundly troubled mother. Now, as I examined it from the sky, my emotions swelled with a love for this place—how the experiences of growing up here made me who I am. Hovering above as a leader in the aftermath of Sandy struck me deeply. Aside from the love I shared with my siblings, this county was our only sense of home—a place that did its best to protect us from the unpredictable. I never could have imagined that one day I'd be called on to return the same security.

WHAT DREW ME to a career in public service was my appreciation for government's purpose: It's the body that decides who receives which resources, and how much of them. My childhood on Long Island gave me a very personal awareness for how people in power can impact the lives of others. Growing up here I faced extraordinary struggles that would have tested any child's strength and endurance. Somehow, with optimism and determination, my siblings and I could usually manage to find someone who was willing to lift us to help.

My cast of resolute characters is composed of my older sister Camille, who is forever my closest confidante; and our three siblings—Cherie, the eldest, who found escape from our childhood in a teen marriage; Norman, fourth in birth order just behind me; and our youngest sister, Rosie. As a scrappy pack of homeless siblings wandering the beach communities of Long Island, sometimes we'd sneak off to the Long Island Sound or the Atlantic's shore—the wild, windy places where it didn't matter who we were, what we wore, or how tousled we appeared. With our hands and empty clamshells as our tools, we'd build sand castles by the water, or etch out all five of our names

Cherie   Camille   Regina   Norman   Rosie

and enclose each with a heart. We'd run, squealing, as the waves roared upon the shore and rolled back in rhythm, unsentimentally washing away our work. Then we'd run back toward the water and create it all anew.

We didn't know it then, but that persistence would become the metaphor to predict how we'd all choose to live our lives. No accomplishment has taken place without trial, and no growth could have occurred without unwavering love. This is the story of how it took a community to raise a child . . . and how that child used her future to give hope back.

1

Bitten Bones

Suffolk County, Long Island, New York
Summer 1980

THE AREA WHERE we live sits between the shadows of the cocaine-fueled, glitzy Hamptons estates and New York City's gritty, disco party culture. Songs like Devo's "Whip It" and Donna Summer's "Bad Girls" blast through the car courtesy of WABC Musicradio 77, AM. Gas is leaded and the air is filthy.

Long Island lacks a decent public transportation system—to get anywhere, you need either a car or a good pair of shoes. Our shoes aren't the best.

Our car is worse.

My mother's thick arm rests on the driver's-side window ledge of her rusty, gas-guzzling Impala—the kind you buy for seventy-five dollars out of a junkyard. Her wild hair blows around the car as she flicks her cigarette into the sticky July morning. The ashes boomerang back in through my window, threatening to fly into my eyes and mouth in frantic gusts. Squinting tightly and pursing my lips hard, I know better than to mention it.

My seven-year-old baby sister, Rosie; our brother, Norman, who's twelve but still passes for an eight-year-old when we sneak into movie theaters; and me—Regina Marie Calcaterra, age thirteen (personal facts I'm well accustomed to giving strangers, like social workers and the police)—are smooshed into the backseat. Like most of our rides, the car suffers from bald tires, broken mirrors, and oil dripping from the motor. If I lift up the mats, I can see the broken pavement move beneath us through the holes in the rear floor.

We rarely travel the main roads like the Southern State, Sunrise Highway, or the Long Island Expressway. For Cookie—that's what we call my mom—the scenic route is the safest because she's always avoiding the cops. Cookie has more warrants out on her than she has kids. And there are five of us.

Her offenses? Where to start? She's wanted for drunk driving; driving with a suspended license and an unregistered vehicle; stolen license plates; bounced checks to the landlord, utility company, and liquor store totaling hundreds of dollars; stealing from her bosses (on the rare occasion she gets work as a barmaid); and for our truancy. And if there were such a thing as a warrant for sending her kids to school with their heads full of lice, we could add that to the list, too!

In the car, we don't speak. It's not by choice—it's actually impossible to hear one another above the loud grunting of the Impala and its broken muffler. Embarrassed by the car's belches, I slump down in my seat. In the front seat next to Cookie, my older sister Camille's doing pretty much the same thing . . . but if our mother detects our attitude, we'll find ourselves suffering nasty bruises. The only comfort is the physical space we now have to actually fit in the car without piling on top of one another as we had to for years. That's thanks to the fact that, at age seventeen, our oldest sister, Cherie, has finagled an escape by moving in with her new husband and his parents, since she's expecting a baby soon.

In the backseat, Rosie, Norman, and I stay occupied, scratching our bony, bug-bitten legs and comparing who has the most bites and biggest scabs. We take turns pointing to them as Rosie uses her fingers as scorecards to rate them on a scale of one to ten. There's never really a winner . . . we're all pretty itchy.

None of us bothers hollering to ask where we're going. With all our belongings packed in garbage bags in the trunk, we know we're headed to a new home. Our short-term future could take many forms—a trailer, a homeless shelter, the back parking lot of a supermarket, in the car for a few weeks, in Cookie's next boyfriend's basement or attic, or dare we dream: an apartment or house. We know better than to expect much—to us, running water and a few old mattresses is good living. We've managed with a lot less.

Most girls my age idolize their sixteen-year-old sisters, but Camille is my cocaptain in our family's survival. She's the only person in my life who's totally transparent, and we need each other too much for any sisterly mystique to exist. For years, the two of us have worked to set up each new place so that it feels at least something like a home, even though we never know how long we might stay there. We just rest easier knowing, at nightfall, that the younger ones have a safe spot to rest their heads. Together. Without Cookie. If we can control that.

Cookie puts the brakes on our wordless games when she pulls into a semicircular driveway, gravel crunching under the tires. We're met by the image of a gray, severely neglected two-story shingled house surrounded by dirt, dust, and weeds. There are no bushes, no flowers, no greenery at all; but the lack of landscaping draws a squeal from me. "No grass!"

Rosie and Norman smile and nod in agreement, understanding this means we won't be taking shifts to accomplish Cookie's definition of "mowing the lawn"—using an old pair of hedge clippers to cut the grass on our hands and knees. Camille and I usually cut the bulk of the lawn to protect the little ones from the blisters and achy wrists.

Cookie turns off the ignition and coughs her dry, scratchy smoker's cough. "This is it," she announces. "Sluts and whores unpack the car." Then she emits a loud, sputtering, hillbilly roar that never fails to remind me of a malfunctioning machine gun. As usual, she's the only one who finds any humor in the degrading nicknames she's pinned on her daughters.

I gaze calmly at the facade before me. It's a house . . . our house. Even if it ends up being only for a few days, I'm relieved that my siblings and I won't be separated.

Since the interior car-door handle is missing, exiting the car is always an occasion for embarrassment. I take my cue as Cookie reaches out her window, pulling up the steel tab that opens her door with her right hand while she pushes with her left shoulder from the inside. It's my job to step out and pull the exterior driver's-side door handle for her, especially when she's too drunk to get the door open on her own. This normally results in me falling on my bony bottom as the heavy steel door comes barreling out toward me from my mother's force. I quickly jump straight up like Nadia Comaneci at the Montreal Olympics—landing with locked legs and arms extended skyward—and look back at the three little judges in the car to rate my performance. As always, this leads to giggles from Rosie and Norman and an *I feel your pain* wince from Camille, whose behind is just as scrawny as mine.

Since my dismount lacks originality, my score is always the same. Rosie is the most generous, flashing ten stretched-out fingers. Norman offers an underwhelmed five; Camille gives me two thumbs-up, which from her is equal to a ten.

Cookie usually just snorts in my direction, but not this time.

Today she's in a hurry. She lurches out of the driver's seat while the car lets up beneath her weight. We all watch her hulking five-foot-two, size-18 figure stagger around the front of the car and toward the gray house with a six-pack of Schlitz beer stuffed under her arm. I rest my hands on my hips and look around, relieved there are no neighbors outside.

The dampness of Cookie's white Hanes T-shirt exposes her quadruple-D over-the-shoulder-boulder-holders and, for God's sake, too much of the boulders—they're struggling to stay in the cups. Her appearance gives me a sudden urge to cover the little ones' eyes, but by now, for them, the sight of our mother's unmentionables holds no shock . . . instead Norman and Rosie are shaking in silent giggles. An old pair of cutoff jean shorts that should be six inches longer and wider in the thighs completes her look. She peers inside the house's window from the front stoop then pushes open the door, which obviously bears no lock. Hastily she turns and waves—"Come on, kids!"—signaling urgency for us to unpack the car.

While our younger siblings remain in the backseat, Camille leans over from the front passenger side of the car, reaches down toward the steering wheel, and fingers the keys Cookie left in the ignition. She looks back at me, and we understand the significance of the keys' position. As usual, Cookie doesn't plan to stick around our new home long.

We spring into action. The faster we unpack the car, kids and all, the quicker our mother will head out on another long binge. We have to move with speed, convincing Cookie our motive is all about setting up our new home. She'd beat us senseless if she ever found out how eager we are to get rid of her.

Through the backseat window I peek at Norman, who's used to my Moving Day choreography. "Take her inside with you," I tell him. He helps Rosie climb out from the middle; his brown, bowl-cut hair uncombed, his face calm. Camille and I work hard to raise him like one would raise any curious, carefree, twelve-year-old boy. His sweet, slanted brown eyes are barely visible below his uneven haircut, and I pledge him a silent promise: *I'll find new scissors for next time.* Sometimes I reason that if I've gotta raise a kid who's only a year and a half younger than I am, then surely I have the right to experiment my self-taught salon techniques on him . . . but that Dorothy Hamill look on a preteen boy is just plain cruel.

Norm shuffles into the house with Rosie, still wearing her pink pajamas, close behind. I pause from unloading the car to take in her presence; a little flash of life scampering barefoot across this gray scene. Her innocence pierces my heart.

After they're inside, Camille scurries around with the keys and opens the trunk, then passes them off to me so I can insert them back in the ignition. We're careful to conduct the move-in with no detail that could keep our mother here longer than absolutely necessary. She's probably inside having a drink right now, which could be enough to disorient her from recalling where she put her keys.

The trunk of the car is stuffed with green garbage bags that Camille, the kids, and I packed: There's a bag filled with each of our clothes, a near-empty bag with our collective toiletries (half a bar of soap; an old toothbrush we share; a bottle of peroxide; and a dull, rusty razor), a bag stuffed with old towels, and a bag packed with all the groceries we cleaned out of our last place. We have a prevailing unpacking rule: You unpack the bag you pick. This way we can't fight about who unpacks Cookie's clothes. I can tell that I'm carrying our nonperishables, which I always make sure travel with us: vinegar, mustard and ketchup, and other essentials like coffee, flour, sugar, and powdered milk. From the other side of the trunk, I can smell Camille's cargo—it reeks of stale cigarettes. She cringes despairingly. "Finders keepers," I tell her. "I have kitchen duty, you're on Cookie duty. Just be glad she likes you better."

It's always been clear that Cookie prefers my older sisters to me. Because we all have different fathers, our last names are as varied as our first names. Cherie is the luckiest. She was named after the Four Seasons' song "Sherry" that hit number one on the *Billboard* charts in 1962, the year she was born. (However, Cookie found the French spelling, *Cherie*, to be much more sophisticated.) My mother named her second daughter after herself—Camille. Her famous line is that she named me Regina because it means *royalty*. "I was right," she always says, "because you turned out to be a royal pain in my ass." Norman was named after his father, and Roseanne was named after my great-grandmother, Rosalia KunaGunda Maskewiez, whom none of us has ever met.

Camille and I shuffle the bags inside. "Whoa," Camille says. "This place actually has furniture."

Rosie's climbed onto a sofa in front of the bay window, and is stretched across it with her feet as far as they can go, mimicking Cookie's position on the couch across the room. "There's even a TV!" she exclaims, pointing to the large unit in the corner.

"Wow," I tell her, crouching down and twisting her pigtail around my finger. "Did you try it out?"

"Yeah, it works!"

I smile and steal a glance at Cookie. She looks pleased with herself, smoking a cigarette with her right arm wrapped across her waist. Mother of the freakin' year.

"My room is next to the kitchen," she says to no one in particular, then waves her cigarette to a staircase behind her. "You kids can fight it out upstairs."

I find three rooms on the top floor. The room to my left is filled with a cot and an old wooden desk. All the desk drawers are missing handles; a broomstick holds up the desk where a leg once stood. The room straight ahead has two windows overlooking the side yard and part of the extension that houses the room Cookie claimed. It has a mattress and a box spring, but no frame. This will work, I calculate, because Norman and Rosie can sleep here. One can have the mattress and the other can have the box spring—kind of like two separate beds.

Although there are no pillows or blankets in sight, this arrangement is an improvement over sleeping three in the back-seat or in an open car trunk, which we've done before. I peer around into the narrow, one-windowed room to the right, which features a mattress and box spring atop a real metal bed frame. Viewing farther inside I find a shelf for clothes. This will be Camille's room. She's the oldest one here and deserves a real bed.

I take the room with the cot, resting my garbage bag on the floor and digging out my plastic Jesus figurines. This will signal to my siblings that this room is mine.

When I turn back toward the door, Norman brakes from running down the hall to stop in Camille's room and looks out over the gray, gravel front yard.

"You like the new place?" I ask him.

"Like it? I love it! Think I can have this room?"

"Nope, it's Camille's. You and Rosie get to share the room at the end of the hall."

He runs there, pokes his head inside, smiles back at me, and takes off downstairs.

"I'll set your room up when Cookie leaves," I yell after him. "Dig out Trouble so you and Rosie can play while we clean."

I find Camille at the car, unloading Norman and Rosie's stuff. "Cookie's in her bedroom," I mutter.

"She better not pass out."

"I made sure she won't. Norman's setting up Trouble outside her bedroom door."

"Genius!" The popping bubble in the middle of the board game, combined with the kids' chatter, will be enough to drive her out.

While getting to work downstairs, it occurs to me that it's

too late in the day for Rosie to stay in her pajamas. While she's playing Trouble with Norman on the living room floor, I sneak over, kneel down, and smooth the wisps of her sandy colored hair away from her moist face.

"*Mia bambina amore,*" I whisper. *My baby love.* "We'll get you dressed after she leaves." She pushes her head back against my hand to acknowledge my affection. Throughout the years, we've sharpened our nonverbal communications in this way, exchanging affection and understanding with the same evolved understanding as some of the wild lion cubs we watch on *Wild Kingdom.* The less we speak, the less likely it is that we'll throw our mother into a rage without knowing why.

Camille and I set out to scrub the first floor of the house, where we'll be spending most of our time . . . but more important, it's where our mother's resting now. The sooner we get cleaning around her the sooner she's sure to leave. I attack the kitchen around the corner from Cookie's bedroom while Camille begins in the living room.

"*Pssst,*" my sister hisses from the other side of the house. I stretch my neck out of the kitchen to meet her gaze. "You'll help me with her room?"

I nod and mouth to her: *After she leaves.*

A white Formica table sits between three cabineted walls and a block of windows that overlooks the dusty backyard enclosed by a chain-linked fence. When I move the scummy dishes, bowls, and pots that the previous tenant left in the sink, I'm met by rivals to our survival.

"WHAT'S WRONG?" CAMILLE yells when the dishes clatter. Rosie's head turns toward the kitchen.

"Nothing. Camille, can you come help me load the fridge?" Camille will understand this code for the cockroach solution we learned long ago: If there's a working fridge with a door that shuts, every bit of our food goes inside it, whether or not it needs refrigeration.

I'm used to ants, mice, and maggots, who, as creepy as they are, will scatter in fear when they sense my presence. But cockroaches! It's not even their spiny legs and long antennae that gross me out; it's the way they work in packs and maneuver in the dark, attacking our food like looters.

I join the others in the living room just as Cookie's emerging from her bedroom, wearing a pair of Jordache jeans, Dr. Scholl's sandals, and a man's Hanes tank top.

Rather than bathing, Cookie tries to mask her cigarette and alcohol stink with a cheap, toxic mixture of Jontue and Jean Naté. As her figure casts a shadow over the room, I quickly work out the cost implications of her ensemble: One pair of Jordache jeans equals one week of oil for hot water; Dr. Scholl's equals eight loaves of bread, four boxes of spaghetti, three bags of wheat puffs, and two weeks' worth of powdered milk. Jontue perfume and Jean Naté *almost* equal bail after a night in jail, since Cookie had Camille and me steal them from the five-and-dime.

Cookie fluffs her hair and rubs her lips together, reminding us how grateful we should be for having a mother who can score such a nice home. "I'm going to find the hair of the dog that bit me. Feed the kids."

"We always do," Camille mumbles.

"What?"

Camille looks up. "We will."

"Norman, you're the man of the house."

In response to Cookie's attention, Norman scrambles to his feet and follows her outside. Rosie, Camille, and I step out to join him on the stoop just in time to observe the car sinking beneath Cookie's weight. "When will she be back?" Norman asks.

Rosie takes his arm. "Not before we finish our game!"

The screen door claps shut as they dash inside. Camille and I turn to watch the cloud of dust disappear as the thunder of Cookie's car motor grows distant.

And just like that, she's gone.

2

Building Sand Castles

Summer 1980

THE KNOT IN my stomach untwists as Cookie's car grinds out of the driveway and heads toward busy Middle Country Road. As Rosie and Norman settle back in to their game, Camille turns to me with a sly smile.

"How long do you think she'll be gone this time?" I whisper.

"Depends on how much money she has," she says, starting inside. "And who she's shacking up with."

In a traditional home, the children depend on the parent for the means to live. In Cookie's world, she depends on us. Her roster of kids means she can breeze into the Suffolk County welfare office and get money for housing, electricity, and food. My angst rises again as my usual question surfaces:

How can they give her this endless stream of cash without ever checking up on where she spends it?

Camille and I figure Cookie must have used the welfare housing voucher to pay the landlord the first month's rent and the security deposit to get us into the house. But she probably took the heating and electric allowance with her. I'd flicked a switch to discover the electricity was already on when we moved in, so the landlord never had it turned off after the other tenant left. Cookie must have investigated that when she looked at the house. And since we wouldn't need heat in the middle of the summer, she decided we could get by with whatever oil is left in the tank if we took quick showers. Cookie actually believes she deserves the heating and electric money for booze. In her mind, she's got us set up pretty good.

The screen door slams hard behind me as I follow Camille inside. "Rosie, honey, let's get you dressed." Rosie rises and lets me shepherd her upstairs.

"I'll scrounge for money," Camille calls from below us.

I stop on the stairs. "Norm, help Camille." He hops off the couch and stacks the cushions to search scrupulously for lost gold that previous tenants may have left behind.

I show Rosie her room upstairs at the end of the hall. I pull the mattress off the box spring to make two separate beds. "You'll sleep on this, okay? Norman will get the box spring. I'll get you each a blanket."

"A towel is enough," she assures me. I wish I could debate with her, but the fact is a towel's probably the best we've got.

We've been trying to get her to sleep on her own, rather than with Camille or me, so enticing her with the mattress as opposed to a less comfortable box spring should help our efforts. I reach into her garbage bag and pull out a polyester romper that I used to wear when I was about the same age. It has blue shorts with a cuff and a light blue sleeveless button-down top that's attached to the shorts. Rosie steps in through the unbuttoned neck opening as I hold it up. We button it up together, taking turns. Then I pull her hair back to help cool her face, fastening it with a rubber band I'd had on my wrist. I kiss her forehead and pat her tummy. "Go help Camille and Norm find money. I'll be down in a minute."

Rosie's long ponytail sways back and forth with her skip. The dirt that's collected in the folds behind her knees and her black-bottomed feet make me cringe as I try to recall the last time any of us bathed in a real bathtub. (Gas station sinks don't count.) Rosie disappears around the corner and descends the stairs to join the hunt for our dinner fare. I fold her pajamas, put them on her bed for later, then move from room to room, opening up the windows in an attempt to cool off the floor. Somehow, I resolve, we'll get to eat *and* sleep tonight.

At a skinny five-foot-two, Camille and I are the same size. Her thick brown hair curls from the summer heat, framing her round face and almond eyes. "Look what I found stuffed into one of Cookie's bras," Camille says, unwrinkling a five-dollar food stamp.

I squish my nose. Her *bra*? "It's a wonder it survived. Have you checked the basement?"

Camille reasons that five dollars will be enough to get us through the grocery store without creating any suspicion. We know that kids as disheveled as we are will be pegged as shop-lifters; but also, if we don't act correctly they'll suspect worse: that we're unsupervised. Then the store manager will call in the police, then the police will bring in child welfare agents, and the agents will instantly see through our lies and realize that we *are* on our own. We'll lose any control that we have over our lives . . . and worse, we'll lose Rosie and Norm. No matter what horrible circumstances Cookie dumps us into, it will always be better than being separated and put into foster care. Over the years, Camille and I have perfected our food-shopping routine because we understand the consequences of any possible misstep.

By now it's three in the afternoon, and all the children's shows are for kids younger than Rosie. I turned the TV knob to our favorite soap opera, *General Hospital*. Camille changes from her jeans into her parachute shorts with lots of pockets, and a long top. I pull on a baggy T-shirt whose bottom falls in line with the hem of my gym shorts.

We kiss the kids. "Stay put," Camille tells them. "We're going to find dinner."

For two teenage girls who don't yet drive, Camille and I have developed a strong sense of direction. No matter where we are, either of us can access any main road on Long Island. Remembering the Pathmark grocery store we spotted on the drive out here, we hike down Washington Avenue and make a left on Middle Country Road. These outings to rummage for food are when I feel most connected to Camille—not just because we're literally partners in crime but also because it's during these moments away, just the two of us, that we can just be sisters.

"After we feed the kids, I want to find a pay phone to call Doug. I haven't seen him in a few days," she says.

"Why? You're staying with us tonight, right?"

"Hey, look," Camille says. "We're almost to Pathmark."

We wander into the store and immediately assume our roles. I head straight back toward the stockroom, where I locate a teenage stock boy and tell him the usual story: We're moving, and my father sent me in to get boxes with lids on them. *Do you have any extras laying around?* By now Camille will be wandering the food aisles to see what she can slip down her shorts and into her pockets.

Since the boxes need to appear empty as I wander through the store, I only slide light things into them: a loaf of bread, a carton of eggs, a few boxes of macaroni and cheese mix, a box of puffed rice cereal, and a package of toilet paper—which is impossible to steal without a box. Even one roll is too bulky to slip down our shirts. Our toilet paper and egg carton–lifting technique requires us to place the items between two stacked, empty cardboard boxes. Casually but carefully, I buzz straight out of the store as though I'm minding my own business with my armful of moving boxes. In the giant parking lot I meet up with Camille, who used the five-dollar food stamp to score peanut butter, jelly, and a half-gallon of milk. We have a strict system of purchasing anything we need that won't fit in our clothes. Camille slides Kraft cheese slices out of her shorts and takes a thin box of Jiffy muffin mix from her pocket, while I shake two little boxes of Jell-O and pudding mix out of my underwear. "We can stretch this for at least two weeks," she says. She places her treasures and grocery bag in one of the boxes, and we take off toward our new home, balancing the weight of our load between us.

As we turn onto Washington Avenue and edge closer to home, I notice our new neighborhood lacks actual *neighbors*. This time of year, residents are either at the local beach or inside where it's cooler, keeping to themselves. There are no kids playing ball in the street or riding bikes up and down the lane. The air is quiet and empty with no friendly conversation or laughter. The few homes we do pass sit with bare lawns and neglected landscaping in a way that suggests passers-by should simply look away and mind their own business. This we appreciate. We aren't comfortable with eyes on us either.

Isolation isn't foreign to us. A few years earlier, we lived together in the town center of Saint James, about eight miles from here. Our apartment then, in a building at 621 Lake Avenue, was on the second floor, above a glue factory. Across the street was the Saint James Fire Department—a giant white building that looked out at us as if it were watching our every move. We lived above the intersection of three major roads, not among the storied homes in the wealthy neighborhoods that overlooked the Long Island Sound with views of Connecticut. Living separate from our better-heeled neighbors ensured that we could stay "under the radar" in Saint James. I would walk through the kitchen door out to the black tar roof of the glue factory, which served as our patio. There I'd observe the townspeople as they hurried along the quaint and preserved main street to the local butcher or Spage's Pharmacy. No matter how long or hard I stared, just daring for someone to catch my eye, no one ever noticed me.

That was actually the home where we lived together the longest as a family.

At that time, Cherie was still with us. She, Camille, and I would stroll up the street to the King Kullen supermarket to collect our groceries, but there was another spot we preferred to gather our meals.

A long walk led us to Cordwood Beach. To us, Cordwood Beach was an amusement park—it had a floating dock anchored offshore, and we'd swim out and jump off of it over and over again. To the left of the dock stood the curved brick wall of a hollowed-out old house that delighted us as a glorified jungle gym and play castle. But the best part was, at Cordwood Beach we got dinner for free! We'd walk home with our shirts hammocking a heavy load of clams, mussels, and onion grass, which Cherie and Camille would steam for dinner. It was a simple way to live, but we were together. That's what was important to us.

"HEY!" I HOLLER. "We're back!" Rosie and Norman are stretched out on opposite couches, watching the news. Rosie looks up, waves to us, and turns back to the TV. Norm meets us with a grin and his arms held wide to help when he sees we're toting food. I take out the dishes I'd found earlier in the afternoon—a few pots, mismatched plastic plates, a few forks, and a spoon—and rinse them in the sink as Camille searches for matches to light the pilot on the gas stove to boil macaroni and cheese.

"How long you think this hot water's going to last?" I ask her.

"Gi, I need to have a serious talk with you," she says. I still myself and look at her, but she's avoiding my eyes by busying herself with drying the dishes. Her voice is low: always a sure sign or trouble.

"What is it?"

"I want to stay at Kathy's for the summer."

"For the *summer*?"

"Yes. I think Doug's parents will let me stay on their couch for a night or two until Kathy convinces her mom to let me stay at their house."

My heart sinks into my flip-flops.

"It's not for*ever*—"

"I thought you would be here more!" I tell her. "Camille, you can't leave me alone with the kids again—you lived at Kathy's the whole last year!"

Cherie and Camille have known Kathy since Cherie was in second grade and Camille was in first. Since my sisters are so close in age, they shared everything, including friends. One afternoon during recess at Saint James Elementary School, Cherie got hit in the head with a baseball. Kathy scooped her up, carried her off the field, and stayed with her until the school nurse came. From that moment, Cherie and Kathy—and Camille—became inseparable. Kathy had a big family and a mother who worked a lot, so Cherie and Camille would just hang out at her house for days, or sometimes weeks. It was during this time that I became the little mom to Rosie and Norman. I kept hoping Cherie and Camille would walk through the door together, but when Camille finally came back, she was alone. Cherie got married and moved into her in-laws' basement in Brentwood.

Kathy and Camille stayed close friends, and Camille lived almost all of last year with Kathy's family after we were kicked out of our last apartment. There was nowhere for the rest of us to go, so we lived out of Cookie's car in a supermarket parking lot on Hawkins Avenue in Ronkonkoma. When I'd see Kathy's younger siblings at school, I'd avoid them. They already had tons of siblings, so why did they get to have mine, too? I pictured Kathy's whole giant family gathered around the table for dinner, my sisters clearing the dishes and helping with homework, when they should have been at home helping me!

"How do you expect me to do this on my own?" By now I'm sobbing muffled words into Camille's embrace. "Huh?"

"Shhh," she says, hugging me again.

"Does Cherie know?"

"Gi," she says, "I need you to understand. I can get a job while I'm living with Kathy and give you money to buy food."

I pull away from her and shove her across the kitchen. I watch her face turn from soft patience to red anger. "You can work here, too, you know! There are stores all over Middle Country Road. You can work at Shoes 'N Things, or the muffler place, or get a job at the supermarket. We just walked by a hundred places, why can't you stay here?"

She wraps her arms around me again, trying to steady me as much as console me. "Because I don't want to," she speaks softly into my hair. "I don't want to be a mom anymore. I raised you. It's your turn now."

"But I've been doing this already." I peel my hair from my face, damp with sweat and tears, in a plea of desperation for her to listen. I think of the possibilities—intruders, landlords, police, social workers, having to manage any of them all by myself. "I need help, Camille. Don't go. Please don't leave me alone again, you don't know what it's like when you're not here, I need you, I need help—"

"Gi," she says, trying to calm me down. "I *promise* I'll be back to check in on you. I'll bring you food. You won't be out stealing by yourself. You'll know where I am and I'll get you dimes to call me."

"I need to call my friends, too, I need something more than this." I gesture into the air to refer to the desolation we're held up in. If I can't negotiate for her to stay, then I have to negotiate for her money.

"I'll bring money every week, I promise," she says, wrapping me again in her arms.

We stand there awhile, just hugging, and I hope that any

second she'll whisper, *Hey. Do you want to come with me?* But her silence cements it: Kathy can't take all of us. When we finally pull away, I look around at the kitchen that's now all mine to manage.

Finally I pull away from her and stand over the stove, trying to concentrate on the macaroni and cheese, blending the powdered cheese with a little milk and coating each of the noodles in the mix. Camille helps me spoon dinner onto three plates—she has plans to eat with Doug, so there will be more for leftovers tomorrow. She pours two glasses of milk and carries them into the living room, while I cover the leftovers and hurry to place the bowl in the refrigerator.

The kids sit up when they see us carrying food, and I notice how loud they have the TV cranked up. It's clear they heard us yelling in the kitchen and turned up the volume to tune us out.

Camille heads upstairs, where I know she will gather her things. My appetite is gone, but if the landlord or police were to discover three children staying here alone tonight, who knows when my next meal could be? I'll eat now. On the bright side, at least we'll have one more bed to sleep in tonight. Camille's room was the nicest, and I'll be able to sleep knowing that the kids are right next to my room.

Norm and Rosie pile their dishes in the sink after dinner, and I wash them right away. Camille chases them upstairs to brush their teeth with the bottle of peroxide Cookie uses to dye her hair. Since we steal food to survive, toothpaste never makes our list. The peroxide is fizzy in my mouth and makes me gag if I swallow even a little. It dries out the corners of my mouth, making my lips crack and scab up in the corners.

"But it sure does make your breath smell fresh!" Camille loves to tease me.

Back in the kitchen, Camille rests the bag of her belongings on the floor and gently kisses the side of my head. "I'm going to the corner to call Doug. You gonna be okay?"

I nod in her general direction. "Just go."

"Love you, Gi."

At this, I turn and watch her make her way to the front door of the house that, just hours ago, I'd been so thrilled for us to share as a family. "Love you, too," I say, trying to force the words through the swelling cry in my throat.

Then she's gone, too.

3

And Then There Were Three

Summer to Fall, 1980

I WAS ELEVEN the first time Camille left and I had to care for the kids by myself. I'm not unfamiliar with the feeling of isolation that comes with this unwilling brand of single motherhood, but every time she leaves, the worst part of loneliness returns: No matter how many times I experience it, it never gets easier.

Gently, throughout my upbringing, Camille coached me for this role. It requires a subtle balance between safeguarding the kids while always giving people around us the impression that it's actually our mother who's caring for us. "Never act hungry, never look dirty," she says, because if the kids are fed, clean, neat, and well behaved, we generally can slide under the radar. The goal is always to stay together and out of foster care.

We admit nothing, and Rosie and Norman know what's at stake. We have to keep quiet and not bring attention to ourselves, no matter how bad it gets. It's our code of silence, and there's a powerful trust among us never to violate it. The system seems content to be complicit in our charade because the social workers of Suffolk County are too busy to keep track of kids in our type of situation. This area that until recently was rural and blue-collar is rapidly increasing in population. People from the city are moving out here, turning Fire Island and the local beaches along the Atlantic Ocean into suburbanized bedroom communities of Manhattan and a playground for the rich and famous. Meanwhile, we've overheard our social workers murmur that almost five thousand kids are monitored by protective services in our county alone. Some of these kids end up in the children's shelter, where we've learned that beatings and rapes are rampant. The stories spread so far and wide that even the people in the city read about it—in fact, I heard about an article in one of the city papers where the reporter referred to the shelter as "the children's jail." So we know to stick to our story. If someone asks us where our mother is during the afternoons, we say she's waitressing. At nighttime she's working as a barmaid. If any authority figure says he didn't see her car in the early morning hours, then it's because she works for a bakery and has to deliver fresh bread to restaurants beginning at three thirty in the morning. Sometimes when we're asked "Well then, where is she during the late morning hours?" we say she works at a deli peeling potatoes for potato salad. Our mother "works" a lot, you see—we have every hour covered.

As long as we keep each other in the loop on the latest story, we can remain in sync and untouchable. And since, at one time or another, Cookie *did* work these jobs and took us along with her to help, we know enough about them to talk intelligently about the details of her work to deter any suspicion.

There have been times, few and far between, when Cookie actually did try to get herself on the right track with a job. She'd fumble around getting herself ready and she'd announce, "I'm going to work," as though it were a normal, everyday outing. We knew not to get excited. Her periods of employment were always short-lived, and often I accompanied her to help. I've spent entire days peeling potatoes behind a deli counter, shredding cabbage for cole slaw, and chopping carrots and radishes for salads. For my work and Cookie's, the deli owner would pay us each fifteen dollars. But instead of giving me an allowance or buying us groceries or new shoes, Cookie would use the money to take Cherie, Camille, and Norman to Adventureland or the movies. "You can thank your father that you're stuck at home watching Rosie," she'd say. I'd stare at the door as it closed behind her. I didn't know what she meant because I never knew my father.

I've always preferred accompanying her when she works at a bar, where at least there's usually music, and peanuts to snack on. When Cookie worked as a barmaid, it was her job to clean up after a long night, and I learned fast that weekends were the hardest! I'd be able to pay our rent if only I had a dollar for every Sunday morning I spent mopping a sticky floor and wiping down tables while the radio system played Elton John's "Levon" and Billy Joel's "Piano Man." At seven, I had no idea what it meant to make love to a tonic and gin, but I sure understood the song's carnival of lonely souls.

My salary for those gigs was as many Maraschino cherries and Shirley Temples as my belly could take. It sure beat the starchy smell of potatoes on my hands.

Once, I asked Camille and Cherie why Cookie turned out so mean, and just as Camille started saying "See, her parents—" Cherie clapped her hand over Camille's mouth. Immediately it was clear there was something they were trying to protect me from. "Trust me," Cherie said. "You don't want to know."

So, as Cookie's primary aim is to put in as little effort as possible to get what she can from whom she can, including the system, my primary aim is to keep Rosie, Norm, and me out of the system entirely. But without Camille to guide me through the summer, to help me think through the day-to-day problems and to keep food on the table, that job is about to get a lot more difficult.

AS NORM AND Rosie get acquainted with their room, I take a quiet stroll through the house. Even though we have no idea how long we'll be here, there's a lot to do to organize the place. The day's events, the move, my mother leaving, our food-shopping trip, and then Camille's departure have worn me out. I step onto the front porch to look at the stars. That's when I realize how my body aches for a bed, and my mind aches for peace, too. I want one night of the kind of sleep you can't get while you're sleeping in trunks, backseats, and, for the short-straw drawer, the back floor of the car, over the hump. Rosie used to fit into the floorwell fine when she was three or four . . . but now she's seven and tall for her age. Her lanky legs and torso don't fold up the way they used to.

I rest my forehead in my hands a few seconds and take a

minute on the porch to daydream . . . not about a boy or even a home for good. I daydream about a *pillow*. They take up too much room in the trunk for us to travel with, so Cookie doesn't let us keep them. I rise reluctantly to head inside. It's time to make my own pillow.

I enter my mother's room with its full-size mattress and box spring. The box spring is ripped on one side and also at the foot of the bed, like someone took a razor blade along the fabric to continue ripping it. I make a mental note to check inside it later for loose change or other surprises. Camille put away all of our mother's clothes before she left, so nothing of Cookie's is left out to rummage through or to smell up the place with stale cigarette smoke.

I walk to the closet to see if there are any old sheets or towels on the floor. A large linen of some kind would be perfect for a pillowcase. Nothing's inside except a few of Cookie's shirts on bent hangers. I crouch down and peak under the bed and dresser for anything I can use. Instead I find ant-, roach-, and mousetraps, and dust-ball tumbleweeds. At least there are traps set, I decide, but they look really old!

I peek in Cookie's dresser to see what I can find in there. The small top drawer contains her huge bras with stretched elastic and broken eye hooks. Her underwear is large enough to serve as a lampshade, if the house had come with any lamps! Although her "privates," as she refers to her under-garments, could definitely serve as the stuffing I was looking for, I cringe at the thought of sleeping with them so close to my face. I continue riffling through the drawer for socks . . . then I happen across something plastic. I pull out two bags: one with "yellow jackets"—uppers that Cookie takes when she's feeling especially low—and the other with two food stamps. I'm shocked that she left home without these, and it quickly occurs to me that she may be home to retrieve them very soon. I put them back for now, exactly as I found them, but I might be back for one or both if I really get desperate for food. Cookie usually keeps an entire traveling pharmacy, including Percocet, tranquilizers, uppers, and downers. Her underwear drawer is a dream come true for any melodramatic, extreme-mood-swinging woman. *She must have forgotten about these few.*

I close that drawer and open the one below it, where I discover an old worn and grayed Hanes T-shirt. I pull it out, and, with some hesitation, I bring it up to my nose. It doesn't smell of smoke, so it's probably not even hers . . . but just in case it is, I estimate I could put a few long stitches in the band of the neck and arms that won't be detected if I have to remove the thread later. The bottom is wide, so I'll have to tie it closed, but it should stay throughout the night. One pillowcase resolved— two to go. I rummage a bit more and, not finding adequate stuffing, I close the drawers, change course, and head out of Cookie's bedroom to the second floor.

First I go to my room, having seen an old, torn towel thrown in the corner. As I go to pick it up, though, I notice the window, which I opened earlier for fresh air. Now, in the evening light, I see it's well positioned for a break-in. Being responsible for two little kids makes you see everything differently—especially windows and doors. It's right on top of a pitched roof that hangs over the back door and the broken concrete patio. From my earlier time in the kitchen, I remember there is enough discarded equipment right near the roof—a rusty dryer, some beat-up-looking motor thing—to act as a lift for anyone who might want to climb on the roof and slither his way into the house by way of that window.

As a reflex, I close the window, then realize there's no lock on it. *This is very, very bad.* I feel my heart pick up its pace: This house is so old that maybe none of the windows have locks. I go to the kids' room and see a window with no locks, and then to Camille's room—same thing. I run into the hallway and see that this window doesn't have a lock, either. I race downstairs, where I find more lockless windows.

I have to switch priorities before I go to bed.

I head outside to collect thick branches that are strewn on the grassless backyard. The pile of junk back there is full of treasure, including discarded broomsticks and a broken rake handle, which I grab. As I shift the pile around, I also spot an old rusty saw. I return inside through the back kitchen door, which—of course—has a push-button lock that even Rosie could pick. I place my makeshift locking devices on the floor and go from drawer to drawer in the pantry in search of an old hammer or anything that resembles one. Finally, I dig out a few old tacks and a screwdriver. Then I race around the house, inspecting the walls for any nails or old tacks I can pull out.

As I walk to the basement door that leads downstairs, I'm still short a hammer and nails. The door sits in a vestibule between the kitchen and the bathroom, where there's a full-length mirror. As I spot my reflection, I lose my concentration. There before me stands a stranger. She's pretty, but so skinny she startles me. *I have to try to eat more.*

I stop and examine my features: my skin that's tanned

dark brown from watching Rosie and Norm outside in the sun; my hair, wavy and somewhat wild, lightened from black to auburn by the sun. My eyes are a bold shade that's more black than brown . . . darker than the translucent brown eyes all my siblings and my mother have. I cringe at the space between my two front teeth and the length of my nose, which is too big for my face.

I open the basement door and ever so carefully take the first three steps down. Fortunately, there's a string attached to an upside-down lightbulb that serves as a light, but when I pull on the string, the bulb is burned out. I take a few more slow steps and notice that a window leading into the basement is broken. That means I'll have to figure out how to secure the inside basement door that leads back into the kitchen. There's no water heater in sight; the basement is dank and empty, except for an old washing machine with its plumbing yanked out in the back and a few boxes containing nothing but old, smelly mildewed clothes and a lampshade. At least, I figure, the clothes can serve as curtains or pillow stuffing. Then I spot gray metal shelves and feel around for nails . . . *yes!* My fingers locate about eight screws and nails to add to my collection. As I put my hardware inside the box of clothes and make my way back toward the stairs, I spot a filthy old iron and I grab that, too.

I lock the back door and lean a chair under the handle so if someone tries to come in, the chair's fall will warn us loudly. Then I move into the vestibule that leads to the basement, where I use the scissors to cut the cord off the iron. Using the iron as my hammer, I bang a nail into the door frame and wrap the snipped cord between the doorknob and the nail, creating a tight figure eight that would slow down an intruder trying to come into the first level of the house through the basement door.

I place all the broom and rake handles and tree limbs on the kitchen table, using the saw to cut them so they'll fit diagonally in the windows and serve as window jambs. After securing all the downstairs windows plus the one in my bedroom, I rummage through the box of clothes I found in the basement. From window to window on the first floor, I pound nails on both sides of the windowpanes. I drape button-down shirts, sweatshirts, and T-shirts across each window for curtains. Closing the windows will cut off any air circulation through the house . . . but it's better to be sweaty than sorry. During this process I realize we'll be sleeping downstairs every night because it's cooler than upstairs, and because we could run out either the front or back door if someone were to break in. With the two living room couches and Cookie's bed, we'll each have our own place to sleep. *Whew: good work!*

Now the pillow dilemma. I stuff the gray Hanes T-shirt and another shirt with the stuffing and close the openings in the shirts. The kids will have pillows for tonight. Mine will wait until tomorrow.

The kids agree to move downstairs. When I check on Rosie in Cookie's room and hear Norm's steady breathing on the sofa, I take the empty couch across from him. The kids sleep long and quietly—they look comfortable for the first time in weeks.

I wait until the sun comes up before I feel safe enough to fall asleep.

In the morning, Rosie wakes Norm and me by turning on the TV. "Can we have some cereal?" she asks me.

"Of course," I tell her, just grateful we made it through our first night alone. "It's in the kitchen."

She hesitates a moment, then twirls her hair around her finger. "Gi, will you get it for us? Cereal always tastes the best when you make it."

I smile, and ruffle her hair as I head into the kitchen. After they eat, the three of us sit down to play our favorite card game to pass the time: five hundred rummy.

I pretend to be engaged as the kids laugh and tease each other. There's dust floating around us in the sunlight, collecting everywhere—on the wood floor; in the corners of the cabinets and shelves. Rosie and Norm look at me with lost eyes when I jump up from the game and yank a towel from inside one of the pillows. I open the front door to let air in and sigh. "I'm tired of being surrounded by filth."

Cookie always wants the place to be clean when she comes home, and chronic tidying up has become a means of keeping peace. Fortunately, I only have the downstairs to clean, because that's the only part of the house Cookie will ever bother to see.

My eyes are on the sink when I march into the kitchen. Dishes are perennially piled up and I hate doing them. My habit of putting this chore off until last is one of the causes of our cockroach problem, but I know that after they've been sitting for a while in the summer heat, this has to be a priority. I grab my bottle of Heinz white vinegar from under the sink. We always have it to clean with, but because it's too bulky and heavy to steal, we have to spend food stamps on it. I splash some vinegar over the dishes, hoping a thorough washing will deflect the army of cockroaches.

Upstairs, I gather our dirty clothes from the floors in our

rooms, run them downstairs to the bathroom, and run the tub full of cold water. I hold a half-bar of Ivory soap underneath the faucet to create bubbles, then scrub the clothes with the soap and rinse them until they feel clean. Normally, I wash only a shirt or two at a time, but Cookie or the landlord could show up any minute, and if we have to take off, it could be weeks before we see another bathtub. After every piece I scrub, I stretch to relieve the strain in my back that comes from leaning over the tub. I'll wash everything except the clothes we have on.

After wringing them out, I carry the damp bunch and hang them everywhere in the house: on doorknobs, hooks, and the backs of the couches and chairs. Then I open the back door and un-jam all the windows to let the air circulate.

EACH DAY FOR the next two weeks, the kids and I walk with a packed lunch to the park or the Middle Country Public Library. The kids moan about the sweltering forty-minute trek and are relieved when we're finally situated at the library, which mercifully blasts with air-conditioning. They don't know that I spent the two-mile trek watching for Doug's brown Chevrolet or any possible hint that Camille's about to return.

At a library table we play Mad Libs and muse through the *Highlights* magazines together. When the kids are quietly wrapped in their storybooks, I find myself living with my favorite characters in the worlds of Judy Blume novels. I don't care that I've already read *Deenie*, *Forever*, and *Are You There God? It's Me, Margaret*. Camille frowned upon me reading *Forever*—"It's not for kids your age," she said—but then, Camille's not here . . . and I'm not a kid my age. Anyway, as I've told Camille, I'm not concerned with the sex. I love the story because of the romance.

I also go through every biography they have on Amelia Earhart, my heroine.

Amelia was brave and courageous. She didn't let others limit her dreams and she never took no for an answer. Amelia Earhart made her own rules.

And unlike Cookie, she wasn't interested in being dependent on a man. In fact, after Amelia broke off her first engagement, she waited until she was thirty-three to marry George Putnam, who actually had to propose to her six times before she finally agreed. Her husband was jokingly referred to as "Mr. Earhart," and on the morning of their wedding, Amelia had a friend deliver him a note that read:

> *I want you to understand that I shall not hold you to any medieval code of faithfulness to me nor shall I consider myself bound to you similarly.*

How thrilling! So fearless! When I'm searching for a solution or scared at night, I've begun to ask myself: *What would Amelia do?* The answer always makes me feel braver.

BY THE END of July, we've settled into a routine I'm confident with, but my worries about getting food never end. With only me present to search for food, my resolution to eat more isn't so successful. Since we don't have enough food to go around, I often skip meals. When I start to feel weak and jittery, I take a swig of vinegar. When I hold it to my face, the smell reminds me of pickle juice, with that salty flavor, I love to drink straight from the jar. Thinking about pickles makes the vinegar more bearable, and for some reason, the vinegar always curbs my appetite. When that doesn't work and I'm still feeling worn down, I know I have backup to keep my energy going: the yellow jackets.

I do my best to ignore the signs of my malnourishment: the bruises that appear in dull purple on my limbs from simple chores around the house, the shallowness of my skin, and the emptiness in my eyes. There's constant pain in my gums, and I can't drink cold water because of the tingling ache in my teeth.

Finally, late one afternoon, Camille comes home for a visit, wearing a huge smile when she steps out of Kathy's mother's car. Through the rolled-down window, Kathy waves as she pulls away.

In my bare feet I step onto the porch and fold my arms, smiling. "Why you looking so smug?"

"Here's why." Camille opens a plastic grocery bag to reveal a whole roasted chicken.

"Where'd you get that?!"

"Today I made ten dollars washing cars with Kathy's brother," she says. "I was worried about you guys."

"No way!" I hug her—quickly, because my mouth is watering with the intensity of a fountain. "What else is in here?" When I take the chicken out of the bag, I find a jar of mustard and a loaf of Italian bread. *Yum!* "Norman! Rosie!" I yell. "Come and eat!"

"Now?" Norm yells from upstairs.

"It's a surprise."

The four of us sit on the floor with the plastic tray of chicken between us. "You're eating so fast!" Camille says, giggling, and poking me in the ribs. "Slow down or you might choke."

We put mustard on our plates and dip the chicken in it. When the bones are nearly stripped clean, Camille sets it aside and we pass around more mustard and dip our bread in it. Rosie and Norm sit back to let their food settle, then run outside to play. Camille smiles at me, seeing how happy they are. I tuck my hands behind my head and smile back in agreement.

With our bellies stuffed, she and I stretch out on the living room couches. I tell her how we've been spending our days and how I lock the house up at night. "Are you going to come back and live with us again?"

"How are the kids doing?"

I understand this is her answer.

Norman and Rosie have always been "the kids," because they're "the kids" to our mother. She'll say, "Who's taking care of the kids?" and I know she means Norman and Rosie. I have never been a kid.

Norman acts like a child, even though we're less than two years apart. He's our mother's little prince, and he loves that we girls take care of him. I tell Camille that, lately, I can see him growing more loyal to me and more willing to help out. "Norm and I are actually close now," I tell her.

"That's good," she says. "We need one another too much to fight like other brothers and sisters."

Rosie, of course, is my solace. She's what keeps me moving ahead when I get exhausted from the library walks, our scant food supply, and living in perpetual, utter fear of Cookie and the cops. Sometimes I grow suddenly overwhelmed to consider what her life would be like without me. What if *I* were to just walk out, leaving Norman in charge? Books are the only escape I have from our struggles. I know one day Rosie will need that escape, too, so I always sign out library books to read to her. My favorites to share are from the Landmark Books series, about our country's founders. Before bed, Rosie snuggles in as I read to her about Betsy Ross, Dolley Madison, and Pocahontas.

I rise to turn on the TV. Camille says the car wash exhausted her, so she's going to sleep on the couch. This gives me an opportunity to run something by her. "Hey, Camille," I say, "I need new pants for school. Will you and Doug be my getaway car at Billy Blake's tomorrow?"

She sighs with inconvenienced hesitation.

"Please? You've left me here alone all summer. I haven't had the chance to get what I need for school."

She concedes. "Sure," she says. "I'll call Doug in the morning."

Normally I'd walk, but it's been so hot and I've been feeling so weak that even just thinking about making the trip by foot makes me tired. I'd already been there twice in July. It's a long walk, several towns away, down Middle Country Road, which is part of Route 25 and always full of traffic, past used-car lots and gas stations and the dramatic complex that's Smith Haven Mall, past furniture shops and carpet stores and Carvel ice cream—miles and miles of exhaust fumes, honking horns, and things I daydream about possibly owning one day.

Later, after I've locked up for the night, even with a house with four bedrooms and lots of beds, Camille and I fall asleep on one of the couches together while the kids sleep opposite us on the other couch.

We spend the next morning watching reruns of *Land of the Lost*, *The Monkees*, and *The Price Is Right*, laughing and guessing the prices of the detergent and furniture that Bob Barker's assistants showcase. In the afternoon, Camille and I teach Norm and Rosie how to play Mother May I (three words we don't often use). Then we feed them chicken salad, using the meat we had pulled off the bones, before Doug pulls up in his father's tan Chevy sedan. After some discussion, Doug and Camille decide to see *The Amityville Horror*, a movie about a haunted house that happens to be a few towns over. As they debate about whether the story is true, I ponder what brand of designer jeans I'm going to choose.

Doug leaves his car at the far end of the parking lot so he and Camille can search for a newspaper that lists the theater show times. I wander into Billy Blake's and head straight back to the juniors' department, where I examine a rack of Gloria Vanderbilt jeans. I find a bright orange pair that I love, imagining how the kids at school will admire my designer duds. I slip them under a larger pair and clip them both to the hanger. On the way to the fitting room I pick up a few shirts; and when the attendant checks the quantity of items I carried in, she hands me a plastic card with the number 4. I smile and close the fitting-room stall door. I take off my pants, step into the Gloria Vanderbilts, and pull my pants back over them. My oversize T-shirt falls past my waist, successfully hiding the double waistband. I pause to make sure the orange hem isn't visible above my shoes. Then I wait a little longer to make it seem as though I'm deliberating, deciding what to buy of all the clothes I'd carried in. When I exit the room, I hand an armful of clothes and my plastic number 4 to the attendant. "Bummer," I say, shrugging at her. "Nothing fit."

It's actually no lie: The jeans are too big on me, but that doesn't matter . . . nor does the fact that they're the same color as a construction cone. I saunter my way toward the exit but inside I'm dying to break into a run. *My very own Gloria Vanderbilt jeans!* Just as I walk out the door, however, a voice bellows in my direction. I sprint out to the parking lot and, hearing the security guard behind me, do the only thing I can think of: duck behind a car. *(I made it!)*

As I try to catch my breath in silence, I feel a growing confidence that I've lost him in the darkness. Just then I spot the glow of a flashlight and hear his hard-soled shoes clicking up and down the rows of cars. I slither underneath the belly of the car I ducked behind, praying the driver doesn't show up. From several rows away, I watch the feet of the man from Billy Blake's walk farther across the parking lot. After I'm sure he's gone back inside the store, I crawl out and, crouching low, quickly make my way to Doug's car across the lot. After I'm safely lying down in the backseat, I swear to myself that I'll never set foot in Billy Blake's department store again.

BY MID-AUGUST, IT'S been six weeks since we've seen Cookie, and one afternoon Rosie and Norm are playing down the road when the landlord comes knocking. *What would Amelia do? What would Camille do?*

Instantly I hide in the kitchen, ready to run out the back if he comes through the front. He knocks loudly once, twice, then three times. I hold my breath in anticipation of the sound of the doorknob turning. When all I hear is the buzz of the refrigerator, I peer around the corner to see if he's still standing there. He's not, but his truck is still perched in the driveway. Unfortunately, I straighten just in time to see him walk past the kitchen window, catching his eye as he catches mine. *Shoot!* I freeze.

His face is creased and round, and what's left of his white hair looks iridescent in the afternoon sun. I steady myself against the wall, bracing for an angry expression, but instead, concern has taken over his face. He motions for me to open the door. I debate it for a second. Then, having no choice, I turn the knob.

"Your mother here?" he asks.

"No," I tell him. "She's working."

"Oh, I see. She must work a lot."

"Pretty much all the time."

He frowns. "The rent is two weeks late," he continues, as though I'd be shocked. "I've stopped by here a few times and haven't seen anybody at home." Now he's studying me, but he makes no move to come inside. I'm blocking the door with my hip, leaving it only slightly ajar. I feel half naked in my striped tube top and cutoff jean shorts. Aware that he appears in no hurry to leave, I cross my arms over my chest to make it clear I don't welcome any physical contact.

"Everything in the house work okay?" he asks, peering behind me.

"Yeah." I peek over my shoulder and nod at him. "No sweat." Something tells me this man won't be easy to fool. *Great.* I'll have to be on the lookout for social services from now on.

"Okay then," he says, starting down the back steps. "Good. Well, tell your mother I stopped by."

I don't say anything, so he turns and walks toward the side of the house. Just before he's out of sight, I call after him. "She works late."

He turns to face me again. "I noticed the oil tank is empty. Anybody been around lately to fill it?"

"I'm not sure, but we don't need it. It's summer. It's not a big deal." After he rounds the corner, I close the door. Then I sit down with my back against it, sighing in relief as his truck pulls away.

The next afternoon, when we return from the library, Norman heads out with his new neighborhood friends to play with someone's skateboard. "Hey, Gi?" he yells. "There's something on the back porch."

"What is it?" I holler, but I know he's already running down the street. I step out on the porch to find a large, brown paper bag. It's filled with carrots with the roots still attached, a pile of potatoes, some tomatoes, and at the very bottom, a huge watermelon. Like the carrots' roots, the tomatoes still have vines attached as if they were just pulled from someone's garden.

This kind of anonymous charity is unusual. What's more, I don't know a single person who keeps a garden: Cherie doesn't, and anyway, she wouldn't drop off something like this without sticking around for a few minutes to see us. *None of our friends from school could have done this*, I think. *They don't even know where we're staying. Could it be from a neighbor?* I crack open the watermelon with my trusty iron—it's become my favorite multipurpose tool—and scoop out some of the center, letting the juice drip down my arms as I inhale the sweet flesh. The sugar gives a wild rush to my empty stomach, and, in moments, I'm so full I could be sick. I load the uneaten part into the refrigerator and turn on the faucet to rinse off my hands and arms. I lift the handle all the way to the left out of habit, hoping it will grow warm enough to melt my stickiness away. Instead the water is instantly scalding hot.

"Oh crap!" I yell. *"Ouchouchouch!"* I slam off the faucet

and shake the sting from my fingers, staring at my hot-pink hands . . . then, it all comes together: the landlord! He must have filled the oil tank while we were gone. What kind of landlord helps people who don't pay their rent? It doesn't make any sense. And he has to have been the one who left the vegetables, too. *Damn him,* I think, skeptical about his motives. *He needs to mind his own business. Why didn't he just call social services and get it over with? Why's he trying to keep us here and buy us food and oil? What does he want?* When you're a kid with no one to protect you, everything comes with a price.

On the other hand, it takes no time to grow accustomed to having a hot shower every day. The best part about having hot water is staying in there long enough to really take in the warmth and rinse the day's dirt off. One afternoon in late August, I step out of the shower and quickly slip on my bottoms and tube top. As I scoot out of the bathroom, holding up my underwear by their unraveling elastic, I steal a glance in the full-length mirror. What I see looking back at me makes me stop and gasp.

I stand there. I try to register what or who it is I'm looking at. I'm shrinking away. The combination of the yellow jackets and the vinegar has taken its toll. Standing completely still, I examine the concave curve of my stomach and the bones sticking out against the skin of my hips. My legs are straight lines interrupted by the bump of my knees; nothing about them is shapely. I'm totally flat-chested, and my rib cage is clearly outlined underneath the blue stripes of my tube top. I have to look harder to see what I've always seen—I can no longer find the pretty girl that used to greet me as I walked by. In fact, there are shocks of gray in my hair in front and in back, and when I reach up and touch the spot where my skull meets the nape of my neck, I find the raw, soft patches of baldness that I've been hiding with what's left of my hair. I stare at myself and, as usual, keep my mouth closed so the huge gap in my front teeth isn't visible in the reflection.

I don't even recognize this girl! She is not me. I'll have to start ninth grade like this . . . *high* school. Even if I could go back to Billy Blake's, there aren't enough designer clothes in their entire girls' department to make me fit in. For the first time, I'm seeing what Cookie says she sees when she looks at me: a rag doll.

Cookie returns before Labor Day weekend. Norman, Rosie, and I are sitting in the living room watching television when she walks through the front door as if she's only been gone an hour. She's carrying a box of Cap'n Crunch, powdered milk, and a six-pack of beer. She's still wearing the pair of jeans she walked out in and her hair is still in a ponytail, with half of it red and the newer parts dyed black. Before, Norman would have run to her, given her hugs, and shouted *"Mom! Mom!"* but today he glances at me with raised eyebrows and then turns his attention back to *The Electric Company*. Silently, I chalk up a point in my favor: These last two months have put him officially on my side. Norman's trust in me is the best thing about my relationship with him . . . and the worst thing for my relationship with Cookie.

"Here's your dinner," she says. Even with such nonchalance, her presence alters the feeling in the room, establishing a weight I can feel in my chest. She waltzes past the stairwell and into the kitchen, where I hear her set the cereal and beer down, rip a can from its plastic ring, and pop it open. "You look like shit," she calls from the kitchen. Then she goes into her room and shuts the door. I'm in awe that, just seconds ago, this house felt clean and safe. Her presence has released a pollution that I can feel settling like grit on my skin.

"COME ON KIDS, let's go!"

The next morning we wake to the sound of Cookie hollering. I hurry Rosie and Norman to dress and shoo them both to the car as Cookie stands with her hands on her hips. "What time of year is it?" she says. "You know the drill." We realize we're on our way to get registered for school.

I have no problem finding clothes big enough to camouflage how skinny I am from the administrators—by now, all my clothes are baggy. I pull my hair back into a ponytail that gathers at the bald spot, tucking the gray pieces under the black hair to hide them from the school attendants' view. Cookie starts the car and sets off toward the back roads.

It only takes five minutes to register me for my first year of high school in Centereach. After the secretary informs us that we arrived late to register and they've already given physicals, they tell me to report to the nurse's office on the first day of school. This I make note to "forget," or I'll be faced with questions about my bag-of-bones build. When Cookie and I walk back outside, I put my head down to avoid being seen with her and her car, even though there are no schoolmates around. I have yet to say a word to her since she's returned to us.

While Cookie walks Norman next door to register him at the middle school, Rosie and I sit in the car. "We won't be on the same bus anymore, will we?" she says.

"No, but you're going to love third grade. You'll learn multiplication and division and how to write *Rosie* in pretty script letters. Isn't it exciting?" When her separation anxiety is still visible, I promise her I'll help her with all of her science projects. "Maybe we'll even build a volcano out of mud!" I tell her.

"Yeah . . ." she muses, then stops and looks up at me. "You don't have to pay for mud, do you?"

"No, sweetie. You don't." She nods and stares out the window watching for Cookie and Norman. My eyes well with tears. At seven years old, Rosie has come to understand that we're poor.

We head home and wait a few hours before going school clothes shopping. Once dusk falls, Cookie flags us back into the car and we head out in search of Salvation Army bins. We know it will take a few dives in these Dumpsters to find enough clothes for all three of us, and we're familiar with Cookie's shopping spree strategy: First she pulls the passenger side of the car next to the Dumpster opening. Then, with the window open, I climb on the seat and stick my head through the hole to look down into the Dumpster. Once my eyes grow accustomed to the darkness, if I see more clothes than garbage and useless debris, I step on the window ledge and squeeze myself through the sloped metal opening in the bin to get inside. I begin throwing clothes out through the hole and into the car.

Using the car's dome light to see, the kids and Cookie root through the clothes to pick out the ones we could possibly use. I locate a pair of jeans and a plaid skirt for Rosie.

"Gi!" she cries. "Look, this pink shirt still has the tags on it!"

"It's brand-new for you to wear on the first day!"

For Norman, I fold a nice pair of corduroys and a couple turtlenecks into a pile, and for myself I dig out a pair of khaki pants that I can make a size smaller by taking them in with a few stitches. Then, once our options are exhausted, I pile all the excess clothes on the floor and climb out, giving myself a leg up as I shimmy out of the bin, back into Cookie's car.

Throughout the weekend, Cookie shares the details of the life she created at her new boyfriend's place as though she's telling us a great fairy tale of which we have no part. "Oh, the meals I cook," she says. "And you oughtta see how well-behaved his daughter is—you three could take a lesson. She's only thirteen, lost her mother to cancer last year . . . treats me like I walk on water. Talk about appreciation. Instead, what do I get from you? I get bullshit." Although I wish someone was taking care of us the way her boyfriend's thirteen-year-old daughter is being mothered now, I can tell Cookie's happy because she's been sober for the entire day. For the first time in as long as I can remember, I'm actually not afraid of her.

After the weekend together, she announces that she's going back to her boyfriend's house. In peace, I begin to rifle through our new wardrobe, sorting the colors to wash in the tub before we start school on Wednesday. As I start my hems and alterations, I flip on the TV, where Ronald Reagan is giving a speech in New Jersey as part of his campaign for the U.S. Presidency:

> *And most of us have begun to realize that, so long as Carter policies are in effect, the next four years will be as dark as the last four . . . I pledge to you I'll bring a new message of hope to all of America.*

A new message of hope to all of America. That includes *my* family. It includes me! I need a new message of hope as much as I need a new wardrobe to start the ninth grade. If my next four years are as dark as my last four years, I'll never make it to seventeen. I hope Reagan, or Carter, or someone, could get me out of this, but I'm not holding my breath.

On the first day of school, it's clear I've made a horrible mistake with my outfit choice. As I walk down the halls, calls from the other students are all that drown out the sound of my baggy denim seams rubbing together: "It's the Orange Ethiopian!" they yell. I know I have more meat on me than the skeletal starving Ethiopians I see on TV, but did I have to go and highlight myself with a pair of fluorescent orange pants? Nothing like blending in at my new school.

Aside from the orange-denim disaster, the first day in this new school is the same as everywhere I've ever been. I don't really mind walking from classroom to classroom by myself—in a way, it's a relief not to have any friends because there's no one who I have to tell about my family. There are assignments to keep me busy and teachers to listen to. I don't say much in class because I don't want any attention directed at me, but I make sure to follow the huddles of students in front of me to each classroom so that I arrive right on time and act alert when class starts. I've learned to give straight answers when the teachers call on me, but that doesn't typically start to happen until the third week of school when the social breakdown between the kids is clear: Teachers take one look at me and go gentle. Leaving the classroom is always the giveaway: If the teacher stands by the door as the class files into the hallway, my trademark is a modest, closed-mouth smile—a well-adjusted, friendly kid.

It's the free times during the day that make my status as

the new girl painfully obvious: lunch and recess, and also gym class, where I use Cherie and Camille's fake cramps trick, even though I have yet to get my period.

Most kids might complain about their teachers, but mine give me a sense of assurance—wrapping myself in my work and obeying their instructions is the easiest, best way to stay safe. School has always been my escape and solace, a place where an independent kid like me finds stability. Because I keep a low profile, my teachers never really know about my life at home. I'm sure some have detected that things aren't exactly as they should be, but most of them have used any vulnerabilities they sensed as a reason to encourage me.

ON SEPTEMBER 17, 1980, just a week after school starts, Cherie gives birth to her first child: a baby boy. I'm down the street, greeting Norman and Rosie from the bus, when I hear Cookie's tires screeching into the driveway and her hoarse voice blaring down the block. "Regina!" she yells. "Your sister had a baby—I'm a grandma!" My first nephew.

"Can I come, Mom? I want to see the baby!" Rosie says. I lace my arm through hers and pull her onto my lap on the porch step.

"I'm not coming back here after," Cookie says. "You can meet him after Cherie takes the baby home to her in-laws'."

Cookie stumbles through the front door one afternoon in early November, holding a box of macaroni and cheese and a half-gallon of milk. "What's going on?" I ask her, meaning, *What are you doing here?*

"Well, by the looks of it, I'd say I'm a single woman again," she slurs. "You could thank me for bringing home dinner.

I'm in a shitty mood. Stay away from me." Lacking the care and the energy to carry the food to the kitchen, she plops down on the couch and promptly passes out—her new pair of clogs falling to the floor with a crack. Rosie and Norm burst into giggles as Cookie's snoring rattles the room. I hush them, stifling my own laughter, and watch her. I thought men liked women who are sweet and attractive, but Cookie's just swollen and angry.

We eat the macaroni and cheese in the living room while Cookie's splayed unconscious on the couch. Together we stand to carry our dirty dishes to the kitchen, careful to be quiet. Rosie rises last, balancing her empty glass on her plate, trailing behind Norm and me. I've just stepped into the kitchen when Rosie's glass falls and shatters on the living room floor, inches from Cookie's ear.

No!

My instinct moves me to her as Cookie jolts from the couch.

This will not be pleasant.

"You stupid little whore!" Cookie shouts, grabbing Rosie's hair in her fist.

Rosie staggers and drops the plate, which falls and cracks in half. Before I can stop her, Cookie slams Rosie's body to the floor, inches from the shards of glass. Instantly Rosie wails—first out of total shock at being pummeled, then as the pain shudders through her body.

Instinctively I jump on Cookie's back, clawing her skin with my fingernails. "You're not her mother anymore," I scream in her ear. *"Let go of her! LET GO!"* My blind rage has filled the room, the entire floor of the house. It's so fiery and fierce I'm sure the entire street can feel its quake. I fight hard to bring her to the ground—if I can just get her down, Rosie can climb away. Instead, she lies stunned and crying on the floor beneath us. Norm sprints over and pulls Rosie toward the bottom of the stairs away from Cookie. There they both stand, screaming at me. "Stop, Gi, stop!" But my mother will not hurt my baby, who's finally thriving under my care. And she isn't going to beat me into submission either, the lunatic! I hardly flinch when Cookie flips me over her back onto the floor, on top of the broken shards of glass.

"You stupid little bitch," she grunts through her teeth, landing her first kick. "You should've never been born, slut! You were my biggest mistake, you stupid little motherfucker."

She's barefoot, but all the weight of her body lands in the small of my back, then on my ribs and pelvis and elbows. I roll on my side, trying to get out from under her. Instead she brings her heel down into the side of my waist, then grabs me by my hair and slams my face into the floor. Blood flows out of my nose, and I can feel it seeping from my back from the broken glass. I roll over on my side into a ball—it's a short opportunity to catch my breath before I use what little energy I have left to stand up and face her one more time. As I turn to rise, her foot slams me full-force in the stomach and sends me flying to the floor again. "You little fucking slut!" she screams, puffing hard and finding another burst of energy to kick me again. I stagger to stand up, about to run at her, when she grips me around the neck and shoves me backward. First I feel my head meet the floor, then my back—my legs and arms had no chance to stretch out and break the fall. I feel the sting of the glass sticking in my head and the blood trickling out of my scalp. But I fight to scramble up fast, knowing that if I stay down, her feet will start kicking blows to my head and ribs.

My will is stronger than hers, but she's drunk and more than twice my body weight. The force of her arms sends me into the railing, where the kids are standing on the other side. I slide to the floor, stunned. When her leg comes in again, I swing at it to trip her, surprised she stumbled. Then I scramble to my feet and dart past her, out the front door.

She turns around just as I make it to the porch, her voice thundering after me. "Get your ass back in here now! I'm not finished with you yet!"

Somehow I've made it across the yard. She can still see me, but so can the neighbors if they choose to open their blinds to the commotion. I slip into the darkness and press myself against the chain-link fence. I hear her voice echo in the cold air. *"You get back in here so I can finish what you started. You're gonna get what you deserve, you little bastard!"*

Four months earlier, I would have obeyed her and gone back inside to take the rest of my beating, especially knowing that if she hadn't exhausted her anger yet, she may take it out on Rosie. But something keeps me from listening this time. She continues to loom a few yards from me. My hair and face are caked with blood, my back stinging from the cuts and aching from the pounding. The only thing keeping me from collapsing is my will not to submit to her again. She yells one more time.

"Get back in this goddamn house!"

I shake my head, pounding from the beating, and whisper: *"No. No!"*

Then I turn from her voice and walk as fast as I can toward Middle Country Road.

The cold concrete wall outside Shoes 'N Things feels soothing against my back. Out of the reach of the streetlight, I pull my legs into my chest and rest my head on my knees. I catch my breath from the tears and dig into one of the green garbage bins for a few boxes. I pull them open and line them up between the Dumpster and the building's back wall to create a bed.

It's probably been an hour when I open my eyes at the sound of her jalopy rolling down the street. I peek out around the corner and see the car turning in the direction of the bars.

I wish these feelings were new to me—the hurt, anger, rejection from the emotional abuse, and the searing physical pain—but for all of the near-fourteen years of my life, this is the only consistent, predictable part of my relationship with Cookie. To me, feeling secure means the opposite of what it means to most kids. Children are supposed to find their greatest safety and comfort in the arms of their mothers. Instead, Cookie's homecoming is our darkest danger, like the worst storm anyone can imagine. I brace myself and lock down my wits as she enters with a stir. We have no control over what comes next as the tension builds, then it's as though the skies open up when she comes down on me in a rage. When she's finished, she goes suddenly . . . leaving the devastation in her wake as the only evidence she's ever been here at all. We're always comforted to know she'll be gone for a while—safe and content, as though it's safe to step out into the sun after a torrid rain. And we recover fast, using our wits and will to stay together and rebuild our home.

I walk into a quiet house. One of the kids has cleaned up the glass, and they're both sleeping toe-to-toe on the couch. My heart swells as I kiss their cheeks good night, and whisper in Norman's ear: "You're a good big brother." I rise and stand there watching them . . . then the tears stream down my face. Not for myself but for how powerless we are over what will happen next. After a minute I secure the front and back doors then head to the bathroom to try and soak away my pain.

4

Breaking Pact

November 1980

THE NEXT MORNING is the fifth of November, four days before my fourteenth birthday. I get the kids up and ready for school and put them on the bus. In the house I close the front door, knowing that, sooner or later, I'll have to attempt to face myself in the full-length mirror.

Because I grew so thin over the summer, the marks from this beating have taken on dimensions I've never witnessed. They're so large and discolored that they cover my entire body like a single mass of blue, black, and red. In some places the marks are so grotesque that it's as though the barrier of my skin has collapsed and my insides are practically exposed.

I ride the late bus to Centereach High School, keeping my

hair down so it covers my face. It takes all of my concentration to ignore the stares I get from the other students. A long-sleeved sweatshirt covers my arms and back. After second period, Mr. Brown, my social studies teacher, pulls me aside.

"Now, Regina," he says, trying to hold my eyes while I stare at my shoes. "I don't want to have to ask you about your personal life—that's between you and your family. You flunked the last test though, and unless some miracle happens between now and the quarter-end exam, I'm going to have to fail you. So whatever's going on, it has to stop."

I continue staring at the floor.

He softens his voice. "If you tell me where all these marks came from, there's a chance I can give you a passing grade."

Mr. Brown is bigger than my mother but not at all threatening. He keeps his hand resting softly on my arm, as though he thinks I might run. But I can't tell him. When I finally raise my head to look at him, he blinks to suppress a flinch. "I'm fine," I mumble. "I can't be late for my next class." Then, I bolt.

When I arrive home from school that afternoon, there's a car I don't recognize in the driveway. The front door is hanging wide open. *Oh no!*

A social worker is rooting through the kitchen cabinets and drawers. She's young and blond, wearing khakis and no makeup. Her face holds a flat expression: She's definitely on a mission. When she notices me, she stops, openly looking at the bruises on my face. I can see she's trying to control her expression when she introduces herself. "Regina," she says. "I'm Ms. Davis." She motions for me to let her look at my arms and gasps as she pushes up my sleeves. "Your school called my office today. I need to know what happened."

My first thought is to give her what's become my natural

reaction when I'm confronted with how we live: I lie. I lie for us. I say, "My sisters and I were roughhousing," or "I fell out of the tree I was climbing," or "I fell off of my friend's bike onto the gravel." I know if I tell her the truth, we'll all be separated. "I fell down the basement stairs holding an iron," I tell her. My toes wiggle inside my shoes, embarrassed to look so awful while she looks so wholesome and pretty.

She looks at me crossly, then comes at me and lifts up my sweatshirt. I don't flinch or fight her—it will only make the pain worse. There's heartbreak in her face when she looks up from my ribs. "C'mon, Regina," she says. "Make this the last time that you fell down the stairs, or into a stove, or out of a tree. I read your file, honey. You are almost fourteen! You can be in control soon—you know what that means, don't you?"

I know. It means I could leave my mother permanently. I've heard this many times before from my social workers, truant officers, guidance counselors, and other street kids. When you turn fourteen, you reach the age of reason. That means you can choose whether you want to stay with your biological parents or choose to emancipate yourself and become a ward of the state. If I opted to become a ward of the state, my mother would no longer have any control over my decisions or me.

All of them—the counselors, the officers, the social workers—seemed well intentioned at first, asking if our mother hit us; if she fed us. They'd give the impression of wanting to help, but then they'd talk to Cookie, who seemed to have a sixth sense about these things and usually returned home when we were in danger of being taken away. It wasn't hard for her to convince them that we brought the bruises on ourselves: For social services, it's easier to keep children with their mother than deal with all the logistics, paperwork, and drama of putting kids in foster homes. And then the cycle would start all over again: Cookie would move us into a different house, using a new combination of names to delay the state in tracking us down, and things would be really bad for a while.

"Regina, she'll kill you if you stay here. Your siblings aren't safe, either." She pauses, watching me, then leans over and puts her arms on the counter. "If you tell me everything, we can get you away. *She will do to them what she has done to you.* Do you want Rosie to look like you in a few years, to feel like you feel? You owe it to them to tell the truth. Stop lying for their sakes and tell me what has been happening here."

"What if I did tell you? What would happen to the kids?"

"They'll be taken away from your mother and go to a foster home, too," she says. "I promise you they will be kept safe."

Before I can think twice, I give in. Without Camille here to run interference, and now, faced with the idea that my silence could put my little brother and sister in danger, Ms. Davis's invitation to finally free us from this hell is too tempting to resist any longer.

Through calm breaths I tell her that the kids cannot go back with our mother. "You need to promise me that they will be safe, *no matter what.*" And then, before I can stop myself, I'm talking and talking and I can't shut up. The stress and exhaustion of the past two years of parenting the kids on my own; the cars, the shelters, and the struggle . . . they break me. It's dusk by the time I'm finished spilling the truth. I don't leave anything out.

The kids arrive just as Ms. Davis is getting ready to leave. Norman eyes her timidly as she places a dime in my hand so I can make a call on the pay phone. "Norm, can you hold down the fort for a minute?"

He watches Ms. Davis exit, still tentative. "Yeah."

I walk to the corner phone booth and dial Kathy's house. "Cookie was about to beat Rosie and I stepped in," I tell Camille.

"Why would she lay a hand on Rosie?"

"Because she accidentally dropped a glass, right next to where Cookie was sleeping. I couldn't hide the marks and my teacher must have called social services."

"Social services came?"

"The social worker was standing in the kitchen when I got home!"

"You didn't tell, did you?"

"Camille—"

"Gi, did you *tell*?"

"You weren't here and I couldn't let Cookie hurt them!"

"I'll be there in ten minutes."

Cookie's beating didn't make me cry, but losing Camille's faith in me has. On the walk back to the house, it sinks in: This did not save my family. Instead, I have violated a pact among our siblings by telling the truth. I've separated us again, and worse, I have exposed Norman and Rosie not only to our mother, should she succeed in getting them back from foster care, but to whomever they'll find in the home they're sent to.

I'm overwhelmed with guilt. When Camille shows up, we stand on the porch facing each other. Tears start flowing until I shake. Because of me, none of us are safe now. Rosie won't survive if I'm not there to protect her; she'll be the only "little slut" and "whore" Cookie will have left. She doesn't stand a chance.

The thought makes me cry harder, hating myself for my selfishness that will make my baby sister completely vulner-

able. Camille and I put our arms around each other, both sobbing. "Do you think there's any way for me to take it back?"

She shakes her head. Says nothing. We both know there's
no going back. I've said too much.

That night I do not sleep. I go to the couch where Rosie
sleeps and watch her breathing. I cuddle and kiss and pray for
her all night, knowing as daylight pushes into the room that
I've crushed any chance of her being protected.

Camille and I put the kids on the early bus in time for the
school's free breakfast. I take the late bus. Camille takes her
post at home, waiting for the inevitable.

It takes every ounce of concentration for me to get through
school. I don't eat my free lunch, nor do I notice whom I've
sat next to in the cafeteria. I pay no attention in class, especially Mr. Brown's, where I keep my head down and pretend
to write in my notebook. I wonder if he was the one who sent
social services to the house, and if they told him what I said.

Three cars fill the driveway when I reach home: two gray
sedans that I know belong to social services; in each, a man sits
waiting behind the wheel. I hurry into the house. The third car
is a familiar orange rust box.

The front door of the house is standing open, and from
the upstairs I hear the creak of a closet door followed by the
slam of an empty drawer.

My siblings are packing.

In the kitchen I find Ms. Davis and another woman with
my mother. Cookie doesn't even look in my direction. "Why
don't you go upstairs and pack your stuff," she says in a sick-
eningly singsong voice. This is the act she always puts on in
front of the social workers. I race upstairs, aware of what's
about to take place.

I find Camille in my room. When our eyes lock, I break again into angry tears. Working fast, I throw my clothes and two Jesus figurines in the green Hefty bag that I keep under my bed. Then I sit on the bed with my siblings. I embrace Rosie, who's also sobbing. "It will be okay, baby, I promise. We'll take care of you." Camille consoles Norman through his heaving tears.

When the four of us come downstairs with our belongings, the social workers lead us outside. They place Norman and Rosie in one car, Camille and me in another. A social worker's cheap guarantee was all it took to lose *mia bambina*—my baby. What kind of big sister gives in so easily?

As they start the cars and prepare to pull away, Cookie lumbers down the steps, pushing her hair back from her face. She's breathless and pale, attempting to maintain her version of composure. At the bottom of the steps, she hoarsely calls after us: "Don't worry, kids, I'll get you back!" Other mothers whose children are being ripped from their homes might proclaim such a promise because they love their kids but I know: That's not Cookie. *"I'll get you back!"* she's screaming through the car window, but not because she's lost what matters most to her. It's because she's lost her meal ticket.

Norman and Rosie's car pulls out first. Cookie runs toward our car and stands staring through the back door of the driver's side where the only thing that protects Camille and me from her is a locked car door. Looking directly at me she yells: "I'll get you back!"

"No," I mouth to her through the glass. "No you won't."

And then we're gone.

5

Failure to Thrive

Ms. Davis and the driver have set the mood with a stiff silence from the front seat of the car. A quick glance from Camille puts me more at ease, but when I turn to look out the window again, the trees and houses grow fast out of focus as tears collect in my eyes and drop down my cheeks. Social workers usually have a sixth sense; almost the ability to *hear* tears fall . . . but when Ms. Davis keeps her eyes locked on the road in front of us, I know she realizes that we're too old for the "This is all for the best" speech. At this point in our foster care career, we know it's not.

We're separated again, and it's because of me.

Because I *told*.

Until now, we've only ever been put in foster care for

slips—for committing tiny errors that gave away our situation. By now, Norm, Rosie, and I have learned that we're stronger together than apart. We've sharpened our instincts and it's kept us together for six solid years, from the time I was in third grade. When I use my sleeve to wipe my eyes and nose swiftly and in silence, Camille reaches across the seat and gently sets her hand on my shoulder. We both understand that our years as a family will probably end today.

As the driver makes a right off Middle Country Road, Ms. Davis finally turns to face us. "You'll be at this next placement for two weeks," she says, "until we figure out another home for you both." *For you both*. Does that mean Camille and I might get to stay together for good? Ms. Davis explains that this temporary foster family has had kids coming and going for more than twenty years, and they've decided not to foster children permanently anymore. But when they heard we were teenagers who lived in the same school district that they did, they agreed to take us until social services found us a new home. I prop my elbow against the car window, partly to block my ear from Ms. Davis's next topic. Through half a muffle, I hear her say:

"This family didn't want young children."

Why would she say that? As if it's not excruciating enough to think of Rosie and Norm on their own—most likely holding each other, sobbing inconsolably, their eyes focused in terror out the car windows, completely unsure of what kind of questions to even ask the social workers.

What did I just do?

Within ten stifling minutes, we pull into the driveway of a tidy, red ranch house sitting on a manicured corner property. Camille nudges me out of the backseat and we edge around to the trunk to unload our Hefty bags. We follow Ms. Davis to the porch, keeping our eyes to the ground all the while. When I look up to the stoop, I'm met by the gaze of a blue-eyed, blond-haired lady, very proper and petite. She appears to be near fifty. Her forced smile turns to a look of horror, then a gasp escapes from her mouth. I suppose this is the first time she's ever met a walking white Ethiopian with cuts and bruises covering her face.

Ms. Davis gestures for Camille and me to stand next to her. "Girls, this is Addie Peterman. You're welcome to call her Aunt Addie." I stare at the clean cuff at the bottom of Addie's pants, at her shockingly white Keds sneakers. It takes all my will to stop from blurting, "Why don't we call you what you are to us: Mrs. Rent-a-Kid." I always hate this Foster Mommy Dearest baloney.

Addie opens the front door, a wreath and a lace curtain hanging from its window. She leads us inside and I gawk around the living room. "Don't touch anything," Camille whispers. As far as foster homes go, this is one of the nicest we've seen.

Addie looks down at our feet and I understand this is polite-lady code for *Please take off your shoes.* My feet leave imprints across the fresh-vacuumed nap of her carpeting. Addie's décor is a quintessential 1970s housewife motif of gingham fabrics and lace; scalloped edges and spindle legs; braided rugs and silk floral arrangements. She leads us down the hall, suggesting for Camille to set down her bag while she shows us into my room.

I rest my shins against the Hefty bag, taking it all in. Addie's generosity with her space does not melt my numbness to her home, nor does her domestic perfection. What's the point? I'll only be here two weeks. A floral wallpaper covers the walls, which are lined with bookshelves and a single bed (that includes both a mattress and a box spring), a dresser and a closet. Next to the bed is a white vanity desk that makes me imagine sitting down with a stack of books and some homework, until my eyes scan up to the huge mirror that's hanging over it:

On second thought, why don't I avoid mirrors for now.

There's also a window—complete with a lock and actual shutters, the wooden accordion kind, for privacy. When Addie leads us into Camille's room, we find her space is just as *Cottage Country*–esque as mine, only a little bigger. I raise my eyebrows at my sister. *Nice, but let's not get too comfortable.*

After Ms. Davis tells us she's posted her number on the pad hanging next to the yellow wall phone in the kitchen, Addie instructs us to make ourselves at home while she prepares dinner. I head back into my bedroom and plop my garbage bag on top of the flowered quilt before it dawns on me that my luggage will dirty the bedding. I take in the delicacy of the patchwork comforter, along with the matching pillowcase covering a cushy pillow.

If Addie thinks she's being generous with all these drawers and the closet space, I'd like to inform her how ridiculous it feels to be finished unpacking in two small armloads. In the bottom of my bag I find my other three possessions: One is a picture of the five of us when Rosie was just a baby, in which we're all sporting matching T-shirts from Lake Havasu, Arizona. Then there are my two Jesus statues. The first is a plastic Baby Jesus from a Nativity scene. The other is the translucent Lucite head of the adult Jesus on the cross. I hold both my Jesuses and tap my finger against them, pondering which surface is the most polished for their display. I turn when Addie walks in and nods toward my hand. "There's a church two blocks away, if you'd like to go and observe," she tells me.

"Observe what?"

"Your religion," she says. "You're Catholic, I take it?"

I glance down at my Jesuses. "Not sure. I don't go to church."

She eyes my figurines and looks back at me, confused. Now I get it. I jump in to clarify my position on God and religion for this clueless woman. "If there was a God, he wouldn't let bad things happen to little kids."

Again her face moves from softness to a look of horror. "Regina, God does not do bad things to little kids—bad people do!"

We look at each other in silence for a moment. I raise my eyebrows, waiting for her to dare say more, before she turns on her heels and huffs down the hall.

I'm strategizing the moment I can put Addie in her place when my stomach rumbles from the smells of melted cheese and toast grilled in butter. Camille comes to my room and says it's time for dinner. "You think I can bring it in here?" I ask her.

"I already asked," she says. "She wants us to eat in the kitchen."

Addie's husband, Pete, is seated with his back to the wall, facing the room while Addie buzzes around the kitchen, placing plates on the table. We join Addie, Pete, and their foster

son, Danny, who's clearly annoyed we're here. It's no accident
that the seat I scoot into is the one that's closest to the front
door—anybody pushes my buttons, I'm outta here! As she
sends the bowl of steamed broccoli around the table, Addie fills
us in on the house rules. "Regina, your curfew is seven thirty
every night," she announces. That sounds fine—besides the
library, where else would I go? Then she adds, "And we don't
approve of your having any boys in the house."

"Boys?" I laugh. "Look at me, I'm less lovable than a
punching bag. Besides," I mumble, "I'm only thirteen."

Addie freezes and looks at me. In silence, Pete places
his wrists on the table. "That doesn't matter," Addie says.
"You'll turn fourteen in three days, and the rule here is that
there's no dating until you're sixteen. We've had that rule in
place for all our foster kids and our three daughters, and it's
worked out very well." Then she looks at Camille. "We know
you have a boyfriend."

Camille places her fork quietly on her plate, as though
she's been caught sliding their good silver into her pockets.

"Tell him there is a curfew of nine o'clock for you, and he
has to come to the door to pick you up and drop you off. No
horn-honking in this neighborhood."

Ouch. One for Addie.

Then she goes on to discuss food distribution. "I'm on
Weight Watchers," she says, "so please, hands off the dietetic
food." Camille and I look at her blankly: Has she *seen* the size
of our waists? We nod. No problem. We're probably the only
two teenagers on all of Long Island who aren't trying to lose
weight.

"And since there will always be someone at home, you

won't need a set of keys." I nudge my knee into Camille under the table, and she nudges back hard: Here it is! The key conversation. Foster kids never, ever get keys. The phrase *There will always be someone at home* is to be translated as *Being Rent-a-Kids, you are guilty until proven innocent, and we assume that almost certainly you are thieves who cannot be trusted.* Addie tells us if there's ever no one home, the porch is a safe place for us to wait. *It's a really pretty porch, too,* I want to gush insincerely, but I stuff my grilled cheese into my mouth instead.

Addie tells us she has three grown daughters, Paula, Prudence, and Penny. I keep filling my face with grilled cheese, finding it hilarious all their initials are P. P. Two of them clean houses in a business with Addie every morning and the third is a nurse. They're all married, and they've all decorated their homes just like Addie's. As she says this, it's clear she's restraining herself from beaming.

She tells us how she and Pete met when they were teenagers and married right out of high school. Pete's frame is short and strong, and he's made a career as a contractor and carpenter—in fact, Addie says, he built the very house we're sitting in. This reminds her of the remaining house rules. Whatever Pete wants to watch on TV is what we all have to watch. *Who cares?* I want to say. *I'll watch anything on cable.* We have to clean our own rooms and do our own laundry, which is no bother to me. "You mean you have a washing machine?" I ask.

Addie looks at Pete and folds her hands in her lap. "Yes, dear. And a dryer, too."

"Then why don't we just do all your laundry while we're

at it?" I ask her, looking between the two of them. "It's no problem."

She dabs the sides of her mouth with her paper napkin. "Don't you worry about our laundry—just know the washer and dryer are yours to use anytime they're free."

Addie informs us that she and Pete had asked to see our report cards before they took us in. Camille and I transact a puzzled amusement: If our most recent grades were acceptable, what kind of kids have they turned *down*? Then Camille helps clear the dishes while I carry the leftover broccoli to the counter. We stand in the doorway of the kitchen and thank them for letting us stay there a few nights, before heading into Camille's room where we shut the door and, sitting arm to arm, speak in whispers. "You want to sleep in here tonight?" Camille asks me.

I nod, getting ready to cry again. "Yes."

We both stare at the ceiling, knowing that somewhere on this island, Norman and Rosie are probably doing the same thing.

We wake early the next morning and enter the bathroom together, mindful not to hog it from Danny and the Petermans. Addie's left us each a toothbrush—"You can have the purple one!" I tell Camille. "I'll take the orange." I squeeze a long strip of toothpaste from a fat tube onto the bristles; it feels like a wild indulgence.

"Don't use so much, or they'll take it away!" Camille says. I smile at her with a mouthful of minty foam.

When we walk out to the kitchen, looking for coffee—a habit I developed to get me through low-energy mornings in junior high, and which, according to last night's rules, is not off limits—we find Addie in the kitchen, stirring her own mug. "You're welcome to coffee, girls," she tells us, pointing to the cupboard.

"Wow," I say, finding all the shelves in the cupboard stacked with dozens of Mickey Mouse mugs. "You're big fans of Mickey, huh?"

"Well, sure we are, we don't drive our RV to Disney World every year to see nature!" She takes a sip of coffee and gets that grave look on her face again. "Girls, you should know, you'll be staying home from school today." Instantly, my stomach tightens—my face must be too scary for the little kids at their neighborhood bus stop. But Addie goes on to explain that, because it's Friday and they want to keep our case moving into next week, Ms. Davis is on her way over to help us write our emancipation affidavit.

"Can we call our sister?" I ask her.

"Right now?"

"Yeah. She remembers a lot of the stuff that happened to us. If the social worker's coming to get our story, we need our sister Cherie."

Addie rests her arm against the kitchen door frame and tells us it's fine, as long as it's a local call. For us, a kitchen telephone hanging on the wall is usually just a good weapon waiting to be dismounted to help smash cockroaches and chase other vermin around the kitchen. "My only request is that before you use the phone, please ask first," she says. "We may be expecting calls and just need to keep the line free."

Addie hands me the receiver and I approach the base to poke my fingers through the rotary holes. Each spin of the dial adds to my nervousness because I know I have to tell

Cherie what I did. As I fill her in on what's happened over the past few days, I can hear baby A.J. murmuring under her chin. "The social worker says the more details I give, the more likely the judge will emancipate me and take Cookie's guardianship of the kids away. Can you get over here?"

I wait for her to respond with annoyance, telling me she has a two-month-old to worry about and her in-laws will give her a hard time about watching him, but instead she says, "Hold on. Give me the address." By nine thirty she's on the front porch, introducing herself to Addie. *See how stable my big sister's life is?* I want to ask Addie. *Isn't she great?* Addie puts on another pot of coffee and some store-brand Oreos on a plate. I fill myself with sugar and caffeine, thrilled that Cherie and Addie are hitting it off with all this mother-to-mother talk. If we were here for any reason other than the affidavit, I'd be disappointed to see the social worker arrive and interrupt our breakfast date.

On the table between my elbows, Ms. Davis places pages and pages of lined paper with carbon sheets in between each page. She explains that there will be two copies of my affidavit—one for my file and one for the judge. She encourages us to start at the very beginning, as far back as we can recall. She instructs me what to write in the very first paragraph of the affidavit

I, Regina Marie Calcaterra, do swear that the information provided is a true description of my time with my mother, Camille Diane Calcaterra. The truthfulness of this affidavit is supported by my older sisters Cherie and Camille. Dated, November 1980.

Then Ms. Davis tells us the rest of the affidavit will be in our own words. At first we search one another's faces for memories and details . . . but it doesn't take long before it's all flowing so fast that my pen can barely keep up with our words.

July 4, 1971
Four years old

MAMA JUST GAVE us each our own watermelon slice and sent us out to the picnic table, promising she'll bring sparklers when we go into town to watch the Fourth of July parade. I take my watermelon under the redwood picnic table to see how many ants I can attract to our picnic. Mama always teases me, saying I'd prefer to live in a mud-pie mountain with ants, beetles, crickets, and lightning bugs as my neighbors over living with clean knees and fingers any day. Four white-sandled feet—Cherie's and Camille's—swing in my direction from the bench above. All their talk about this new mom and a new home distracts me from my ant collecting.

"If they adopt her, then we won't see her ever again," Camille says.

"They can't adopt her," Cherie says, "because Mom won't let them. Either way, it's bad for all of us."

"How can Mom say what happens to Regina? Regina doesn't even know Mom."

"I know, Camille."

"Mrs. G is her mom. I mean, how do you take a baby away from the person she thinks is her mom? She even calls Mrs. G 'Mama.'"

"Camille, knock it off. Mrs. G is not her mom. And Regina's not a baby—she starts kindergarten this year."

"She shouldn't even be in kindergarten yet, she's only four!"

"Well, it's that or she stays home with Mom all day!" Cherie says. "It's safer for her to be at school! Stop arguing with me, wouldya? Regina belongs with us." Cherie pauses from all her insisting to sigh. "I wish Mrs. G would adopt all of us," she says. "I wish we could stay here."

"Me too," says Camille.

"Me too, me too!"

From above, my two sisters laugh at how I've chimed into the conversation. Cherie's nicknamed both Camille and me "Me Too" because everything our older sister says, we younger sisters agree with. "You learned 'Me Too' at the Happy House," Cherie says, leaning down and brushing dirt off my face. "Do you remember the Happy House?"

I shake my head. "What's the Happy House?"

For as long as I can remember, I've lived with Mama, Papa, and their teenage daughter, Susan. I love my mama and papa, but I spend every minute I can around Susan. She reminds me of a princess in her long, flowery dresses. I like to snuggle up with Susan and play with her silky light brown hair or let my tiny fingers get tangled in her long necklaces of leather and wood.

Cherie picks me up. She and Camille take my hands, and we walk to the house to find Mama. "This is the Happy House," I tell Cherie.

"No, Gi, this is the Bubble House."

"Huh?"

When we walk inside, Mama and Susan are crying in the kitchen.

"Why you cry?"

"You're going to go live with your new mom now," Susan says through her tears.

My head tilts with confusion. "I have a mama . . . you mean I have another mama?"

"You have two mamas. And a little brother, too!" Mama says.

"His name is Norman," Cherie says.

I sort of remember calling someone else Mommy because she wanted me to call her that. I visited her house last Christmas. Mama dressed me like a princess in a crimson velvet dress, patent-leather shoes, and clean white stockings. Susan called the other mommy my Christmas Mama, because she wanted to give us Christmas presents. But I don't know why I have to see her now—you don't get gifts for the Fourth of July. "Is it Christmas Mama?"

They all start laughing until it seems like Mama might start to cry. "Yes, honey," she says. "It's your Christmas Mama."

I smile around at all of them. "I get Christmas presents?"

Susan and Mama pack for my visit with Christmas Mama. I wonder why I need so many clothes? As Mama tucks stacks of folded laundry in a suitcase, she explains that, even though it's summer, we need to pack warm clothes, too.

"Why?"

"Just in case you stay with Christmas Mama."

"Until Christmas?"

Mama stays quiet a moment. "Yes."

I move in to help them pack my bag of clothes, my dolls and stuffed animals, and my toy Baby Jesus, resting in a pile of plastic hay.

In the car, Cherie and Camille are silent. I chat away, bubbling over about Christmas Mama and hoping there will be new toys, baby dolls, and maybe even an Easy-Bake Kitchen so Mama and Susan can show me how to bake when Papa comes to pick me up from Christmas Mama's house.

Papa slows the car, then pulls into a lonely building in the middle of a three-road intersection. "This is it?" he bursts. "This is where she'll have them living?"

Susan whispers in a way that confuses me even more. "This is only a Christmas visit, Dad, remember?"

Papa snaps back. "Enough with the fairy-tale talk, Susan." His voice is starting to sound like he's choking, like a frog. "She'll figure out what's happening as soon as we leave."

"No leave," I say.

Everyone climbs out of the car, leaving Camille, Cherie, and me in the backseat while they unpack the trunk. I watch closely as Papa walks in the front door of the building and comes back out with his face all red. His neck is bulging. He looks scary. Then he yells. "This is a goddamn glue factory!" he says. I've never seen Papa so mad. "The apartment . . . is upstairs . . . from a goddamn glue factory!"

"Dad, shhh—"

"She couldn't have found an apartment in a normal complex? She had to pick a damn glue factory in the middle of all this traffic?"

He tucks in his shirt like he's trying to calm down, and he directs Mama and Susan with our luggage up the steps. Then he walks us to the side door. Papa stoops down and wraps Cherie and Camille in each arm. He hugs them with all his might, until he's crying, and he collects himself to stand over them. "Stay strong and take care of one another," he says. "Especially Regina. She needs her big sisters now more than ever." Then he turns to me, scooping me up off the ground and letting me nuzzle my head in his neck and shoulders.

"Papa, why do you look so sad?"

"You know you'll always be my princess, right?"

"I know, Papa," I tell him, cupping my hand around his neck. "And you're my king." He squeezes me against him, and Mama and Susan turn their faces away. Papa gently places me next to my sisters and tells Mama and Susan in his froggy voice that he can't go upstairs and he'll be waiting in the car.

Mama clears her throat and takes Cherie's hand, then Camille's. The three of them navigate the narrow staircase together, their shoes on the hollow steps the only noise. Susan holds on to my right hand, and I hold the wooden banister with the left. "Hey, Susan, watch!" I do what she, Cherie, and Camille have taught me to do whenever I get scared or sad—I count. "One step, two steps . . ."

When I reach the platform, I look up at Susan. Why isn't anyone skipping or smiling, or excited at all? Then a door opens. Christmas Mama is standing there.

She's thin, and her very black hair is in a tight ponytail. Her eyes have a lot of makeup like a lady on TV. Her dress is long and black with a belt around the waist and no sleeves, and when I look at her feet, she has on sandles with a little heel. She seems pretty, but something about her is spooky, too. A tall, skinny man pops up behind her. Behind him walks a big, gray, hairy dog. I hide behind Camille. The dog sits next to the man.

Cherie and Camille allow Christmas Mama to hug them. "Welcome home, girls," Christmas Mama says. Then she looks at me and points into the kitchen past a yellow Formica table with aluminum legs. She says, "Regina, I am your mother. I love you, and here is a Big Wheel."

A Big Wheel?

My mother?

I hold Susan's hand closer. Nobody here seems happy, and everyone is watching me. Like a robot on a cartoon, Christmas Mama stands there smiling, blinking, waiting for me to say something. Susan leans down and whispers, "Say thank you, Pumpkin. Look at your present."

I look at the Big Wheel bike and then down toward the floor. I start whimpering, then it's a full-fledged cry into Susan's flowing skirt. "But I don't want it," I say. "It's not Christmas." My whimpers continue until Susan grasps me tighter. Finally, I turn toward Christmas Mama. I'm afraid to look at her so I don't, but I tell her through my tears, "Thank you for my Big Wheel present."

Mama says it's time to go. She shakes Christmas Mama's hand and tells her to take care of her little gifts. After we all get fast big hugs from Mama and Susan, they hurry down the stairs and disappear.

This visit feels different than the other Christmas visit did. I want Mama and Susan back, and I start to yell for them. Christmas Mama shushes me and takes us into a room with two little beds. My cries turn into a piercing wail. "*Mama! Mama! Mama!*"

Then it lands on my right cheek: a sharp front-handed slap. My head jerks toward my left shoulder but is jolted back with a backhanded slap to my left cheek that knocks me to the floor. "Stop crying or else I'll really give you something to cry about, you little bitch!" she howls. "I'm Mom. You got that? *I'm* Mom."

No, no, no. I look at Cherie and Camille. "This is our mom," Cherie tells me. She looks sad.

"Listen to your big sister, you little whore. She's right. You came from me, see this? From *this* belly. I'm your mom."

No.

No.

No. I don't want her for my mom. "I want Papa."

"Oh, you want your father?" Christmas Mama says. "Well, he didn't want you, and it's no wonder, you goddamn little waste of skin. And he didn't want me, either, so you just shut the fuck up about any *papa*. You got that? You do not want to get me started on that man, the arrogant, self-absorbed piece of shit."

I almost cry again but Camille runs and puts her arm around my shoulders. Christmas Mama commands her and Cherie to go outside and bring up all our stuff. "I'll deal with this bastard," she says. She looks mad at me, and I want to cry again. I haven't done anything bad. Mama and Susan never yelled at me this way.

Cherie and Camille stand in the door, staring with fear in their eyes. "You two go, goddammit!" she screams. When they run for the stairs, Christmas Mama tells me that she wishes I was dead, that I should have never been born. Then she bends over and grabs my right arm to yank me upright. She slaps both my cheeks again, then slams the door and locks it behind her.

I'm locked in that room for days. I'm only allowed out for potty, baths, and to eat. If I start crying, my sisters come running in and beg me to stop. They lead me in counting. We count. They leave. I sleep. I wake, and I sit there bored. I count. I count. I cry. They come back. I count.

The room is hot, so I take my clothes off to try and get cool. I climb on top of one of the beds and open the second-floor window, waiting for a breeze. Outside that window is a view of a big building with noisy red trucks that come out. Every afternoon there's a loud, scary alarm that comes from a big yellow horn on top of the building. I stick my head out the window and look for someone to rescue me. When it's clear that no one's coming, I rest my chin in my hands and see what else is around: lots of parked cars along the tarred drive-way downstairs, a forest across the street, a traffic light, and lots of cars with families driving by. I count the cars parked downstairs, and the ones driving by, and the shiny red fire *frucks*—a word Cherie and Camille taught me. I say it a lot because every time I do, they laugh until they fall on the floor, and that makes me laugh.

Christmas Mama finally tells me I can come outside and play with my Big Wheel, as long as I stop calling her Christmas Mama. "For Chrissakes, I told you! Just call me Mom," she says. I nod.

Together my sisters carry my Big Wheel downstairs, where I can play on the sidewalk with cars whizzing by. I learn to stay quiet and just count, and this way I can stay outside all the time. When it gets really hot, I take off all my clothes and climb back on my Big Wheel, riding around in big circles to create a breeze to cool off. The glue factory workers run out and wag their fingers, stretching their necks for my mother or telling me I'm too young to play Lady Godiva. Then my sisters dash down the stairs and outside, chasing after me with my clothes in their hands.

But I guess I've shown Mom how well I can take care of myself because one day she tells me I'm going to live in Baby

Norman's bedroom. She says she's tired from all the work she has to do with three messy girls living in her house now, and someone needs to take care of her little prince. Mom tells me I'll need to clean Norman's diaper and give him baths and teach him how to go potty like I learned. If he goes in his diaper it's my fault, so I make sure he lives on the potty. When he stands up and tries to run away with no pants on, I chase him down the hall and lure him back with the toys Mom got him at the thrift shop. Mom teaches me how to wash and wring out his cloth diapers in the tub. "You never know, I might need them again," she says.

We all have chores. Cherie and Camille have to cook and do the dishes. I have to dust and clean the bathroom. All of us take turns caring for Baby Norman.

At night, Mom's husband, also named Norman, comes home and stumbles up the stairs in the dark. If he's with Mom and they're happy, they go to sleep and the house is all quiet. But if Norman gets mad, he beats Mom up, and then we have to be really, really good. If we don't clean the house or change Little Norm's diaper the right way, she beats us just like Big Norman beats her.

After a few weeks here my sisters stop playing with each other. They don't even talk anymore, and nobody laughs together. If dinner's not ready or a dish is still wet, Mom wants to know whether it's Cherie or Camille who should get the beating. My sisters point their fingers at each other, and Mom stands with her hands on her hips, considering which one of them she'd like to hurt. Cherie and Camille don't try to cheer me up anymore, and when I cry, they yell at me. "Shut up!" they say. "Do you want Mom to beat you again?" It's every kid for herself, except for Little Norman. Mom loves Little Norman.

This isn't my family anymore—they're like strange, scary ghosts. I used to love Cherie and Camille more than anyone in the world, but in Mom's house they're different people. I'd rather be by myself than with them, so when Mom and Big Norman are out one night, I decide I don't want to live with all the sad people anymore. I sneak out the door, down the thirty-six steps. I run across the street and deep into the woods. I hide. I stay hiding, even when I hear the voices of Cherie and Camille calling out for me. Then Mom and Big Norman join them, and I close my eyes. I'm never coming out. They keep calling and calling, but I know they'll never find me. I drift off to sleep under a pile of leaves . . . until . . . do I hear the sound of Susan's voice calling for me?

"Little pumpkin! Fairy princess!"

I hear her, again and again. I jump up. Susan's come to get me to bring me home! I just know it. I dash out of the brush and run toward her voice, racing into her arms. I hear Cherie and Camille yell, "She was in the woods, we found her!" Susan carries me back toward the street where I see Papa's car is parked . . . oh, I knew they'd come back for me! But she doesn't stop at the car to put me inside. Instead she walks past it, carrying me toward the glue factory. "No!" I scream.

She carries me into the hallway up the steps, stopping at the platform where Mom is standing. "I'm so happy you're okay!" Mom says, smiling at Susan. "After a nice bath I'll give her some oatmeal and put her to bed." She looks at me adoringly and says, "You could have gotten attacked by a wild dog—or even worse, hit by a car, you silly girl. You scared all of us!" Susan kisses me good-bye, again, and walks down-stairs. I sob as she closes the outside door behind her.

Mom stands there with the phony smile on her face. Then it turns mean. "Cherie, are they gone?"

Cherie stands by the window and nods. I beg her, "No!" Doesn't my big sister know what will happen now?

In an instant Mom turns her energy toward me, grabbing me by my hair and slamming me to the ground. It feels like my hair is being pulled all the way out of my head, and the skin on the top of my head is being ripped open. I try to put my arms in front of my face, but she punches them down and grabs me around my waist. Then she picks me up and throws me into the wall, denting it. As I slide down to the floor and land on my back, she grabs my right arm and leg and flips me over on my stomach. Then she kicks my legs, back, and stomach until I'm all weak and my head turns heavy. There's a loud buzzing sound ringing from my brain. All I can see is white, and I can't fight back or move my body anymore.

When I awake, I'm naked. I try to sit up, but my arms can't cooperate. I raise my head to see why I can't move, and I notice my arms are clasped together on my side and tied to the radiator. My legs are bound together above my ankles and tied to the rails underneath my bed. When I see this, I have to rest my neck. My brain feels like it's swollen. I close my eyes.

I feel something cold. When I open my eyes again, Camille is holding a rag that feels like it has ice inside. "Where's Susan?"

"Gi, Susan is only our foster sister. We don't live with her anymore."

"Can we go back?"

"No." Then she whispers, "Not unless the police find out

that Mom hurts us." Camille tells me, still in a whisper, that while Mom was tying me up, she made my sisters take all my clothes out of the room so I couldn't run away again. "This is what happens when you don't listen to Mom," she says. Now I want to spit in Camille's face, but I can't lift my head.

After that, Big Norman tells Mom that having a baby was enough, he didn't bargain for three little girls and their crazy business, too. He starts spending more time away from the house, and one morning Mom's crying at the kitchen table, smoking a cigarette, saying Big Norman left her for good.

She says she needs more time to herself and I'll start kindergarten in a few days, even though I'm only four. My birthday falls in November, a few days before the cutoff, so she says I'll probably be the youngest in my class. She also tells me that I have to use her last name when I go to school because I don't have a daddy like Norman does. "Because you're a bastard, remember?" she says. "Your daddy didn't want you. And I can't blame him. You're a smug little snot, just like him." Cherie overhears Mom saying this, and later she tells me not to worry about having the same last name as Mom—Cherie has the same one, too, and that makes me feel better. I like sharing a name with Cherie. "Cherie, where's my daddy?" I ask her.

Her only answer is this: "I think he's at the Happy House."

Where *is* the Happy House? "Can we go there?"

"Well, maybe someday when you're bigger we can find it again."

I want to find the Happy House now.

Because my school day is shorter than Cherie's and Camille's, I have to stay in the school library until they're ready to walk me home. That seems okay because I flip through books all afternoon, but it doesn't work so well when my sisters start getting held up in detention all the time. They miss school to take care of Norman, and they're not turning in their homework, and they said that it doesn't help that the man who's been sneaking in our house at night likes Mom more than his wife, who happens to be a teacher at our school. When they're in detention and I stay too long at the library and can't watch Norman, my sisters realize we're all in danger of Mom's beatings. They tell me I have to walk home alone, as long as I cross with the crossing guard and walk along the storefronts.

The next fall, Mom meets a new man named Vito, who always wears a black suit and a thick belt around his waist that we're not allowed to touch. Vito is nice to us, way nicer than Big Norman, but the two friends who are always with him are weird. They're really quiet, and they're always wearing sunglasses—even at night. I know this because when Vito sleeps in Mom's room, his friends sit down in the car and wait for him so he always has a ride somewhere.

Mom begins to stay out with Vito all the time, and we love to play house without her. When the snow melts from winter, we collect our change and bundle Norman up and take a long walk to the Saint James General Store, where we treat ourselves to apple, grape, and watermelon swirled candy sticks and candy necklaces.

Then on the way to the local King Kullen supermarket we drop Norman off at home, securing him in a room by himself so we can go shopping with Mom's food stamps. Camille and Cherie take two different carts, and I stand on the outside edge of Cherie's with my feet on the bottom rail, adding up the cost of the food items as they're placed in the cart to make sure we have enough food stamps to cover our groceries. When we bag our food at the cash register, my job is to hide an extra stash of bags in our cart. Then Cherie tells the cashier we have to go find our sister, and she wheels me back into the store to look for Camille, who takes the contents of her cart and stuffs it all in my bags when no one's looking. Camille's cart is always better—she grabs Fluffernutter, peanut butter, frozen jelly donuts, and lots of cake mixes. Then we zip out the door with our stash.

We prefer to be left alone. We watch *Sesame Street, The Electric Company,* and *The Flintstones* without any interruption from my mom's boring shows like *Guiding Light* and *As the World Turns.* When it's cold or raining outside, we take out the games that Mom gets from the Salvation Army for Cherie and Camille. We play five hundred rummy, chess, checkers, Connect Four, and Battleship. We take turns feeding Norman and teaching him words for the objects around the apartment. *Couch,* we tell him. *Television. Lightbulb.* Of course, we also continue his potty training.

When spring breaks, Mom's away even more, so I go out to the side yard to make mud pies and chase worms and ants. We miss school more days than we attend, which finally brings a truant officer to our door. Then we start attending again, for now.

When the weather heats up, Mom starts coming home more. She's always groaning that her back hurts. "You'd better get prepared," she says. "You'll have a new little brother or sister by Halloween."

Mom says she and Vito want to plan a vacation together, so she begins working across the street at the deli. On weekends she brings me to stock the freezers. Her tummy is too big for her to climb around, but I'm small enough to crawl on the ground and stack juices, milk, and sodas on the bottom shelves. Then I stick around and clean the counters and mop the floor before the deli opens.

After school lets out in June, Cherie, Camille, and I put Norman in his walker and walk two whole miles to our favorite spot: Cordwood Beach. We stroll past homes that look like palaces with big wrought-iron gates, finally arriving at the beach. On sunny days it's filled with kids—splashing around, building sand castles, and screaming when they see a horseshoe crab or a jellyfish. We spatter in the sand and water with them, taking breaks to climb the remains of an old brick house that looks like a castle and jumping off the floating dock. Even on gray days, we'd prefer to get caught in the wind and rain than stay home bored in the glue factory. We squeal, digging in the wet sand for clams with our hands and feet, hunting out mussel beds, and loading up our arms and pockets. On the way home we pick onion grass for a special treat at dinner.

Right after I begin the first grade, our baby sister is born. We're all thrilled to have a baby girl in the house. Roseanne doesn't look like any of us, with her pale skin and blond hair—just like Vito has.

Sometimes I like to imagine that my daddy has dark brown hair, just like mine.

For Rosie's baptism at Saint Philip and James, we dress Rosie in a long white gown. Vito looks funny in his dark suit and sunglasses, and his two friends stay by his side during the ceremony—even for the photos. After Rosie's christening, we get to take care of her ourselves while Vito takes Mom on a celebration "baby trip" to Lake Havasu, Arizona. It's Mom's first plane ride. When they come back, Mom tells us she and Vito had a great time on his "going away" trip but that he won't be seeing us. "Vito had to go live somewhere else for a while," she says.

It doesn't take long before Mom disappears, too. She begins to spend more time away at night, and when she returns from her binges, she brings home a man or a hangover . . . or both. We learn to stay out of her way, because especially when she's sad or not feeling well, we'll catch a serious licking. As men come into our home, though, they always comment on what pretty little girls she has. We look down and walk away: If only they knew the trouble their compliments cause. When the men leave, Mom makes sure we all know that we're just sluts and whores, and Norman is her prince. "You think you're so pretty?" she says when her visitors leave. "Get over here. You won't be pretty when I'm done with you."

Months after Rosie arrives, our mom doesn't look like our mom anymore. She locks us in her room and cries that, at age thirty, her old go-go dancer body is gone forever and all the stress of raising kids is making her face lined and puffy. "My life amounts to nothing, and it's all because of you kids!" she screams. As her unhappiness worsens, so does her drinking; and as her drinking increases, so does her weight. It's Cherie, Camille, or me who take a beating during these tirades. And we never allow her near Norm or Rosie, but Mom's usually too tired to fuss with the baby anyway.

We teach Rosie to talk and walk and play games, and we shower her with beautiful expressions of love like *mia bambina amore* and *je t'aime*. We don't know how they're so familiar to us, but we use them a hundred times a day.

All our fawning over Rosie frees Mom up even more, but

instead of bringing men home, she's started bringing in animals to try and cheer herself up. We tiptoe around, cautioning
Rosie to avoid the monkeys, turtles, and chickens that Mom
attempts to hide from the landlord. The three squirrel monkeys are kept in a cage, and Mom reminds us to put on gloves
to feed them—otherwise they'll eat our fingers as appetizers.
Unfortunately, our yellow dishwashing gloves aren't exactly
appropriate for primate-caretaking: One of the monkeys bites
off a rubber fingertip and chokes to death, and Mom leads us
in an emotional burial service in the side yard. We clean up
poop from the donkey that lives up on the tar roof, where we
sometimes shower with the hose since we can't use the tub—
it's the home for our land turtles. They're our favorite. When
any of us gets grounded in our rooms, we take a couple turtles
out of the tub and line up bits of food to pit them against each
other in a turtle race. But since we only have one bathtub and
need it for five baths and clothes washing, the turtles finally
make a mystery escape in the middle of the night.

The chickens only last until the landlord finds out about
them. I envy all these animals for their easy exits from our
mother's domain. Pepper, Mom's German shepherd mix,
is the only creature in this house who's always happy and
loving. We take him to the school yard to run around for exercise, or on long walks past the local farms. Occasionally we
stage a disaster scene as though he's run loose into the fields,
and while we go "looking" for him, we snatch corn and potatoes for our dinner.

By December of my second-grade year, Mom has gone
roaming again. The glue factory workers, crossing guards,
and firemen are suspicious. In fact, sometimes we see a parked

police car outside, and Cherie says we need to be careful because they're watching us.

WE ARE READY for the cops when they come up the stairs. We
realize they caught Norman wandering outside in the dark,
at night, in the cold, and that they'll be the ones to bring him
back to us. We know they are watching and waiting to catch
us doing something wrong, and Norman innocently gave
them a tip. The two cops come in and grab all five of us, still
in our pajamas. They put Norm in the front between them
and all us girls in the back, with Rosie on Cherie's lap. They
ask us to stay silent, but we are five kids in a police car without
our mother, and we don't know where we are being taken. We
aren't silent. We are children.

It's mid-December and they've decided to put the four of
us older kids in a home together so we're not separated for the
holidays—but Rosie, just a year old now, is going to another
house.

The foster family sets up four sleeping bags for us on the
living room floor. The parents and their two teenage boys
force us to lie in the sleeping bags all night and day, never
moving or complaining. If we do, they close the bag around
us by zipping it up over our heads, and they beat us while
we're inside of it. If we cry too loudly, the punishment turns
even worse. One day the foster mom grabs me by the head
and cuts off my long curls with a giant pair of scissors. When
the social worker checks on us and asks what happened, she
answers that I got gum all stuck in my hair so she had to cut
it out. I haven't chewed gum since the last time my sisters and
I went to the Saint James General Store.

One day a package of Yodels cakes goes missing. The boys force me to open my mouth so they can smell my breath, and they agree that I'm the Yodels thief. I'm beaten again, this time by them and their mom, while Cherie, Camille, and Norman are forced to watch and stay silent. If we try to defend one another, the kid getting the beating will only get it worse.

One night, while I'm sleeping, I'm suddenly cold—somehow I've gotten out of my sleeping bag. I wake to the realization that my pajama bottoms have been removed and the two boys are looking at my private parts. I begin screaming, but by then Cherie and Camille are nowhere in sight, and Norman—despite the boys' threats—starts kicking them and screaming for them to leave me alone. As they drag me into their room, they yell to Norman to shut up, telling him they'll lock him outside in the freezing cold all night like they just did to my sisters. I'm alone with no one to help me. I watch the slice of light from the hallway disappear as they close their bedroom door, trapping me alone with them inside. I begin counting.

By NOW I understand what foster care means. Susan, Mama, and Papa weren't my real family—they were people who wanted to give us a nice home after the cops found out Mom hadn't been taking decent care of us. Now, after the bad home, the five of us are separated into three different foster families. To me, being a foster kid is a little bit like being a dog: You have no control over the kind of family who will take you. Even if you're treated badly, it's possible no one will ever find out the truth and come rescue you.

Rosie stays where she was originally placed, and Camille and Cherie are placed with a family named the O'Malleys.

Norm and I move to the Tenleys' in a town called Dix Hills, with little houses on tiny lawns, that's thirty minutes from where we used to live. The Tenleys' house is all wood paneling, and Mr. Tenley's hair matches the gray button-down shirt he wears to work every day. Right away Mrs. Tenley gets into an argument with the social worker—"Someone needs to buy these kids some clothes!" she says, but she insists she'll save the receipts and would like the county to reimburse her for the purchases.

When the social worker introduces me, she informs the Tenleys that I'm the troublemaker and Norm is an angel, and that they'll have to keep an extra eye on me. The Tenleys relay this information to my new teacher, who introduces me to my second-grade class on my first day of school, right after Christmas break. "Class, this is our new student. Her name is Regina, and she may not be here for very long—she's a foster child." I look at her, shaking my head. She's just ruined any chance I might have had of getting invited to my classmates' birthday parties. "We'll welcome her for the time she's here, and she'll start in the lowest reading and math groups."

That's where I cut her off. "But I don't belong in the low groups," I insist. "At my old school I was in the highest group."

After a week, she sees I was right and I'm placed in the advanced class. The kids at school don't know what to say to a foster kid, so I spend most of my free time in the bedroom reading my favorite Judy Blume book, *Are You There God? It's Me, Margaret.* That, and every library book with Amelia Earheart I can get my hands on.

I finish second grade while at the Tenleys' and only see my sisters one day every other month when social services coordinates a visit between both pairs of foster parents. By the time I see them in late August, Rosie's moved in with them. She'd been losing weight and getting extremely ill because she refused to eat. She'd also been hospitalized with dehydration. I overhear her foster mom tell Mrs. Tenley that the doctors said Rosie was suffering from Failure to Thrive, a condition that makes it difficult for her to absorb nutrition because, emotionally, she's too upset about being separated from her family. The social workers hope Cherie and Camille can comfort her and nurse her back to health. They said they hope that with the love of her older sisters, she'll gain weight fast.

Mr. Tenley's always talking about Walter Conkrite, his favorite newsman, whom he refers to as the "most trusted man in America." He never lets Norm or me watch anything except the evening news, and I sit on the edge of the couch shifting my weight, staring blankly at the TV set.

One night, after I've started the third grade, Mr. Tenley calls me into the living room. "Nah," I tell him. "That's okay, I'm busy with homework." That's when he comes into my room, picks me up, and carries me down the hall, planting me in front of their wood-encased television set. "This is an historic moment," he says. "President Ford is pardoning Richard Nixon. Pay attention. You will always remember this."

There sits the president, looking friendly but serious, wearing a black suit behind a desk with a grand window behind him:

I have come to a decision which I felt I should tell you and all of my fellow American citizens . . . I have promised to uphold the Constitution, to do what is

right as God gives me to see the right, and to do the
very best that I can for America.

I feel that Richard Nixon and his loved ones have
suffered enough . . . Now, therefore, I, Gerald R. Ford
. . . have granted . . . a full, free, and absolute pardon
unto Richard Nixon for all.

This Thanksgiving is the first time I see Mom since last December when the cops found Norman roaming the streets. Mr. Tenley drives us to Saint James, and I make him pinky-promise he'll pick us up after dinner.

Mom tells me she won a visit with Norm and me at her fair hearing. She talks all about a new guy named Karl and how she's planning to buy a house in Smithtown so we can all live together again. I imagine having earplugs in my ears, until I'm helping her prepare dinner and she starts asking me about Master Bate.

"Master Bate?" Maybe she means Mr. Bate? But none of my foster fathers were named Mr. Bate. None of my teachers are named Mr. Bate. I don't know any Mr. Bate! Mom asks me why I've been touching Mr. Bate and my privates at night, and when I stare at her in confusion, she tells me to stop with Mr. Bating.

"Mrs. Tenley told the social worker, Regina. And the social worker told me. You're only nine—that's too young to touch yourself down there. It's a dirty thing for a little girl to do."

I nod my head, but I'm still lost. The only time I touch myself down there is when I hold my privates to protect them from ever being hurt again like in my last foster home.

6

Houses of Sand

March 1974 to 1977

IT SEEMS LIKE every few months we get a new social worker, so it's not surprising when a new lady shows up to get Norm and me. While I'm helping her load our bags into her trunk, Mrs. Tenley stands at the front door. She calls behind me, "Regina, it's not spring quite yet! Come put on your coat." But Mrs. Tenley told me that all my sisters and I are about to be reunited in a new home, and the anticipation of this has made me fearless against the cold . . . and pretty much everything.

As I whiz past Mrs. Tenley with the last of our things, she says, "Regina, the way you move, you seem like you can't wait to leave here."

I look up at her. "It's not that," I say. "I just can't wait to see my sisters."

In the backseat I hold my newest plastic Jesus figurine while Norman plays silently with a G.I. Joe. We stay quiet even as the social worker pulls into the smooth paved driveway with fresh-cut grass of a stunning colonial-style house with a double door entrance, large brass knockers, and two story-high columns flanking the front door.

"What are we doing here?" I ask the social worker from the backseat.

"This is the address your mother gave me."

Norm and I look quizzically at each other. "You might wanna check that again."

"Can you help me get your bags out of the trunk, please?"

I sit still in the backseat for another second. Then my fear of embarrassment to present my garbage bags of luggage in front of this magnificent home propels my plea: "The address—please check it again. They're going to tell us we have the wrong place." Right then, the door opens.

Standing in the entrance is my mother.

I take in her face, then her outfit. She's wearing a floral shirt and gauchos—with *pleats*. Her hair's been let down from its messy ponytail and colored a single shade of pure red, curled into a careful lilt at her chin. It would have taken an actual hairbrush to create such poofy, neat waves. I remember her telling me when we lived above the glue factory that the only good thing I got from my father is my hair, but for the first time ever, hers actually looks pretty, too. And she's thinner than I remember. Could this really be the same monster who lived with us in Saint James?

Anxiety from my confusion begins to rise in me until an unassuming, tall man appears in the doorway. From the first moment, I can sense that he's gentle. His hair starts at one temple and is combed neatly across the front of his forehead and pasted down to the other side. Thin arms fall from a short-sleeved button-down shirt, and polyester pants are fastened around his belly button with a brown leather belt. Black-rimmed glasses frame his face. Given our mother's romantic history, I'm cautious to get my hopes up about him. I slump back in my seat and mumble to Norm: "Guess that's the new guy."

As they exchange a few seemingly polite words with the social worker, Norm and I file quietly out of the car. When our mother's eyes scan to us, she fixes a smile on her face, like the mom in a Hamburger Helper commercial: *Oh, you silly, adorable kids.* The man extends his hand to me when we reach the porch. "I'm Karl," he says. "Pleased to meet you."

"You too," I tell him. "Nice house."

"Well, after I passed the real estate exam," Mom interrupts, "I worked fast to close this deal. You should've seen the pack of Stepford wives lined up the block, licking their chops when I pulled the Century 21 sign out of the ground. *Inside deal*, see. That's what happens when you have the right connections."

Mom acts as though we've all enjoyed a cheerfully prepared breakfast of French toast, eggs, and bacon together every day for the past year and a half as she shows Norm and me through the house. *What do you think of the boyfriend?* I'm dying to whisper to my brother. Instead, I ask the more urgent question: "Where are Cherie and Camille?"

"The bus should be dropping them off from the middle

school any minute. And don't even ask—you're already registered in third grade at Branch Brook Elementary. I took care of everything." Her voice echoes through the expansive foyer when she says, "By the way, you two can thank Camille for your bedrooms. She helped pay for the house."

"Camille?" I ask her. "How?"

"With her broken legs. Don't you remember the story? She got run over when she was two. The driver put money in a trust fund for her to use when she grew up."

We start up the grand wooden stairs, following behind her. "So where is the trust fund money now?"

"You're standing in it, darling."

Darling? Getting sober turned her into a different person!

"I talked the trust's lawyer into handing over the cash because I told him—get this—that the whole point of buying this house is to raise Camille and her siblings in a safe environment. Smart Cookie, right?" Aha . . . the old Cookie Calcaterra peeks through the Beaver Cleaver facade. "Come on outside, I'll show you the swimming pool."

Norm and I follow her in silence, ogling at the inground pool with an awkward fusion of excitement and hesitation. I can't predict how likely it is that we'll even live in this house through the summer to enjoy swimming in it.

"You want to know the best part?"

We look up at her.

"I own the house with the bank. I don't have to pay *rent* anymore."

The part of me that loves this house cooperates easily with my mother's happy-family charade. While she's at work in the afternoons, Cherie, Camille, and I make dinner and then help Norm with his homework. At dinnertime Karl sits at the head of our rectangular kitchen table, coaching us to say *please* and *thank you* and indulging our requests for stories about his work as an engineer at Grumman Aerospace. "Don't ask Karl too many questions," Mom chides. "His work is top secret."

"It's not that secret, Cookie," he says. "It's good for them to learn this stuff." Then he turns to us and says, "Right now we're building a military aircraft that America needs to keep us safe from the Communists in Russia. We're in a Cold War, see. They can attack us with their nukes any time so we need to be prepared."

Karl thinks the reason I listen in awe is because his stories are so interesting, but really I just can't get enough of having his attention. Sometimes I think of asking Mom and Karl, "Say, how'd you two meet anyway?" but it's a more pleasant fantasy for all of us to make like they've been together all along. Mom is much calmer these days—she says it's because Karl's such a good father to her kids, but Cherie and Camille say her maternal demeanor is thanks to the fact she's not drinking anymore and that her doctor has her on the right medication. "Doctor?" I ask. "Is Mom sick?"

Cherie and Camille exchange a sarcastic glance. "She's sick all right," Camille says. "Sick in the head."

The possibility that Cookie's been faking us out makes me uneasy, like the day she showed me the swimming pool out back. "You know what they say," Camille says. "If it seems too good to be true . . . then it probably is."

At night, Mom and Karl watch TV in the family room or Mom makes real estate phone calls in the kitchen while Karl reads the paper in the recliner. Meanwhile, Cherie, Camille, and I all help one another put Rosie, who's already two, to bed in her crib that's positioned against the wall in my bedroom. Then I settle in for long talks in Cherie and Camille's bedroom and help them tape *Teen Beat* photos of David Cassidy and Leif Garrett on their walls. Sometimes we invite Norman to come in, under the condition he'll agree to put on purple socks so he can be my Donny Osmond as I play Marie. Cherie and Camille join in singing and dancing, and the four of us carry on just like the old days at Cordwood Beach . . . together.

I notice that not having been able to rely on Cherie and Camille at the Tenleys' house brought out a grown-up side to me, and sometimes I find myself still acting like a mom to Norm . . . and even though my brother's the only person in the whole house who doesn't have to share a bedroom, he still appears mindful that it's his sisters who taught him survival. In an effort to make up for the year we lost, the five of us do everything together. After school we take walks to Branch Brook Elementary's playground and spend hours swaying gently on the swings and talking, or squealing as we balance the weight of all five of us between both sides of the seesaw. On cold or rainy days we take advantage of the fact that Mom has yet to find enough abandoned furniture to fill our house. We set up our radio inside what Mom calls "the great room"—our step-down giant living room with floor-to-ceiling mirrors—and dance like maniacs as the songs on Casey Kasem's Top 40 countdown echo off the hardwood floor. When Frankie Valli's "Swearin' to God" comes on, we crowd around the radio to listen carefully to all the words and scribble them down. Mom always wants to be the first person she knows to memorize all the lyrics to the new Four Seasons songs. She says she has a special connection to them from her time as a go-go dancer when they were just an up-

and-coming band from New Jersey playing the Long Island club circuit.

One day she arrives home from work and nonchalantly invites us out to the front lawn to help her unload the car, where we find three bikes, and a new Big Wheel for Norm, in the front yard. "Mom, wow!" we exclaim, instantly taking off for the park on our new rides. We whiz past Karl, who's standing there, quietly beaming with his hands in his pockets. I shout over my shoulder, "Karl, thanks!"

He shouts back: "You got it, kiddo!"

This is when Mom suddenly gets wrapped up planning a new project: having a portrait taken of her with her five kids. As a hobby, she's started sewing dresses for all of us, having purchased cotton fabric with raised crushed velvet in yellow, pink, and blue. She sits in concentration at her sewing machine, creating tea-length dresses with scooped necks and dome sleeves. She grows so possessed by the endeavor that when she hears us walking past where her sewing machine's set up in the dining room, hints of the old Cookie begin to reveal themselves. "Stay the hell outta there!" she shouts. This is my cue to begin spending my afternoons in the school library. That old familiar undercurrent of uncertainty is back.

Mom insists that Cherie's and Camille's hair remain straight and long like Marcia and Jan Brady, while my natural waves are styled in a trendy shag—short at the ears, long in the back. Mom cuts Norman's hair to highlight his intense almond-shaped eyes and chiseled cheekbones. Rosie's wispy blond locks are always in little pigtails. We keep taking bets on when she'll grow out of her blond hair, but so far she hasn't. "She'll always be a blonde," Mom says, lowering her voice in a way that makes it hard to decipher between melancholy and bitterness: "Just like her daddy."

Karl's still at work when the photographer shows up. "Do we need to wait for your husband?" the woman asks.

Mom's only answer is this: "He's not my husband."

This simple phrase is the pin in my balloon, a careless reminder: We're not a normal family at all. Suddenly I'm nauseated as Mom commands us into position on a bench by the great room's shiny wooden stairs: "Look happy, kids!"

When the photographer leaves, Mom turns as dramatic as a soap opera star, gushing about her excitement to have a family photo to add to the last one—the one taken three years ago when we were all wearing our Lake Havasu T-shirts. I know this is another excuse for her to mention Vito.

"Where is Vito anyway?" I ask her.

"He's locked up," Mom says. "His enemies figured him out." She tells us Vito's garbage business was so good that he didn't have to share his routes with anyone else, which pissed off other garbage men, who told the FBI on him. Then he went to jail. Mom brags that Rosie's daddy is famous because he was the boss of the garbage men. "Before they put him away," she says, "he was in all the newspapers." There's a faraway twinkle in her eye when she says, "He always reminded me of a husky Robert Redford." When we ask her if the cops tried to put her in jail with Vito, she rolls her eyes and laughs. "God no. Everybody knows girlfriends and kids are always left alone—we're protected by the Mothers and Fathers Italian Association."

Later that night, Camille asks me, "You know what the Mothers and Fathers Italian Association stands for?"

I shake my head.

"Think about what the first letters spell out: M-A-F-I-A."

"*Ohhhhh . . .*"

The next day I ask Mom out of curiosity: "How long will Vito be in jail?"

"Jesus, Regina, I don't know. Stop asking questions," she says. Then she takes a long drag off her Virginia Slim. "Maybe another two years—what will Rosie be, five? But it doesn't matter anyway," she says, using her bare ring finger to scratch her cheek. "Karl is Rosie's daddy now."

WHEN OUR FAMILY portrait arrives in the mail, Mom flings it on the kitchen table. "Look at this," she says. "All that work I did—for a bunch of fucking clowns." When she adds "What a goddamn disgrace," it's impossible to tell whether she's referring to the photo or her life.

In it we're lined up in two rows, Cherie, Camille, and Rosie in the front and Norm and me kneeling on a bench behind them. The only one smiling is Norm. Cherie's arms are straight out, holding a hysterical Rosie like she has a dirty diaper, and Camille is looking over at the two of them as if she just sensed it. "And look at Regina," Mom says. "Could you *pretend* to listen to me for once?" I didn't bother to smile in the picture; I never do. My haircut is boyish and my gapped front teeth look like mini Tic Tacs screwed into my gums. My expression shows an intolerance to participating in a picture meant to capture this facade. I know that, just as fast as the photographer's flash, soon this will all be gone.

While Mom and Karl are working overtime trying to keep our home, we get to spend more time alone, in this big house, entertaining ourselves. So we bake. We bake muffins, bread, rolls, cakes, and cupcakes. And when we can't bake because the pilot light is out, Cherie leans her head into the oven with a lit match, while Camille turns the gas on. Luckily it's almost summer when Cherie's eyebrows, lashes, and hair are singed, so we stop baking and move on to more outdoorsy hobbies. We dive into the green pool water and scrawl our names on the algae-covered walls.

Regina Marie Calcaterra, I write.

Regina + Donny Osmond

Mrs. Regina Osmond

All the letter *O*'s are formed in the shape of hearts.

We swim to the bottom of the pool in search of treasures sitting on the floor, waiting like shipwrecks for someone to discover them.

NORM AND I arrive home one afternoon in June to find a padlock and tape barricading the front door. All of our stuff is piled on the lawn. "Oh no," I tell Norm. "Mom and Karl must've had a fight!" When we run around back to try to get in, Cherie's fishing our inner tubes out of the pool. She sees us and rests the net on the ground . . . signaling she's about to share bad news.

"What's going on?" I ask her.

"She forgot to pay the bank," she says.

I slump down and sit at the edge of the pool, somehow having known this was coming. For almost a year I'd managed to convince myself that this life was really ours. But just like that, it all went up in smoke. I should've known better than ever to count on Cookie Calcaterra.

Mom finds a house a few blocks away on Terry Road so we can stay in the same school, but Karl never shows up.

"Don't look so fucking miserable, you little whores," she tells us, swigging from a can of Budweiser as we struggle through the front door of our new house, heaving Hefty bags. "It was good while it lasted."

It's not long before she's fired from Century 21, and she starts spending her days at the bars again. If she comes home to Rosie crying or to a cold dinner on the table, or a front yard that hasn't been properly cut with our dull scissors, then the drinking turns into beatings. The new house gets broken in by my body as it makes dents and holes through the paneling and Sheetrock walls. I avoid her because I never know when she'll feel like grabbing me by the back of the head and slamming my face into the table, causing relentless nosebleeds. I begin to run away again, hiding in the woods near my school or up in trees where no one can find me. Sometimes I disappear overnight, and at lunchtime the next day I tell my teacher I'm walking home for lunch. Then I head straight for the woods to search out safer hiding spaces. When I find them, I stash books wrapped in plastic bags there for me to read when I arrive later.

When I've finished a book faster than I'd anticipated, I pass the time spelling *antidisestablishmentarianism*, the longest word in the dictionary. My goal is to get all the letters in under seven seconds. Then I shorten it to six seconds, then five, and when I conquer that, my mind begins to ponder how else I can keep it busy.

Every few weeks Mom brings my siblings and me with her to her mandated psychiatrist visit. When we were in foster care, she spent time in what she called the loony bin—Pilgrim State Hospital. They only discharged her on account that she was good about taking what she calls her "happy pills," and because she agreed to fulfill regular visits with a psychiatrist that would include a few visits with us kids. Before we walked into his office for the first time, Mom bent down and wrapped her hand around my arm so tight her fingernails dug tiny pink half-moons into my skin. "So help me Christ, if you blow it, Regina . . . He reads body language for a living. Lie good."

"About what?"

"You know about what—about the little tiffs you and I have sometimes." She leans in so I'm breathing the cigarettes from her breath. "Or else, you know, Regina. You know what will happen next."

I knew: The state would take us away again. I sit quietly in the psychiatrist's office, looking at my hand against the blue canvas couch and insisting with my nods and smiles that life with Cookie Calcaterra is a day at the beach. The psychiatrist seems to watch me closer than he does my siblings, and I know he knows I'm lying.

People look but don't see, why?
People hear but don't listen, why?
People touch, but don't feel, why?

After I write a poem titled "Why?" my fourth-grade teacher, Ms. Muse, suddenly seems to take a special liking to me. She asks me to read it to the class and then invites the other teachers from our corridor to hear me recite it a second, third, and fourth time. She begins to ask me, when the other kids are busy, "How are things at home, Regina?" The day I tell her I'm moving, I'm stunned when her eyes suddenly fill with tears. "Promise me you'll never forget that you're special, Regina."

Special? I usually get *dirty, ugly, poor, bastard, gross, nasty, slut, rag doll,* and *whore* . . . but never *special.* Ms. Muse continues, telling me I need to always make sure I have a library card, that reading will help me wherever I end up. "Stay smart, stay sharp, and never, ever stop reading," she whispers in my ear. She hugs me so tight I think I might cry, too.

"THE MORE EAST you go in the cold months," Mom tells us, "the cheaper rents are." As we drive near the shore, I notice construction workers securing the bulkheads to protect the beaches from another harsh winter. I try to imagine the bungalows we pass in Sound Beach bursting in summer with families, block parties, and barbecues . . . but when Mom finally moves us into a place in Rocky Point, it reminds me of a camp's dark bunkhouse. The kitchen is a tiny galley with a two-burner stove and the furniture is broken and cushionless. I can see through the worn wooden floor planks to the dirt and weeds below.

Mom leaves for a few weeks, telling us she's "going to get warmed up by the Red Devil." We know the Red Devil because he's spent the night here before—he's a pale, freckled, lanky guy with a long red goatee that comes to a sharp point.

"Good, go," Cherie says quietly when the front door slams behind Cookie. "We like our freedom without you anyway."

"Yeah," I join in. "And don't bring that crusty scruff back with you, either." Cherie and Camille burst out laughing.

In the house, the only source of heat comes from the semiwarm air that's pushing through one floor grate in the hall that adjoins the bathroom to the one bedroom. From the house's front windows we watch icy snow fill the road, wondering how we'll get a ride to school—our only source of meals and warmth—when our bus driver inevitably gives up on attempting our narrow hill.

In between alternating as caretakers for Rosie, now age four, we go digging in enclosed steel bins outside the Salvation Army and St. Vincent de Paul charities for items to stuff between the floor planks, insulating us from the wind and door drafts, and any semblance of towels or blankets to pile on top of us when we sleep.

"Snorkels!" Camille hollers from inside one of the bins.

Cherie snorts. "Get real, it's winter. What the heck will we do with snorkels?"

"No, no, look," she says, climbing out with her arms full. "They're puffy coats with hoods that cover everything but your eyes." Camille is our aspiring fashion designer, so we take her word that such ridiculous-looking coats could be named after underwater face snorkels.

We wear the snorkels home with newfound mismatched gloves, hats, and scarves, while we stuff our pockets and pillowcases with undershirts, towels, sheets, washcloths, and socks.

When the snowdrifts eventually grow taller than us, we tunnel a hole through the snow to the street, then walk twenty minutes in the drifts to get to Route 25 where our bus driver said she'd pick us up for school. Some days, though, the weather is so bad that we don't even bother. At home, we wear our snorkels all day with our other findings piled on top of us for warmth. At nightfall I unlatch the exhaust hose on the back of the washroom's clothes dryer, then position the dryer so that the back of it points toward the center of the room. After I make sure the dryer door is closed so Rosie can't crawl inside, I press the on button. Warm air blasts into the washroom, and we generate more heat between us by cuddling up with our arms around each other in our snorkels piled with stuff. When we finally get sick of sipping the sugar water we boil on the electric stove to fill our stomachs, Cherie, Camille, and I wake up around four in the morning to wrap whatever we're sleeping in around Norm and Rosie. Then we venture out in search of food.

Our snorkels make it easy to hide stolen candy and snack cakes, and we realize how much more we can smuggle by cutting a hole in one pocket then ripping through the coat's lining to the other pocket. We know the bakery's delivery guy arrives at the town market just after five in the morning. The minute his van has disappeared around the corner, we fill the lining of our coats with warm rolls, donuts, crumb cakes, and soft bagels. Then we head to the deli that's past the road to our house, to see if the milkman has made his delivery so we can feed Rosie. We're able to eat for several days after one outing. On the walk home, we snack as we savor our successful hunt, and sing "Ain't No Mountain High Enough"—taking turns being Marvin Gaye and Tammi Terrell—since it symbolizes the lengths we'll go for one another.

Each of the girls have to miss at least one day of school a week since someone always needs to be at home to take care of Rosie, who doesn't start kindergarten until next year. She'll be the smartest in her class since her schooling on pictures, colors, and numbers is inspired by our boredom—when she counts to twenty, it's a victory for us all.

When it's my turn to watch her, I fill her day with songs

about optimism by teaching her the lyrics to *Annie*'s "Tomorrow" and my very favorite, "Ooh Child."

Oo-ooh child things are gonna get easier. . . .
Oo-ooh child, things'll get brighter. . . .

We fantasize about the song's promise of walking in the rays of a beautiful sun, in a better brighter world.

I don't care much for my new fourth grade teacher, who's nothing like Ms. Muse. Instead of listening to her, I daydream, and on the days I'm actually present, my classmates and teacher act like I'm not. Rosie's not the only factor that keeps us from going to school: We've also been dealing with heads full of lice, ultimately followed by a family decision that it'd be better to stay home and build snowmen, make snow angels, and go sledding down the road on pieces of cardboard. If the library were closer we'd be there finding books of games, reading to Rosie, and teaching her more colors, bigger words, or how to stay inside the lines with crayons. At home, of course, all this is tougher to do since our fingers, numb inside our mittens, have a hard time turning the page or holding worn-down crayons.

Inside, we spend our days watching *The Six Million Dollar Man*, *The Waltons*, and *Happy Days* on our eleven-inch, black-and-white television. Maneuvering with our mittens makes games like five hundred rummy last longer. We save our new favorite, The Game of Life, for last and play until keeping ourselves warm all day has exhausted us enough to sleep again.

One morning Cherie tells Camille and me to go looking for food without her. "It hurts when I breathe," she says, worrying us by adding, "I feel like no matter how much I sleep, I can't stay awake." Her coughs are deep and long, and she feels hot with fever as her perspiration soaks the clothes and sheets we wrap her in. Somehow, though, she can't stop shivering.

When we get outside in our food-hunting gear, I ask Camille, "Do you think it's the flu?"

"I don't think so," she says. "You don't cough like that with the flu."

Over the next few days and then weeks, Cherie's cough grows stronger while her body grows weaker. "Be the man of the house, Norm," we tell him as we snorkel up—but this time not in search of food. Our younger brother has to care for Rosie and an eldest sister who can barely lift her head off the couch. When we leave, he's positioned himself by her side to monitor her breathing.

Camille and I follow the road into town, relieved all the taverns have their signs lit up now that night falls so early. We find one called The Cornerstone that we've heard Mom talk about before. "Hey, mister," I ask the bartender, "have you seen Cookie Calcaterra or the Red Devil?" The bartender turns to us, clueless. We walk in and out of every pub we find, telling the managers and bartenders that the Red Devil says he knows everybody in all the bars in Rocky Point. Finally, one of them lets us behind the bar and stands over the phone book with us, pointing out numbers to all the other pubs and dialing the phone for us. "Our sister is sick," I tell each one. "Can you please see if Cookie Calcaterra is there?" After a few hours of searching, we finally give up, but on our way home, snow starts to fall . . . and something about this makes Camille wonder out loud if Cherie is going to survive. "You think she's dying?" I ask her. The look on her face tells me enough.

We turn back and head for one of the bars where we remember seeing a pay phone hanging on the wall. I fight the butterflies in my stomach when Camille dials 911 and tells the operator in a shockingly steady voice, "Our sister is very, very sick. She's weak and she can't breathe." I purse my lips in worry as she answers the dispatcher's prompts. "Yes, we need an ambulance. Our mother is working."

We run home in time for Camille to climb in the ambulance with Cherie . . . and just as the police are pulling in. They question me about our mom's whereabouts. "Where did you say your mother works again?" one asks.

"Some real estate agency," I say with a shrug. "I don't remember the name."

The paramedics rush Cherie to the hospital, where she's admitted for severe pneumonia. When Camille returns late that night, getting a ride from a social worker, she tells me she had to keep herself from fainting when the doctor told her we waited so long that Cherie could have died. "Her lungs are damaged worse than any pneumonia case I've seen," he told Camille. "If she ever gets her lung strength back, it will take months."

We know what's coming when two social workers pull up to the house in two separate vehicles. Camille and I are driven to one foster home; Norm and Rosie are placed in another. We're separated again . . . but this time without our oldest sister, who usually knows what to do when we don't. Worse, she's by herself, with no one there to hold her hand while she fights for her life. "Can thirteen-year-olds get Failure to

Thrive?" I ask Camille. Her face is expressionless when she shrugs. "I hope not," she says. "I'll be thirteen next year." Then she turns and wipes the frost from her window.

Camille and I are obsessed with what will happen to Cherie when she's finally released from the hospital. "She's a sick woman," my older sisters say about our mother, and I'm coming to understand that's the only explanation for her choices in her manner of raising us. Beyond her heavy drinking are her violent mood swings and unpredictable outbursts, which we've been trying for years to accept as part of who she is. Sooner or later she always found ways to repent by taking my siblings to the movies or bringing us to a bar and giving us all the money we wanted for the jukebox and Shirley Temples. But the ruthless abandonment of us in midwinter in a desolate neighborhood—with no heat, no food, and limited contact with the outside world—has changed Camille.

The first outward sign of her contempt of our mother is when we're placed in our new foster home in Brentwood. "I don't want to be called Camille anymore," she tells me.

"What? Why?"

"I don't want to share a name with Mom." After a few days, Camille announces that she wants me, and everyone, to call her by her middle name: Deanna.

My task of having to call my sister by a new name after a decade knowing her as Camille is only further confused by the fact that our foster parents, Nancy and Frank, named their son and daughter Nancy and Frank. Nancy and Frank, Nancy and Frank, Deanna . . . and Regina.

Like most twelve-year-olds, Deanna is allowed to play after school with friends from her new school, go to dances, style her hair, and eat whatever she wants as long as she goes to class and does all her homework.

But Frank treats me like his second son. He shares his love of boxing and Sugar Ray Leonard with me, and I find myself liking Sugar Ray's baby face . . . and having someone who acts like my dad. We constantly watch boxing matches, interviews, and news on Sugar Ray, and as we prepare for a match, we talk about it for days leading up to it. Then we warn Nancy, Nancy, and Deanna what they're in for if they dare to join us for the fight. This is the first foster home for as long as I remember that we actually *don't want* to leave.

Anytime Deanna mentions Mom, she refers to her as Cookie. "She doesn't deserve to be called a mom," she explains. I begin to call Mom "Cookie," too—after all the months and years of growing up without her, she feels too unfamiliar and detached for the name Mom. Nancy tells us that Cherie's being released from the hospital and the court has permitted Cookie to take Cherie back, as long as Cookie lives in the same residence as Karl. Deanna and I roll our eyes.

Not long after that, Nancy learns Cookie's won back guardianship of Norm and Rosie, too. Nancy explains that the court only wants Cookie to take care of a few kids at a time, and if she proves she can, then we can return to her, too. "We're not in a rush," I tell Nancy. "Trust me."

Our summer's been filled with inground swimming pools, Slip 'N Slides, and water balloons. Frank takes us to the community celebration parade and shares our amazement over a fourteen-year-old Romanian gymnast named Nadia whose score showed up as 1.00 because the Olympic scoreboard makers never imagined that they would need room to post a fourth digit, since before her routine, no one had ever scored a perfect 10.00.

As our summer of Olympic-size fun comes to a close, so does our stay with Nancy, Frank, Nancy, and Frank. With a new school year coming, the court has ruled it's time for us to return to our mother . . . or, as we've made a pact to refer to her from now on: to Cookie.

Deanna and I hatch a plan to write a letter to the court, asking them if we can please stay with the Nancys and Franks, but we finally reason that Cherie will need our help taking care of Norm and Rosie until her lungs get better.

September 1977

THE MONTH BEFORE fifth grade starts, Cookie and Karl reunite. They find a nice two-story home to rent, directly across the street from the Saint James Episcopal Church. "Does this mean I'll get to go back to Saint James Elementary?"

"No, Regina," Cookie says. "I'm gonna send you to school in Timbuktu."

The house is nestled off of busy North Country Road, surrounded by dense woods that hide a secure tree house built high into a group of trees. Norm and Cherie are settled in bedrooms on the second floor by the time Deanna and I arrive. Cookie puts me in a bedroom on the first floor with Rosie, right next to the bedroom she shares with Karl. "I remember your little tendency to run away," she explains. One night, very late, when I hear strange noises coming from Cookie and Karl's bedroom, I knock on the door. "Is everyone okay in there?" I yell. Instantly the noises cease, and the next day Cookie tells Camille—whose new name was dropped the day we arrived here—to help me move my things to the spare room upstairs.

I'm excited when I return to Saint James Elementary, the school I loved attending from kindergarten to the middle of second grade. My fifth grade teacher, Ms. Van Dover, is known for being nice, and my old friend, Beth Nadasy, sits in the desk right next to me. "I'm sorry I never got to say good-bye to you in second grade," I tell her on the first day of school.

"That's all right. Where'd you go?"

Of course I can't tell her that we were taken away in a police car in the middle of the night because my little brother was found wandering the streets in his pajamas, or that we've been living with strangers for the last three years. But what I tell her is still the truth: "I thought of you all the time."

Cherie begins high school with her lifelong friend Kathy, and Camille is in Nesaquake Middle School with her old friends. The single advantage about being forced to live with Cookie again is that, for the first time in our lives, we don't have to walk into a school on the first day and fear whether anyone will sit with us at lunch or invite us to play on their dodgeball team. This makes going to school easier for all of us, and now staying home is easier, too: Karl's insisted that the only way he'll stay is if Cookie stops drinking. So she does.

We're even in walking distance from our favorite spots like Cordwood Beach, Saint James General Store, Wicks Farm, and Saint Philip and James Church where Rosie was baptized. It strikes me how strange it is for life to feel so normal. Then, one night at dinner, Mom announces that Vito, Rosie's biological father, has been "wasted."

"Wasted?" I ask. "You mean he's drunk?"

"Wasted," Cookie says. "Smoked. Rubbed out. Murdered by the enemy."

I shut my eyes and hope that the Mothers and Fathers Italian Association is still watching out for us. Then I turn and look at Rosie, whose blond pigtails bounce as she claps and laughs in her high chair. She'll never get to know her real dad, which makes me lose my appetite. My wish to meet my father one day sometimes feels like the only thing I have to look forward to.

Cherie and Camille begin studying foreign languages. When Cherie asks her teacher about the phrases we've been using for as long as we remember, we learn that *je t'aime* means *I love you* in French, and *mia bambina amore* means *my baby love* in Italian. Both are much sweeter to hear than Cookie's old foreign words like *vaffanculo* (which I'm pretty sure means something about the F word) and *puttana* (which, based on Cookie's context when using it, we've translated to mean *whore*). I begin writing *je t'aime* and *mia bambina amore* all over my notebooks and then in the daily love letters I share with Justin James, a boy whom I rarely speak to, but who tells me he thinks I'm pretty. For a girl who thinks her teeth look like Tic Tacs screwed into her gums, this is irresistibly wooing. Every day I hide his letters in a shoe box under my bed, tucking them in a dark spot so Cookie will never find them.

When my classmates ask me where we lived over the past few years, I answer, "With my grandparents." Then I quickly change the subject. And even though I think of this as my school, I sometimes can't help but feel like a visitor. I observe others in the class—while they haven't changed much, I definitely have. I wonder if I would be as content and confident as they are if we'd never been taken away that night. Would I feel differently about myself—pretty, clean, and carefree, like my classmates? I love to watch Kathleen Totter in her dresses, knee-high socks, and Mary Jane shoes, how her silky blond hair is neatly parted into two perfect ponytails that are tied with matching ribbons. But even if I had nicer clothes and polished shoes, none of it could cover up the past few years of turmoil. So I dress like I feel inside: stained, torn, wrinkled, and mismatched. The school made me get these big silver-rimmed glasses when they figured out I'd been hiding my strained vision by memorizing the eye chart every year, and my haircut makes me look more like my brother than my sisters. But for me, this actually works: I want my awkwardness to be clear to the other kids. Pretty much the only comfort I've ever felt is when I've been living in my own world, sending signals to others to keep away from me so they never find out the truth about my life.

Rather than bothering to hint to my classmates that I'd love to be invited to their homes, I spend my afternoons studying in the school library or napping in the tree house. I also spend endless time in my room listening to my little vinyl records on my phonograph, always playing over and over the funny songs on the *Dumb Ditties* album we got from the Salvation Army.

Since Karl was able to retrieve what few possessions we'd left at the Rocky Point house, I still have my Jesus figurines. Now, with a church across the street, I'm intrigued to find out why I've been carrying them around with me for as long as I can remember. So every Sunday, I cross the street by myself to attend all three morning services at the Episcopal church, retreating to my tree house after each one, until I see people filing in for the next service. I discover in the weekly bulletin that they also hold a Saturday-night service, and I begin attending that as well. I have no idea what I'm reading or singing about, but I take comfort in the safety of this space. It's also the only place I've ever been where you can be a stranger and people still smile at you.

Fifth grade is going great because my teacher thinks I'm special. The closer I get to Ms. Van Dover, the more I want to please her. Even in winter she smells like fresh flowers, and her red curls and creamy white skin make her brown eyes stand out when she smiles. Even though she treats every kid in the class nicely, I'm convinced that she finds moments to spend extra attention on me. She holds weekly spelling bees, most of which I win; my prize being the choice between a Twinkie or a Ring Ding, which I always scarf down on my walk home. At the end of the year Ms. Van Dover announces we'll be voting for "superlatives," and she gives me an inconspicuous wink when my class votes me "Nicest."

Unfortunately, my budding confidence is shaken when the end-of-the-year spelling bee turns into a showdown: me versus Susan Kominski, the president of the fifth grade class (whom the class voted Most Popular). She's crowned the fifth grade spelling bee champion when I misspell *vacuum*, which I really should've known, because my classmates are always singing the "Regina Hoover Vacuum Cleaner" jingle to me. (Also, because of the *Understanding Puberty* video that we all had to watch after Memorial Day weekend, I take note that at the next school I move to, I will change my name to something that sounds nothing like *vagina*.)

After school's out, Karl comes home exhausted from

working long days at Grumman. He tells us work is stressful because of the Communists. Cookie's out working later as well . . . back behind a bar. Although Karl threatens that she better not drink, she comes home every night smelling like booze. When he starts to follow her, she sticks me in her car, telling him she's taking me to the mall or to visit my grandparents.

"Grandparents?" I ask her. "I don't even know my grandparents."

"Shut the fuck up and cooperate."

Finally, in the heat of summer, I come down with the chicken pox. Cookie takes me to the doctor, who simply instructs me to bathe in oatmeal to soothe the itching. Karl tells Cookie he's not convinced we went to see a doctor, and they both flee angrily in their separate cars.

Karl's the first to finally return. He flicks off the *Donny & Marie* show and sends us out to the front yard so he can use the living room to sort through his belongings. Cookie comes home drunk, screeching and flailing when she sees his packed boxes lining the entryway. Their argument spills out to the front yard, where he tries to take her car keys away so she can't drive while she's smashed. He wrestles her to the ground to calm her down, and just then she starts screaming, *"Rape! Help, he's raping me!"* A stranger stops and opens his car door, and Cookie throws herself inside and shouts obscenities from the window at us. When they speed off, Karl hurls his things into his car. "Take care of yourselves," he tells us, resigned. "I tried to make this work, but your mother's a goddamn hopeless case." All five of us stand on the front lawn for a while, knowing the only thing we can be certain will come next is chaos.

When Cookie finally goes off the deep end, we're not sure if it's thanks to Karl's departure or Elvis Presley's death. When she hears on the news that the King died in his bathroom, she locks herself in ours. For the next week she consumes jars of peanut butter, known to be one of Elvis's favorites, while sending us out to buy all of his albums, which she plays through the house on full blast.

Shortly after I start sixth grade at Nesaquake Middle School, Cookie stops paying rent. I hold Rosie as I walk into Ms. Van Dover's classroom. "We're moving again," I inform her.

"Be safe," she tells me, crouching down to sweep my long bangs out of my eyes. "And if you ever feel scared, look back at what I wrote to you in last year's yearbook, where I told you that you were a bright girl with lots of talent and that you should never stop your quest for knowledge. I meant every word."

And just like I thought, Ms. Van Dover goes on to tell me how special I am to her. "The only thing that will get you out of your situation is to stay in school, Regina," she says. Then she looks at my hand clasped tight around Rosie's, and tells me, "Make sure you teach Rosie what you've learned—she needs a teacher who cares about her as much as I care about you."

This time I just smile.

Then Rosie reaches up to be held . . . and again, we're gone.

7

Keeping Pact

1977 to Summer 1980

THE FIFTH WEEK of my sixth-grade year, the temperature reaches ninety-eight degrees, which feels even more suffocating in the back of Cookie's station wagon. I wish Long Island's scorcher Indian summer were our only source of discomfort. In the driver's seat, with a beer between her legs, Cookie stays mum about our new destination, only directing us to smoosh ourselves and all of our belongings into the car: garbage bags stuffed with clothes, our black transistor radio, towels, sheets, cups, silverware, pots, coffee, beer, sugar, vodka, peanut butter, whiskey, jelly, flour, five kids, and one Cookie. We know the drill.

With all the bedding, housewares, and food, this is by far the most crowded our car has ever been . . . and this brings me to wonder whether Cookie ever thanked Karl for being such a good provider for us. She made me leave my phonograph, records, and books behind, but inside my shirt I hid my two Jesuses and my fifth-grade autograph book, plus some picture books for Rosie. I also grabbed a deck of cards for Cherie, Camille, Norm, and me to play with.

Cookie pulls into a gas station and parks next to the Dumpster. "This is humiliating," Cherie says. We watch our mother approach drivers as they're sliding the nozzle inside their tanks to fill up. However, we quickly learn our cue: When Cookie points to us fanning ourselves with hands of cards, we wave and put on expressions of misery and desperation . . . which is not all that challenging, under the circumstances. Finally, her shameless strategy gets us a full tank of gas.

As she takes the expressway ramp, Cookie announces: "We're going to meet your grandparents."

"Our grandparents?" I ask her. "You mean the ones you fibbed to Karl about?"

"You mean I have grandparents?" Norm says.

"I thought they lived in another state," Camille says.

"What'd you think," Cookie says, "that I was born from apes?"

I watch Camille dig her knee hard into Cherie's, and with all our might the three of us try not to explode into laughter.

Forty-five minutes later we pull into the driveway of a blue ranch house with a garage attached and small, trimmed evergreen bushes lining the front bay window. Cookie puts the car in park and stares at the house with an awareness I've never seen her have before. "Get out," she finally says, her eyes still fixed on the house.

We sit silently.

"I said, *get out*," she growls through her teeth. "This'll be a lot easier if they see you."

The four doors of the car slowly move ajar, and simultaneously the house's front door opens, too. With the help of a walker, a thin woman in a pink floral muumuu shuffles onto the porch. With dark, slanted eyes she stares at us, and at her side arrives a wrinkled, tanned man with navy Bermuda shorts met by knee-high black socks. My eyes are drawn up to his belly, which is as round and bare as a newborn elephant's. There's a showdown of eyes until Baby Elephant Belly speaks up. "Get the hell out of here," he says.

We all look at Cookie, paralyzed to budge.

"Nobody move a muscle," Cookie says. "We're gonna do this my way. Kids, these are your grandparents—the grandparents who turned their backs on you, especially when you needed them the most." She turns her gaze toward the two elderly figures on the porch. "Mom, Dad, meet Cherie. She's fourteen. Camille is thirteen, Regina is ten, Norman is nine, and Rosie is four. These are your grandkids . . . do you get that? They have no place to stay, and unless you stop acting like careless fucks, they'll be sleeping on the street tonight. Is that what you want?"

From the stoop, they peer at us, and the muumuu wearer tells her, "For God's sake Camille, put your children in the car. Kids don't need to witness all this." Hearing Cookie called by her real name makes me curious about how she must have been raised. I can see that she and her mother share the same strong cheekbones and wide hips, but my grandmother appears much less combative than Cookie. I'd like to call her Grandma and ask her why she thinks Cookie is so mean.

"I have to go potty!" Rosie cries, and when everyone

pauses to look at her, I whisper to Cookie: "I need to go, too." The muumuu wearer looks at her husband and reluctantly opens the front door.

We all file inside.

When Camille approaches the bathroom with Rosie, Baby Elephant Belly takes her shoulder and says, "What the hell are you doing? That baby's four years old now, she can go peepee on her own." Rosie runs for the bathroom, then Baby Elephant Belly turns to me. "And you," he says, piercing me with his eyes. "You better not take anything."

"Oh sure," I reply, surprising myself with my sass. Whatever this guy did to make Cookie turn out so nasty, there's no way I'll let him push me around. "You want me to give back the piece of toilet paper I use, too?"

"*No*," he says squarely. Then he straightens up. "You can place that where it belongs."

Their living room is a museum of wooden and glass curio cabinets featuring shelves and shelves of cherub-faced porcelain collectibles. On one wall I spot a photograph of a man who must be my mother's brother, Nick, who once invited us to his Lions Club holiday party for poor kids. I nod toward his wedding picture. "Is that Nick?"

"Yes," Cookie's dad says.

I look back at the picture. "Any kids?"

"Nope."

Darn. I was hoping for cousins.

"Lots of attempts," he says, "but so far nothing's stuck. Better off, if you ask me. They got a pack of Doberman pinschers . . . real handfuls."

I push myself to pee fast, anxious to exit the bathroom's unloved, soiled motif. Now I see where Cookie gets her lack of taste in décor: Her parents' bathroom boasts the color brown from floor to ceiling, plus a sliding glass shower door so covered in film you can't see into the tub.

Suddenly I think of my uncle's photo again and get a shiver. It occurs to me that with his sharp chin, black eyes, and short but ear-to-ear facial hair, it seems almost possible he could actually father a Doberman.

Cookie's mom stands nervously inside the front door. "Thanks for the bathroom," I tell her.

Baby Elephant Belly watches from the stoop as we surf over our belongings, squeezing into the car again. Cookie stuffs the twenty her mother slipped her inside her pocket, satisfied that our presence helped her seal the deal. She backs out of the driveway and drives just a few blocks before pulling into the back of the Waldbaum's supermarket parking lot off of Sunrise Highway. She waddles into the store and emerges a few minutes later with a six-pack of cold Budweisers, two packs of Virginia Slims Lights, a loaf of bread, a jar each of peanut butter and jelly, and a roll of toilet paper. "We'll sleep here for tonight, kids. Don't worry. I'll hit up their friends tomorrow . . . turn up the heat a little. They're not going to get away with ignoring me that easy."

Cherie, Camille, Norm, and I move a few garbage bags out of the station wagon to make room for all six of us to sleep. "Leave the important ones in here," Cookie says from the front seat, "just in case we need to make a quick getaway." Rosie climbs into a backseat floorwell, and Norm tucks himself in the other. Cookie relaxes against the headrest of the driver's seat and cracks open a beer, and I huff silently when my sisters decide I should sleep on the passenger-side floor. "I'd rather sleep in the trunk with the bags," I whisper to Camille, who uses her eyes to suggest I go with the flow. Then she and Cherie stack heads-on-shoulders in the backseat, lounging against each other with their eyes closed.

We wake to a car stinking of perspiration and cigarettes. Cookie rubs her eyes and announces, "I gotta go pop a squat." After we've hauled all the bags back inside the car, she takes off down the highway and pulls into a McDonald's.

"Mom, are we eating here?" Norm asks, his eyes wide as pancakes.

"What do you think, Norman? Huh?"

He says nothing.

"Are we eating here?" she mocks him. "Please. It's for the bathroom and free napkins. We'll need them later when we're out of toilet paper." She holds the restroom door open for us to file inside. "Try to look nice," she says. "We've got a real important mission today."

When she pulls into a post office, we all pile out and into the building. "Is Mike here?" she yells up to the clerk from the line. The clerk looks at Cookie like she's a madwoman. "Mike Calcaterra?"

"He's out on his route," the clerk replies.

"Well let him *know*," Cookie says in defiance, "that his grandchildren were here today, looking for him."

At the butcher, she props her elbows high on the deli counter. "Hey, any of you guys seen Rose Calcaterra?" When the men working the slicing machines turn to her with bewildered eyes, she continues her pursuit. "I'm Cookie, Mike and Rose's daughter."

Her explanation does nothing to aid their understanding of what she's doing there.

"I know, it's been a long time since I've been in here. See, I stopped by their house earlier, and they weren't home. I'm just trying to track them down— Oh!" she says. "And by the way, these are their grandchildren. I wanted to introduce them to their grandparents."

Camille whispers to Cherie. "What in the world is she doing?"

"Just watch her," Cherie says, and before long we begin to see the point. We troop into every grocery, deli, and liquor store in town, watch Cookie snow the workers with her harebrained story, and retreat to the aisles when they set us loose, telling us with pity to get what we need. Soon we have enough cigarettes, vodka, deli salads, beer, soda, bread, and toilet paper to last us days. At each stop, as the bell jingles to mark our exit, Cookie tells the clerk: "Just put it on Mike and Rose's tab."

ON NOVEMBER 9, I imagine that one day, when I'm an adult, a friend or my husband will ask me, "So, Regina, tell me: How'd you celebrate your eleventh birthday?"

"Oh, you know, like any kid," I'll answer. "Living as a parking lot gypsy and bathing in a gas station sink."

We've spent the past two months sleeping in Cookie's car, while she's been cruising all over Suffolk County to stay under the cops' radar since she never registered us for school this year.

But just as the stores and houses we pass are putting up Christmas decorations, Cookie finds a landlord who will rent to us with a welfare housing voucher. The problem is that his property is close to our grandparents' house, and by now, our food supply in their neighborhood has already been cut off—except for the butcher, who feels sorry for my mother. He tells her to come in either first thing in the morning or at night, when there's no rush of customers. Then, with clean white paper, he wraps up pigs' knuckles, liver, and tripe.

"What's tripe?" Norman asks.

"It's cow intestines," Cherie says.

"At least we're eating healthy," I joke with my sisters. Norman looks like he'll vomit. But when we set the food on the table, we're so hungry that we inhale tripe in its broth, and liver smothered in ketchup and mustard. This helps get it down without gagging.

The most thrilling feature in the new house is its portable washing machine. Cherie and Camille wheel it up to the kitchen sink and attach a hose to the spigot while Norman and I search the house for every piece of clothing we've worn since September. The excitement fades, of course, when we see how many times we have to run each load before our clothes actually look clean; and it takes no time to learn the washer's other issue: The water inside never gets hot enough to kill the lice we picked up from one of the gas station restrooms.

Thanks to the lice, none of us pass the health exam that's required to register for school in West Babylon. We spend our days at home with our heads under the sink, sudsing up with the lice killer we lifted from the pharmacy, then combing the eggs out of each other's hair. When the neighbors learn the reason we never seem to be at school, we pack up yet again . . . leaving behind our clothes, blankets, towels, socks, and any ounce of self-respect that wasn't compromised by lice and liver. I wonder how any landlord will ever house us again if word gets out how we left the place.

As their 1978 New Year's resolution, Cherie and Camille have decided to make a change. "We want to move out," Camille informs Cookie.

"Out where?"

"Out of the *car!*"

Cherie tempers the conversation by adding, "I would like to go back to school." *I would like to go back to school, too,* I'm seething to say, but I don't dare utter a sentence that could leave me without allies.

By late January they're both living at Kathy's and it's clear I'll probably miss the sixth grade altogether on account of the fact that we'd need an address to register for school. While Cookie spends her afternoons in bars, Norman, Rosie, and I take short walks in the snow or stay huddled together in the car with garbage bags of belongings piled on top of us and layers of socks covering all our limbs for warmth. Sometimes the bar owners invite us inside to sit in a booth as long as we don't run around; other times they let us split a hamburger if we wash dishes and mop the floors. One of them tells me, "You're a good big sister, you know." At first I'm confused when she slips me a five-dollar bill and puts her finger to her lips . . . then I get her point: If I don't protect the money meant for the kids and me, Cookie will spend it on herself. "I like to work," I tell the owner, delighted by her praise. It's true—it keeps us warm and occupied, and we get to eat for free.

There's also something in it for us when Cookie meets a guy at the bar: Either we get to sleep in his living room (taking savvy advantage of the chance to squeeze toothpaste onto our fingers for a long-awaited brushing) or we get the whole car to ourselves while our mother spends the night in a hotel.

Around town Cookie hears there's a deli in Commack with an open cashier position. She agrees to take the job for less money than usual, since her new boss is giving her a perk by allowing us to move into the apartment upstairs, and for me the perk is that Cherie and Camille have agreed to move back in with us now that we live in a normal place again.

In February we all go to visit a school in Hauppauge . . . but since we don't have records for the first half of the year, we're not able to register. "We'll climb on the bus every day anyway," I tell Norman and Rosie, and the plan quickly proves successful.

One day, while I am eating the school's free breakfast, Mrs. Young crouches next to my cafeteria table. "Would you like to come with me to the office?" she asks, and I oblige her, feeling safe that we have the same thing in mind. Together with the principal, we fill out registration forms for Norman, Rosie, and me so we can get credit and finish out the school year.

The only thing that will get you out of your situation is to stay in school, Regina.

I remember Ms. Van Dover's words, so I perform well on Mrs. Young's tests and participate not *like* my life depends on it, but *because* my life depends on it. I keep to myself during free time so that none of my classmates will ever ask to come to my house. When Mrs. Young sees me reading at recess, she gives me work sheets to practice long division and encourages me to take a stab at the challenge questions in our science books. The more work I have, the safer I feel.

Holding it together with a job is stressing Cookie to proportions we've never seen before. Making it worse is the fact that summer's fast approaching, and the taste of independence that Cherie and Camille had living on their own is inspiring them to lash out. "I've got five kids, a household to manage, and a paycheck to keep!" Cookie says. "And now you sluts want to give me attitude?" Cookie stays out all night at bars or rolls out of bed just as we're heading out the door to school. On the rare occasion she's home when we are, the beatings are guaranteed and more brutal than ever. We all go into full-fledged survival mode and stay out of the house as much as we can when she's home.

On the school bus, Camille adopts the nickname "Dancing Queen," swaying and boogying to kids' boom boxes and starting impromptu dance parties, in an attempt to preserve her fast-fleeting days as a teenager. When I ask her whether she ever flirts with boys when she goes to dances at the community youth center, she looks at me dubiously. "Haven't you seen how Cookie behaves with men?" she says. "Believe me, I'm not dancing to meet boys. I dance so I can be me. It's the only time I can really be a teenager."

One night, I pray Camille will have beat me home when it takes me until almost seven to arrive from school. Instead I open the front door to find chicken cutlets frying on the stove, and Cookie, who turns to me with her eyes blazing. "Where the hell were you?" she says.

I hesitate, until I blurt it out. "I was looking for my coat." She burns holes through me with her eyes, spurring me to share more. "It disappeared from my locker today."

"Good goddamn job, you dumb shit. It's gonna be a cold, wet April. What the fuck, Regina—is your head up your ass?" She pauses a second, but I say nothing. "So where's the coat now?"

I shake my head. "I don't know. I think someone stole it."

Camille walks in just as Cookie hurls the pan of bubbling grease at me. My sister runs to me just as the hot grease splatters all over my forearms that I raised to protect my face, but Cookie grabs Camille by the neck and drags her to the front door. Then from the second-floor deck, she throws her down a flight of stairs, where Camille now lies hollering in pain. Cookie runs down the stairs and kicks my sister in the back. "That'll teach you to interfere!" she roars.

"Great job, you sluts," she says, walking toward the car. "You ruined my dinner." She puts the car in reverse and leaves.

I throw on a sweatshirt to hide the instant blisters on my arms and run into the deli downstairs, pleading to Cookie's gray-haired coworker Helen. "Call an ambulance, quick! Camille fell down the stairs!"

"Did she fall, or was she pushed?"

"Helen," I beg, *"please, just call."*

Later that night when Camille is discharged wearing a neck brace, the two of us phone Cherie from the hospital. Kathy picks us up, but when we arrive home, we have to curl up in the stairwell because the door is locked. When the sky begins to light up, Rosie pops her head out. "Norman and I were scared last night," she says. "We were all alone."

Camille shoots me a glance. "No you weren't, sweetie," Camille says. "We were here the whole time."

We're brewing coffee in the kitchen when Cookie's car pulls up. Hearing her clamor up the stairs, Camille and I stiffen. I take a deep breath and prepare to play it cool. "So, I imagine you told the doctors what a horrible mother I am." This is her hello as she eyes Camille's neck brace and the bandages on my hands.

I take a moment to torture her with my silence. Camille seems to be in on the tactic.

"Well?"

"We didn't say anything," I tell her. "Just that I dropped a pan of grease and then Camille fell in it."

"And you expect me to believe they bought that crock of shit?"

Camille and I look at each other and shrug. "Yeah," Camille says. "They bought it."

"We'll see about that. You two clean up the mess you made last night. Camille, you better stay up here and rest today," she says. "But Regina's gonna help me at work. We don't want any nosy teachers asking what happened to you two."

As the school year winds down, it's completely clear that Cherie and Camille have no intention of hanging out here this summer. I ask Hank, Cookie's boss, if I can start helping at the store. He looks at me with hesitation, and then thoughtfulness. "Your mother *has* had some trouble keeping up," he admits. "How old are you again?"

I fold my arms across my flat chest to hide the prepubescent evidence. "I'm thirteen—and a half."

He looks at me suspiciously. "Weren't you eleven last week?"

"I'm a good worker, Hank, ask anybody."

"All right," he sighs. "But I'll have to keep you hidden in the back. You've got to be older than fifteen to work in this state."

"I'll hide," I promise. "I'm small, see?"

"And you'll have to listen to your mother."

I nod. Being with her in public is safer than being with her at home.

The first week, I come in every day after school and head back to his kitchen—a long galley with steel tables, a sink, and a big, industrial fan mounted on the wall over the oven. I slip on plastic serving gloves and roll up my apron to make it shorter, the way I've seen Cookie do with her skirts before she goes to the bars. Until six o'clock I work, shredding cabbage for coleslaw and peeling carrots and potatoes, then I clean up and take out the trash in time for the store to close at eight. After my first Friday on the job, Hank hands me fifteen dollars cash in an envelope. When we get upstairs, Cookie wiggles her fingers at me. "Hand that over," she says. "Hank's little pet, huh? You wouldn't have gotten this gig without me getting you a foot in the door."

I look at her in disbelief . . . and then I hand over the money. She opens the front door for my siblings to head out to the movies, leaving me at home by myself. "I'm sure you'll find some way to occupy yourself," she tells me. "You're so goddamn resourceful."

The next morning I put on shorts and a tube top and march back downstairs to the deli. "As long as you don't mind," I tell Hank, "I'm going to take deli orders from the cars while they wait in line for the pump."

He looks at me in amazement.

"What?" I tell him. "I'm trying to earn a little extra cash, I didn't solve the gas crisis."

"You just solved *my* gas crisis," he says, pointing to the traffic lined around the corner. I head out from car to car with a pencil and a tablet of order checks. "Hey folks," I say through their windows. "Can I get you anything from the deli?" I schlep their cigarettes, chips, and sodas, gratefully accepting tips of a dime or whatever spare change they tell me to keep. Soon I've got the system down so well that I start pumping their gas for them, too, popping an average tip of twenty-five cents into my pocket after every fill-up. When Cookie comes downstairs for her shift, she looks at me suspiciously . . . but when she steps out back for a cigarette break, I spend some of my newfound salary to scarf down a sandwich and hide some snacks in the deli kitchen to give Rosie and Norman later.

I find work not only helps provide for my siblings and me—it also keeps my mind distracted from how my family is crumbling. When I'm idle, I'm in so much pain wishing my older sisters wanted me; or that just once, my mother would tell me she loves me. When Cookie's working and Norm and Rosie are watching TV, I lock myself in my bedroom and cut my arms with scissors. I watch the skin give way, then the blood comes to a swell, and for a second there's some release to the pain deep inside me. Sometimes when Cookie and I are working together in the kitchen, I try and flaunt the gashes just to see if she cares at all. One day, she finally throws me a bone. "You got a little problem with your arms there?" she asks me.

Behind her in the distance I see Hank working the register. I shrug.

Cookie laughs. "Next time, if you're going to do it, do it right," she says. "You cut on your wrists. Not your forearms."

A few days later, I'm startled from my thoughts of this conversation when a man wearing a black T-shirt, jeans, and work boots appears at the deli's Employees Only kitchen door. I take in the vision of him—dark curls framing a tanned, handsome face and eyes shining pure as onyx—then I get back to peeling potatoes. I pause, waiting to see whether he'll say anything.

He stares.

"Can I help you?"

He examines me, taking in all my features. Finally, silently, he shakes his head. I look back down to peel the potatoes; when I move my eyes to see if he's still there . . . he's gone. Although I don't recall ever meeting him, something about his eyes is eerily familiar. I can't shake the certainty that I've seen them somewhere before.

"HIS NAME IS Paul Accerbi." The flicking sound of Cookie's lighter collides with the ding of the dishes I'm setting on the table for dinner. "He comes waltzing in, digging through his wallet, then looks up at me—a deer in friggin' headlights."

I stop setting the table to stare at her.

"God, what I wouldn't give to capture the look on his face when he saw me. *'Your daughter's in the back,'* I tell him. Do you know how long I waited to deliver that line?" She takes a drag of her cigarette. "Well, actually, I'll tell you how long: eleven *looong* years." She laughs, a cackle then a hack. "The look on the son of a bitch's face, I thought he was gonna shit a bagel."

I've just seen this man for the first time five hours ago and already I'm planning how I'd like to decorate my bedroom in his home. *Dad*, I'd ask him, *will you hang a shelf where I can place all my Jesus figurines?* He'd install blinds on my bedroom windows and check their locks every night at dark. Then he'd tuck me in, pushing the edge of my comforter between the mattress and box spring to make sure I'm safe and secure.

"See that?" Cookie says. "He took one look at your sore ass and left you again. Good thing you have me to care about you."

But nothing she says about my father can bring me down from what I've just learned about him: *that he exists*. There's someone else in the world with me . . . I'm not alone anymore. I've always wondered, Who *is* this man? Is he even alive? He's not just alive, he's handsome . . . and looks *normal*.

My universe has shifted.

Paul Accerbi. I had heard those words, but they have new meaning now. In our first apartment in Saint James, Cookie would tie me to the radiator and invoke his name as she beat me. *"Paul Accerbi!"* she'd scream, yanking my hair to pound my head on the floor or whipping my back with a belt. *"He hurt me the MOST,"* she'd wail. *"So YOU will hurt the most!"* I knew this from the first night that I met her when I was four, and she never let me forget it.

Cookie shared her stories of who each of our separate fathers were. Some we knew to be true; when she talked about Rosie's dad and mine, her stories never changed about Vito and Paul. But the details always got blurred with the identity of the fathers of my other siblings—she claimed they ranged from famous pop singers from her go-go dancer days to gas station attendants she met on the rebound. What was shocking for me to learn about Paul is that he lived close enough that stopping in the deli for lunch could have been part of his normal routine.

After Cookie's gone out for a drink, I grab the Suffolk County phone book; my stomach is doing flips as I near the first page of *A*. I scan the listings . . . until I reach the only name that matches his:

Accerbi, Paul & Joan

My father and what appears to be his wife live in River-head, which, if I'm reading the phone book's map correctly, is probably a forty-minute drive east of our house. I flip back to the *A*'s and close the cover, staring at the no-nonsense yellow and the black text. Of everything I've ever read, who could have known that the book that would give me all the hope and answers I've prayed for would be the White Pages.

IN OCTOBER OF my seventh-grade year, Cookie is arrested again for driving drunk, with no registration and a suspended license. When they run her name through their records they discover she has outstanding warrants for bouncing checks all over Suffolk County. "How much money do you think Mom has bounced checks for?" Norm asks me.

I shrug. "Maybe a couple hundred," I tell him, even though it's more like thousands.

The cops come to our door, reporting Cookie's trying to get out of jail by sobbing that her kids are alone and in need of their mother. It takes Cherie and Camille some very practiced skill to answer all their questions. "Have you looked after your siblings for days at a time before?"

"Not really," Cherie says. "But we babysit them a lot."

The cops ask Rosie and Norm to come chat. "Do your big sisters take good care of you?"

The two of them nod enthusiastically. Within a couple minutes we've convinced the cops that we'll be fine until Cookie makes bail. But just as they pull out of the deli parking lot, Hank comes knocking. "When your mother gets back, tell her she has a week to get out of here," he says. The next few days, I work morning, noon, and night at the deli to earn as much cash as I can. Hank drops a couple jars of peanut butter and jelly in a bag along with two loaves of bread. "That should last you kids awhile," he says. "Right?"

I nod. "Thanks, Hank."

That night, a cop car drops Cookie out front, and they set a court date for later in October.

We've always avoided apartment complexes because their management companies conduct background checks on the renters, but this time it's the only thing Cookie can find that will accept a welfare voucher.

She's been paranoid about the "pigs" ever since she left jail, so we all stay shuttered inside with the shades drawn tight and all the lights off. Cookie refuses to register us for school in case the authorities would use us to track her down. The first two weeks, she sends Cherie or Camille out every other day for cigarettes and food, until they deflate me with a joint announcement that they've decided to move back in with Kathy's family permanently.

Norm, Rosie, and I are stuck—yet again—with Cookie in a cold, unfurnished apartment. It's my job to get her cigarettes and food with our food stamps, but when I meet a friend my age down the hall, whose parents have an apartment that's completely furnished, I catch a beating for taking the risk to draw attention to us. My embarrassment about the bruises makes me half-relieved when there's a knock at our front door at the end of our first month. "Shit, the pigs!" Cookie hisses in the dark. "Regina, you answer it!"

"We know you're in there!"

Calmly, I loosen the chain on the door to find two men in button-down shirts standing in front of me.

"We know she's in here," one of them says, wearing a shirt with the complex's water fountain logo embroidered on the pocket.

"She's not," I answer, "and I'm not allowed to let you in when my mom's not home."

"Well, she better get here fast because the police are on their way."

When I latch the door, Cookie lights a panicked cigarette. "What the hell am I gonna do now? They must've found out about my record and reported my whereabouts to the police . . . the motherfuckers."

"Norm, Rosie," I tell them, "get all your clothes. Towels and blankets, too."

Cookie takes a load of our luggage out to the car. "I skipped my hearing and lost the bail money," she confesses, as though we're suddenly friends. "They probably have another warrant out for my arrest."

"Then let's hurry up and get out of here," I answer.

She rolls out of the complex's parking lot, chanting this rhyme:

We were here, but not to stay.
We didn't like it anyway.

WHEN THE LEAVES start changing, it looks as though I may spend my twelfth birthday the same way I spent my eleventh: We live in the car while Cookie sits in bars. If she finds a man with enough class (or a wife) who will take her to a hotel for the night, she asks him to get us a room right next to theirs. I take baths so long I nearly fall asleep in the tub while Norm and Rosie stretch wide on the bed, watching TV like little kings. We live it up on these nights, knowing that in hours we'll be back in the car, sleeping behind a nondescript supermarket or in the parking lot of the Smith Haven Mall.

In November, Cookie meets Garcia, a compact, kind-faced farmworker who frequents the pub that's just down from the mall. When she tells him her kids are living in her car, he offers for Norm, Rosie, and me to sleep in an empty farm trailer all winter, if we're willing to muck out the horse stables every morning. "He said there's no heat in the trailer," I tell the kids, "but it's better than living in a parking lot all winter."

In the hours of the morning when most kids are still slumbering before their parents wake them up, we're rising from a shivering, teeth-chattering night to wash our faces using the hose inside the barn and a bucket of water with soap. Shortly after we've supplied the horses with water and hay is the best part of the morning: that's when the workers arrive. They bring us breakfast of warm rolls from a nearby bakery or Hostess cakes, and sometimes they walk us to the pub for the soup and sandwich lunch special . . . but we always hurry to exit before Cookie parks herself at the bar for the day.

As far as caretakers go, I'm partial to Garcia, who looks out for us so well I don't bother to wonder why he would never date Cookie.

He promises that after the horses get used to us, he'll give us riding lessons. A few days in a row he teaches me to practice saddling up Dixie, a sweet nutmeg mare. After half a dozen lessons in the saddle, Norman, Rosie, and I take turns trotting her around as if she were our own, until one afternoon when both Rosie and the horse find themselves surprised. Apparently Dixie's being sought after by an overly enthusiastic stud, causing all the farmworkers to crowd around in terror. One runs to rescue Rosie from the reins, while the two horses go on to give us all a lesson in horse mating so thorough I'm tempted to write in to *National Geographic.*

Garcia informs us that Cookie's been living with a guy from the pub, so for Thanksgiving, the workers call Salvation Army to bring us a warm dinner. When the food arrives, the kids and I slip socks poked with holes over our fingers and open the Styrofoam containers heaped with turkey, stuffing, mashed potatoes, and cranberry sauce. We scurry to take seats around our trailer's folding table. "Let's say grace," I tell them. We bow our heads as I lead:

> Bless us O Lord,
> And these Thy gifts
> Which we are about to receive from Thy bounty
> Through Christ, our Lord.
> Amen.

When my sisters first taught me this prayer, they gave me permission to bless myself with the sign of the cross, even though none of us are sure whether I was ever baptized. I watch as Rosie and Norman dig into their dinners, reminding them to chew slowly. After dinner we eat the pumpkin pie the Salvation Army brought us, then we lounge on the floor to play board games with our stomachs so full we can barely move. "Does your belly hurt?" I ask Rosie.

"No," she answers. "It feels delicious."

As the weather continues to chill down, the workers begin to arrive earlier, allowing us to sleep in and stay out of the cold. The three of us begin to spend our days hanging out at the mall, watching shoppers' carts fill up with gifts as little kids climb onto Santa's lap. "Do you think Santa will ever bring us presents?" Rosie asks me.

"One day, sweetheart. When we stop moving around and we're finally home for good."

It's almost Christmas when Cookie shows up again. She says welfare has a room for us in the Los Biandos shelter in Patchogue. There's no mention of my going back to school, and part of me would prefer to stay on the farm with the workers who look out for us, but at the shelter we'll get heat and three meals a day, plus running water in the shared bathroom.

I find my preferred spot is the shelter's laundry room, where it's warm and easy to strike up conversations with our neighbors. That's where I finally meet a new friend. Just like me, Karen is twelve, and she loves to read like I do. We hang out, paging through magazines from the shelter's shelves; or often Karen's family invites Rosie, Norman, and me to sit with them at dinner in the shelter's dining hall. I love this, because her mother is married, and her stepdad teaches us new words when we play hangman and Scrabble after we help with dinner cleanup.

Karen's stepdad sits in one of the wooden-frame chairs in the shelter's TV room, urging the baby as she practices walking or talking with Karen and me about what's happening in the news. He's the only man I can think of who has ever treated me like an adult, and he's one of the only decent dads at the shelter.

One day when the laundry room is almost empty, Karen tells me her stepdad's been asking her where I get all my bruises and cuts.

"It's from my brother, tell him," I reply. "You know boys, they love to wrestle."

Then the man who runs the shelter starts watching me in the laundry room. When I'm in there alone, in the corner of my eye I watch him take a seat next to me.

"Regina," he says. "Can you tell me where your mother spends her time?"

"Around," I answer. "You see her sometimes, but usually she just sleeps a lot." I pretend to concentrate on my magazine, an issue of *TV Guide* I've read a dozen times, aware that he knows my mother hangs around the shelter long enough to make herself appear present before she takes off for days to go hopping between bars and beds.

"I need you to tell me where the marks on your body come from."

I freeze.

"Your family's room is right next to the administration office, and some of the staff have reported hearing shouting, or often the TV's on full blast." When she is around to beat us, the loud TV is Cookie's number one tactic.

"It's my brother," I insist. "You've seen how he plays."

"Regina."

I put down my magazine with a huff.

"If you don't tell me the truth, I can't let you eat at meal-time."

"*It's my brother,*" I tell him. "If I were getting beat, don't you think you'd hear it?"

I'd survived worse than not eating for a few days, and not telling and going hungry was better than the risk of telling and getting separated.

At Christmas, the shelter workers invite us kids to help them decorate a Christmas tree. Rosie, now six, gently takes my hand and looks on with a shy smile when Santa arrives carrying a sack on his shoulder. The shelter director encouraged me to make a wish list, so I asked for new Mad Libs game pads and *Highlights* magazines to share with Rosie and Norm. As the gifts are being handed out, he also tells me to write a list of books appropriate for seventh grade, and he'll sign them out of the library for me. I jot down a dozen Landmark history books to read to Rosie, and a couple Judy Blumes. I figure, why not load up? You don't have to pay at the library.

Then a few months later, in March of 1979, Cookie returns to the shelter and announces that she's registered us back in school and rented the top unit in a duplex in Ronkonkoma. She drops us there and takes off immediately, which suits Rosie, Norm, and me fine: After having lived in the shelter for a few months, the three of us are so used to having friends around that every day after school we invite the neighborhood kids to our house. But the fun's over one afternoon when Cookie decides to come home, taking me by the hair and dragging me into her bedroom. Our friends tear down the stairs and outside as Cookie grabs a belt then rips off my shirt. She lashes my back, over and over. I try for the door but end up huddled in the corner, and as she takes a break to regain her grip on the belt, I start fighting back. She fights for her breath as she hurls the belt and screams, "The more you fight it, you skinny little whore, the longer it's going to take! You have boys over, you stupid slut? This is for your own good. You want to end up pregnant? Who's gonna take care of your baby? Huh?" she demands. "Me?"

When she's finished, she drags me to my room by my arm and tosses me inside. Quickly I put on a different shirt and shimmy down the back of the house, running out of the yard, dodging the commotion on the back porch as the neighbors point her to where I've gone. All one-hundred-eighty pounds of Cookie come heaving after me, and again she takes me by my hair and tugs me back to the house.

"Take off your jeans and your top," she says.

I glare at her.

"Take off your fucking clothes, you whore. Rosie, Norman," she says, "I want you to see what happens when you try to run away." I make eye contact with Rosie, who's looking on in fear as Cookie spins me so that my back's facing her. I stiffen, hearing her arm rise high in the air. She whips me . . . and whips me . . . and whips me some more. I squeeze my eyes shut and bite my lip and then finally cry out in pain as my entire body feels like it's swollen and red. Then she ties my hands together. She binds my ankles, and wraps my wrists around the closet rod. Once I'm hanging helpless inside the closet, she slams the door shut. I kick the door and scream, not able to control myself from giving her such satisfaction. The afternoon light streaming under the closet door begins to disappear swiftly, and the sensation is as though I'm being buried alive—chained up and shoved into a small space, the way she'd do when I was little. When my voice is gone and I'm certain my wrists must be sprained, I have no choice but to give up fighting. I struggle to keep my mind from panicking as the numerous incidents of being tied or chained up caused my intense claustrophobia. I fight off a panic attack by counting, then praying for any image that could possibly slow my pounding heart.

Then, I'm there: walking on the beach with my sisters and the kids, writing our names in the sand, floating in the water, and lifting up rocks to discover clams for dinner. I can taste the onion grass, feel the sway of the beach weeds bending against my knees in the breeze as we head out to swim on the floating dock.

IN THE MORNING Norman comes in to cut me loose, and I direct him as he gets Rosie ready for school. "You two cannot miss the bus," I tell him. "You have to eat today, and I can't go to school like this." Not only are my wrists scarred, but my image is, too. I work my stomach into knots wondering what I can possibly say to my friends after they witnessed how my mother treats me.

Days later I've got bigger problems when the landlord opens the door and marches right past me, carrying our belongings out to the lawn.

"But it's hardly even spring yet!" I tell him. "You're expecting us to sleep out in the cold?"

"I've let you stay here three months," he says, "which is two months more than your mother's paid for."

I turn to the kids, trying to keep my cool for their sake. "You stay here with all our stuff. I'm going to call Cherie. I'll be right back." At the convenience store up the road, I beg the clerk for a dime to call Cherie.

She shows up in her boyfriend's car to get us and sets us up to sleep at Kathy's house for the night. I dread her call to Cookie . . . who has no choice but to turn up the next morning with some BS story to try to rectify herself in front of Kathy's mother. "Oh, just wait until they hear from my lawyer. I'm gonna sue their shorts off!" she says. We spend the summer and fall living out of cars, bars, and hotels, and my thirteenth birthday is just like my twelfth . . . which was just like my eleventh. Right before Christmas, Cookie finds us a place in Smithtown with a landlord who likes to pay her visits late at night in lieu of accepting rent.

But it's all going as smoothly as I can hope when I'm able to register for eighth grade in the middle of the year, not revealing that I never finished seventh. Also, Camille moves back in when I persuade her during another pay phone call. "Smithtown's close to Hauppauge!" I tell her. "You'd be close to all your friends!" She moves back in, and we stay through the spring . . . but at the beginning of summer, the landlord's wife comes knocking when she finds out how the rent is being paid.

And then, before I ever see my eighth grade diploma . . .

We're gone.

8

Empty Emancipation

November 1980 to Summer 1984

I SHAKE THE cramp from my hand and look at Ms. Davis over the thick affidavit on Addie's table. "Emancipation," I ask her and Addie, "means that I will never have to answer to Cookie again . . . right?"

Addie glances at Ms. Davis, who says, "That's exactly what emancipation means, Regina."

In exhaustion, I want to rest my head on this document. Completing this affidavit will change everything, but based on every event we've experienced in the foster system up to now, we can never predict whether the change will be better or worse.

The story of how we grew up is finally revealed to the

authorities. Inside Addie's kitchen on that Sunday in November, four days after my mother bruised me with her kicks and bloodied me with broken glass, Ms. Davis primes us to sign the affidavit by explaining that nobody can access a report where child abuse is involved, especially not the accused. She also assures us our statements will only be used to proceed with my gaining freedom from Cookie.

"And—you swear, the county is going to do everything it can to make sure Cookie can *never* get the kids again?" I turn to Camille, making sure Ms. Davis knows the hardness of this next statement is all for her: "Because I would suffer these black-and-blue marks all over again—I would spend the rest of my life sleeping alone behind a grocery store to hide from Cookie—if it meant I'd never have to see my little sister's and brother's faces in terror inside a social services car again."

"I understand," Ms. Davis says.

"Well then, promise: You and everyone you work with will fight for the kids' safety from the second I put my pen to this page."

"Regina, I promise."

I look at Cherie and Camille. "I'm ready."

I put the ballpoint pen to the line reading *Signature* and in loopy, feminine strokes, sign:

Regina M. Calcaterra

Then I flip the pen toward Camille. "You're up."

She gently slides it from my grip and, with the confidence of a maestro, scrawls her name beneath mine, and then Cherie follows her lead before she heads back home to her young family.

"Now that you both determined you won't return to your

mother's care," Ms. Davis says, looking at Camille and me, "you need to begin planning how you'll live on your own as soon as you turn eighteen. The state only covers your foster care costs until then, unless you go to college."

"College?" I asked.

"Granted, that comes with its own challenges—in fact, I have yet to see a foster kid go to college."

"What? Why?"

"Well, think about it: It's tough to hold down a job and make rent when you're working hard to study. In any case, we'll start teaching you how to live independently. Then, hopefully, one day you can make it on your own." I glance at Camille, who's giving Ms. Davis a look of daggers.

After she leaves, Addie stands aside to let Camille and me pass from the kitchen. "Will you be joining us for dinner?" she says.

"No thanks," we call behind us. We close ourselves in Camille's bedroom, and I stare up at her ceiling. "I don't know how to feel," I confess.

She collapses with her head next to mine on the pillow. "Me neither."

Then as if on cue, we turn to each other and burst out laughing. We laugh so hard we begin to hyperventilate in tears until we roll off the bed, making two bony thuds on Addie's floor. Eventually, I'm able to compose myself enough to mock our three full days of social workers and legal talk. "Congratulations!" I declare. "Now that you've just dumped your mother, you'll be homeless again at eighteen . . . if you survive until then!"

Camille wipes her tears and folds her arms across her bust as Ms. Davis is apt to do. "Listen, girls," she says with fake empathy, "really, you don't stand an icicle's chance in hell. Just try not to end up a drug addict, an alcoholic, pregnant, a prostitute, or in jail."

"Like your mother!" I wail.

That night Camille kisses me on the cheek and smooths my hair behind my ear. "What are you thinking about?"

I sigh. "Rosie and Norm. Tomorrow after school I'm going to ask Addie if we can call them."

"I'm worried about them, too . . . but this is your day," Camille says. "Do you think our birthday girl is going to get her wish?"

I smile. All weekend we'd been trying to stay out of the way at our temporary foster home while also racing against Ms. Davis's deadline to get the affidavit completed and signed on time . . . but through all the chaos, my sister remembered that today I turned fourteen. Tucking my hands behind my head, I lie back on my pillow. "I think I just did."

MONDAY'S SCHOOL BUS ride is still buzzing from last week's presidential election with Ronald Reagan defeating President Jimmy Carter. "Are you better off than you were four years ago?" Reagan famously asked Carter in their final debate, a week before the election. *I'm better off than I was four* days *ago,* I figure.

In the halls of the high school I keep my hair in my face and my head down, hoping that if I don't meet the gaze of my peers, then they can't see me, either. I spend my time in class doodling *je t'aime* and *mia bambina amore* on the covers of my notebooks.

I begin to eat more, and within a week at the Petermans', my clothes start to fit differently. Because I'm a foster kid I get free lunch at school, then dinner every night with Camille, Danny, and the family. The more I eat, the more I want to eat—"Putting some meat on those bones for the winter!" Pete says—but Addie makes it clear that her home is no place for me to make up for all the meals I've missed in the last fourteen years. She's constantly on a diet, so eating between meals is discouraged for all of us . . . and I catch myself craving the Ho Hos and Twinkies I'd make a meal out of when we were living on our own. Camille, too, is obviously strained by all the restrictions—suddenly our entire lives are structured around the Petermans' meal schedule, TV-viewing schedule, homework, and curfews. At night, whispering in her bedroom, Camille begins to prepare me: Even though the Petermans have invited us both to stay permanently, she doesn't want to live in a way that's so restricted. She tells me she'll stay with me through the holidays, but by spring she wants to find another situation.

"Spring," I say. "Great. You're going to leave me just when we're about to go to court in April to make my emancipation official."

"Regina, I'm seventeen," she says. "You want to live this way forever? Speaking only when you're spoken to and always feeling paranoid that our foster parents are talking about us when we're not in the room—about our futures, our behavior, the way we hold our forks? Huh?"

I say nothing.

"Do you want the only love you feel to come from snuggling with your plastic Jesuses and pictures of the kids dressed in Lake Havasu T-shirts?"

Ouch. One for Camille.

"No matter where we've had to make a home for ourselves, we've always shared a lot of love." I know she's right—even when it was just Norm, Rosie, and me shivering inside the horse trailer, I'd learned from living for years with my sisters how to create an atmosphere of laughs, comfort, and ease. And when Cookie was around, we'd somehow establish a small space among the chaos for solace, where we could go and be together to talk and snuggle or play games. "By now I know how I want to live my life," Camille continues, "and it's not by learning to obey new rules in a strange house. I've already raised myself."

She gets a job at Wicks 'n' Sticks, a candle shop at the Smith Haven Mall. In turn I begin making friends at the bus stop. Sheryl and Tracey make it clear they're talking to me because they're really interested in coaxing me out of my shell, and it doesn't take long before I'm spending all my time outside school at their houses. They both have fathers and mothers who live together, two cars in the driveway, swimming pools in the backyard, closets stuffed with well-fitting clothes and, most important to me, refrigerators and pantries stocked with snacks and soda. I find it's much more comfortable to play the guest outside my foster family's home than in it.

It's fascinating to observe how normal families interact. With a mother and father in the house, it's as though everyone has a distinct role in the family: Dads work full-time at offices, moms work part-time or run the kids around; we kids can just hang out . . . and be kids. It's a totally new experience for me. We spend weekday afternoons watching MTV and doing homework and weekends at the movies, the bowling alley, and playing Pac-Man and Centipede at the mall arcade. Tracey giggles at my pronunciation. "It's Centipede, not Centerpede!" I just shrug and smile.

These families think they know me well, that I live at my aunt's house. I never share my story; the details of how I grew up, that I have younger siblings I'm trying to save, or that I have a mentally ill, alcoholic, promiscuous mother who won't be my mother much longer.

Camille and I are allowed a once-a-week phone call with Rosie and Norm, who cry in hushes when they tell us their new foster mom never hugs them and then disciplines them with hits and cursing. Over and over they say they've tried to tell their social worker, but instead of the sympathy or solutions they need, she tells them they ought to be better listeners. Camille and I tell our social worker that the kids, especially Rosie, would never lie about being hit. We beg Addie to please allow the kids to come live with us. Each time, however, she sadly tells us that she just cannot take them as well. She says she's already stretching her energy and resources; and besides, Rosie and Norm's social worker isn't convinced they're not just making up these stories because they're homesick for us.

As Christmas approaches, a social worker named Ms. Harvey is assigned to our case now that the Petermans have invited us to stay permanently. Her lack of cooperation to help us see the kids causes Camille and me to grow even more reclusive and rebellious, staying out of the house until curfew then locking ourselves in our rooms for the night. When Addie gets our monthly welfare check, she gives us each the county designated amount of sixty-two dollars of the two four-hundred-twelve-dollar checks she receives to use as our personal allowance for clothes, toiletries, books, and school field trips.

Then in early December the social workers inform us that we'll get to see the kids for a Christmas visit. Realizing we've spent all of our first check on warm coats and snow boots for ourselves, Camille takes a second job selling fragrances in the mall while I begin walking door-to-door to Addie's neighbors, offering to clean leaves off their lawns before the first snow for ten dollars each. Addie sees how hard we're working and recommends me to neighbors who need a babysitter who's willing to clean house . . . and on top of that I make an extra five dollars per week dusting Addie's furniture.

When Camille and I go Christmas shopping for Rosie and Norm, my sister follows my lead around the kids' clothing stores at the mall. "I'm a pro around these parts," I tell her. "They've got sizes that fit me, less expensive than the juniors section. Where do you think I've been doing all my shopping?"

"Save money shopping for kids' clothes while you can," Camille says, gesturing at my body. "I can already tell, you're starting to take some shape. The same thing that happened to me is gonna happen to you: You wake up one morning and—va-va-VOOM!—you need a bra. A *real* bra," she whispers. "We oughta place a bet on how much longer you'll fit into kids' turtlenecks."

"Just help me," I tell her. She pushes a cart and we load it with gloves, hats, scarves, new underwear, socks, winter boots, some jeans, and a rainbow array of cable-knit sweaters.

On Sunday, December 23, at one thirty in the afternoon, Cherie picks us up from the Petermans' and drives us thirty minutes to the kids' foster home. "Don't be surprised if they're not blown away by the gifts," Camille says. "Cookie's visitation was from nine to one today, and if she tried to win them over with anything, I guarantee it was toys."

"At least her car's not here," I say when we pull into the driveway of a dump of a house. The social workers were wise to give us an hour gap so we wouldn't have to cross paths with our mother.

Cherie turns off the ignition and helps us unload two stacks of presents so high we have to coach each other to navigate our eager approach to the front door, where we're met by a woman in a velour jogging suit and giant hair who, instead of welcoming us or introducing herself, tells us Cookie hasn't returned with the kids yet.

"Of course she hasn't," Cherie says. We look at each other, wondering how long it will take her to invite us in. We finally break the awkwardness and trudge back to the car. Cherie starts the car and flips on the heat full-blast. Then she walks to the corner phone booth to call her husband and tell him she'll be home later than she planned.

We sing to the radio and take turns knocking on the front door to ask whether Cookie has called with an update. Hours pass. Cherie tells us she's running low on gas and has to go home to feed her baby.

She drives Camille and me back to the Petermans'.

Every hour we call Rosie and Norm's house, and the answer is always the same. Hoping she'll respond first thing Monday morning, we leave a message for Rosie and Norm's social worker, whose number Addie agreed to pin on the corkboard by her phone.

We stay up through the night. When Camille's alarm clock flashes 6:00 in bright red digits, we tiptoe out to Addie's kitchen and pick up the phone again. Their foster mother's voice is groggy and irritated, and Rosie and Norm are still gone.

Ms. Harvey believes our conclusion that Cookie's run with the kids. "But it's Christmas Eve," she says, "and there's really not a lot we can do besides wait until the county's back from the holiday. I wouldn't worry, though—"

"Our mother has our eight-year-old sister and our twelve-year-old brother holed up in a car behind some grocery store, or in the house of whatever scuzzball she's sleeping with this week. And you wouldn't *worry?*" Camille yells into the phone. I fold my arms across me, sick to my stomach. When Camille gets upset, the weight of my guilt for coming forward multiplies.

"With the state watching over your mother's shoulder, it doesn't seem very likely she would do Norman and Roseanne any harm."

"She just *kidnapped* Norm and Rosie," Camille says. "And you don't think we should call the police?"

"They would have to have been abducted by a stranger to warrant my calling the police."

"Our mother is more dangerous to those kids than any stranger," Camille says. "You're fools if you don't track her down."

"Merry Christmas, Camille," Ms. Harvey says, ending the call. "Tell Regina, too. Enjoy your time off from school. When I'm back from holiday vacation, I'll look up your mother's most recent address in the files. I'll get back to you when we have something."

It's after New Year's when social services finally finds

Cookie living at her boyfriend's house. "My children told me they were being beaten at their foster home. You think I was going to deliver them back to that hell on earth?" she told the workers. "I am their mother. They're happy with me. Go piss up a tree. I'll see you in April."

Ms. Harvey said that, from everything Norm and Rosie's social worker reported, the kids were living in a nice house in the same school district and seemed content living as a family with Cookie's new boyfriend and his teenage daughter. "They've decided to let the situation be for now," Ms. Harvey explained. "But as long as the judge grants Regina's emancipation at the April hearing, then it's almost guaranteed the court will determine that Cookie is an unfit caretaker and most likely will remove your brother and sister from her care."

Camille's skeptical. "And why would that be?"

"Your case hasn't gone to court, so your mother gets the benefit of the doubt. But once the judge reads your statement, he'd be crazy to let her keep Norman and Roseanne."

"Sure, go ahead and wait," Camille says. "But Cookie knows what's coming. By April, you watch. She'll be long gone."

WITH COOKIE'S ABDUCTION of the kids looming over us, even our February vacation to Disney World in the Petermans' RV is hard to enjoy. Our teachers sent a list of reading and homework for us to do on the three-day trip down the East Coast, but instead we play Scrabble and the license plate game . . . and even then, my mind drifts to thinking about what Rosie and Norm must be going through. Every time Pete stops at a gas station, I eye the phone booth. I've got change to make a

long-distance call and Ms. Harvey's number memorized . . .
but considering the results of all the calls up to now, I figure
the money will be better spent on Mickey souvenirs for whenever I do see the kids.

In March, Cherie shows up at the Petermans' house in a
tizzy. "Cookie was arrested for stealing from her boyfriend's
house," she says. "She called me to bail her out."

"Did you do it?" Camille and I ask in unison.

"Yes, I did it. I couldn't think of what else to do, I was so
worried about what would happen to Rosie and Norman with
no one there to protect them if the cops showed up. I can't ask
my mother-in-law to have them stay here. So I said to Cookie,
'If you want me to get your ass out of jail, you better tell me:
Where are the kids?'

"'The *kids*,' she tells me, 'are in a hotel that I went to after
Jeff kicked us out.'

"And I go, 'Oh, *Jeff*?'" Cherie says. "And I'm just supposed to know who Jeff is? So she gets all snotty: 'Who the
fuck do you think he is, Cherie? He's the guy I've been living
with the past couple months.' I thought I would throw the
phone at the wall. 'Norm is there, watching Rosie,' Cookie
says. 'He's twelve—practically a young man now!'"

"Oh crap," I say. "Did they see her get arrested?"

"That's what I asked her," Cherie says. "Cookie tells me,
'Nope,' all dismissive. 'They busted me in the pub parking
lot. See, I went to meet Jeff so we could talk it out, but he set
me up. Next thing I know, I'm in cuffs.'" Cherie explains that
the cops had social services track down the kids, who were
staying in a motel.

I march to Addie's kitchen phone. "I'm calling Ms.
Harvey."

When she answers, she explains: "The cops decided Norman is old enough to watch Roseanne while Cookie is incarcerated for assault and battery."

"Wait, Ms. Harvey, let me get this straight: Cookie is arrested for trying to beat up her boyfriend—in jail for the weekend—and our little brother is watching Rosie by himself?"

"Regina, I'm just telling you what the police told me."

"Who's paying for the room? What if they get kicked out? Then what?"

"Well, in that case they would be homeless and we would place them in another home. But until then, the authorities have decided that they're both safe and secure. Besides, now that your mother's bailed out, she'll probably be back with them in a few hours."

Camille and I have devised a plan: The only way we can watch out for Rosie and Norm is to convince Cookie that all's forgiven and we still want her in our lives.

"She's a lunatic," Cherie says. "You sure you want to go through with this cockamamy plan?"

With Daisy Duck and Goofy ball caps in a bag as souvenirs, we wait at the motel room's outside entrance until Cookie answers with a cigarette between her fingers like some Hollywood vixen. "Well well well," she says, holding the door as though she has to consider letting us in. "Just like always, you two come crawling back."

Camille occupies Rosie and Norm while I sit down on the bed, across from where Cookie's seated at the motel room's desk. Without looking at me, she says, "I see you're starting to come into your own. Shocker with those little tits, nobody's knocked you up yet."

"I didn't come here to be the butt of any insults," I answer. "I really want to work this out."

"Well, don't try to buy me with any sweet talk. You ratted me out to every official in Suffolk County when all I've ever done was work hard to give you kids a good life."

"Ratted you out?"

In the background Camille turns on the TV for Rosie and Norm.

"You are required by law to attend the emancipation hearing of Regina M. Calcaterra," she recites. "What are you, fucking Queen Elizabeth? I got friends, you know. I know what emancipation means."

Camille slides to sit on the bed next to me. Cookie lights another cigarette. "There's been a lot of confusion," my sister says. "But Regina and I are always talking about how we miss being a family."

"What the fuck do you two want?"

"We want to see you. And Norman and Rosie."

I pipe in. "And you know, it won't be long before I'm eighteen." I remember how Ms. Harvey suggested I try to maintain contact with Cookie in the event I need a place to go when I age out of foster care. I tell Cookie: "I'll have the choice of who I want to live with. Who knows, maybe we'll want to be a family again. Maybe things could be normal."

"Regina, you've been running away from me since the day you sprouted legs," she says. "If you think for half a second that I'll support you when you're an adult, then you better quit whatever it is you're smokin' now."

"We just want you in our life . . . Mom." The word tastes like vinegar in my mouth.

"Well, you little assholes should have thought of that before

the county asked me to RSVP to the Regina Calcaterra Independence Day Parade." She takes a drag off her cigarette. "Is
Cherie waiting for you in the car? Get the fuck out of here."

Camille and I exchange a glance, rise, and approach the
kids to hug them good-bye. When Camille takes off outside,
I follow, slamming the door to Cookie's motel room so hard
the windows shake.

IN APRIL, CAMILLE is watching me closely. I'm not eating
again, thanks to the nerves the emancipation hearing is kicking up in my stomach. "You don't even have to go," Camille
says. "Ms. Harvey is your court-appointed guardian, she'll be
doing all the talking."

With how poorly she's protected the kids these last few
months, unfortunately that information is zero comfort.

The afternoon of the hearing, when Camille and I arrive
home from school, Addie's in the kitchen tapping her finger
on a cup of coffee. "What?" I ask her. "The news isn't good?"

"It's good for you," Addie says. "You won by default."

"Default?"

"Your mother didn't show up to the hearing. The judge
made a default judgment against her."

"Regina!" Camille says. "You did it!"

"Wait," I ask Addie, pulling back from Camille's hug.
"Rosie and Norm: They're free from her, too?"

"Regina, that's the bittersweet part," Addie says. "You
don't have any control over what happens to your brother and
sister. For now, the court decided to leave them with your
mother."

I stare at her, indignant. I don't have any control? I look at
Camille, whose eyes are welling with tears. We can't be happy

for my freedom while there's any ounce of possibility that our younger siblings will be forced to suffer with Cookie. I flee from the kitchen and slam my bedroom door. I grab everything I can get my hands on and throw it: the only outlet I've ever found effective when I'm in a blind rage.

ONE MORNING IN May, Addie and Camille exchange a knowing glance when I come out to the kitchen with stomach pains so bad I think I might throw up. "Maybe you should stay home from school," Addie says.

Camille knocks on the bathroom door just as I'm discovering a spot of blood on my leg. "Honey," she calls, "why don't you let me help?" She inconspicuously edges inside the bathroom and shows me how to adhere a maxi pad. "And here's where Addie keeps our stashes. Always make sure you have extras in your bag . . . especially if you visit Cookie."

"Why?"

"Because she doesn't buy these. She'd rather spend the food stamps on beer and cigarettes. Remember the bloody washcloths she used to leave around the house?"

I grimace. "Oh, Camille!"

"Yeah. I know. It was gross."

In the kitchen, Addie's looking through the phone book. "I'm going to make you an appointment at the doctor," she says.

"The doctor? I'm not sick, I just got my period."

"Well, there are precautions certain young women should take when their bodies grow capable of bearing children." Oh, that's what this is about: Addie's afraid she'll be raising a foster grandchild if she doesn't get me on the pill. "Birth control helps regulate a woman's cycle," she says.

I want to tell her to cut the crap. I could teach sex education at my school better than any teacher who actually studied it. At the age of eight, I learned how one gives a blow job thanks to Cookie's demonstration on one of her boyfriends when she thought we were all asleep. At twelve, I walked into my mother's bedroom to find a huge pink dildo and a magazine called *High Society* laying open to a letter from a man detailing his one-night stand with a female gymnast so skilled that when she swung from the chandelier, she landed in a split, directly on his erect penis. Thanks to my mother's graphic language and her casual displays around the house (like how she would grab Karl between his legs in front of us), when you grow up witness to such sexual behavior, nothing about it is very fascinating. In fact, it shuts out any desire whatsoever.

Still, with Addie's incessant urging, I make a trip to the gynecologist. The county bus system is so infrequent and confusing that I arrive late, alone, and even more stressed out than I'd prepared myself for. When the nurse calls me into the sterile gray room, I follow her instruction to lie on the table. "Slide your feet into the stirrups, please," she says, and I feel the blood rush from my face when the doctor walks in the door. After barely an introduction I feel the heat of his examining light between my legs, and my body clenches with the touch of his medical instruments. Suddenly I'm back in that foster home seven years ago, on the winter night when my sisters were locked out in the cold and Norm was banging on the door. *"Let my sister go!"* he'd screamed. This doesn't feel much different. I feel violated, isolated, and quite certain that this makes it official: I never want to allow a boy to touch me again.

It seems like no one besides Camille will give me a straight talk about womanhood, although some adults do seem to care enough to fumble through a few tidbits. On the last day of freshman year, I go home with my friend Sheryl, whose mom takes us to the park at the Wood Road School. I catch her eyeing my orange tank top before she says, "Girls, this is probably a good time to bring this up, and I'm only going to say it once: Never sit on the same swing with a boy."

Sheryl and I look at each other bewildered. "Mom, why?" she asks.

"Because there are two swings: one for each of you. So you can swing, and he can swing, and you can even swing at the same time . . . but separately, you see. Never together."

We break into a fit of laughter. "Mom," Sheryl says. "What about the teeter-totter?"

"Girls, I'm serious: There will be no bumping on the swings."

"Thank you very much for that informative birds and bees talk, Mrs. Z," I say, and Sheryl and I run for the swings, wrapping our arms around our shoulders with our imaginary swing-bumping boyfriends.

That summer, Cherie is tied up with the baby. Camille's still at the Petermans' but often working twelve hours a day. I spend my days babysitting the kids on Addie's street or with Sheryl and Tracey, taking the nine A.M. bus to Smith Point Beach and hopping the five P.M. bus home. We buzz about the thought of entering tenth grade and trying out for gymnastics. Secretly, I'm also excited because it's the first time I'll start the school year with a close-knit group of friends and a wardrobe I'm actually not embarrassed to wear.

The first week of school I'm dumbstruck when the gymnastics coach reads my name off the list of girls who made the cut. "Coach," I say, while the other girls are busy in huddled squeals. "I couldn't even take a stab at the bars."

"Your upper body needs some strengthening, but your legs are cut and you're strong on the beam. I'm going to start you with the junior varsity team."

Instantly, I begin to structure my days around a full day of school followed by gymnastics practice until six thirty, then babysitting and housecleaning jobs. In study hall, while the other kids sketch the logos of Van Halen and AC/DC on their notebooks, I doodle *Rosie* and *Norman* in hearts and bubbles with *mia bambina amore* and *je t'aime* scribbled around them. Any homework I don't get done at school is a good excuse for me to maintain my privacy when I get home in the evenings.

One night in early October, Addie knocks on my bedroom door. "You have a visitor," she says. Cherie appears behind her in the doorway, and Camille pops her head out of her bedroom.

"What are you doing here?" Camille says. "You never stop over without calling first."

Cherie looks at the ceiling as if she's praying to save her last nerve. "Cookie was driving drunk and she got into an accident," she says. "She left the scene, and the police were looking for her . . . and . . . she skipped town with the kids."

Camille asks, "Wait, I didn't hear this part. What do you mean 'skipped town'?"

Cherie says, "I got a call from Cookie's friend Jackie Sones. You remember her? She lived near us in Saint James."

"Jackie Sones—the one who moved to Idaho?"

"Yeah," Cherie says, clearly dreading what she has to

reveal next. "She told me Cookie is heading out there so she can live in Jackie's trailer and work with animals on a farm. So, with the kids, off she drove."

We walk out to the kitchen, where Addie gives us permission to call Ms. Harvey at home. "Girls, there's nothing anybody here can do if your mother left the state."

"Oh, big shock," I say, "considering how much you did to protect them while they were here."

It's close to Halloween when Jackie Sones calls Cherie to tell her Cookie and the kids have arrived.

"They stayed with Jackie a few weeks until Cookie found a bowlegged old man named Clyde who lives on a farm in some town called Oakview," Camille tells me.

"Let me guess, so she used her ways to convince him that he would be better off if her brood moves in."

We learn that, to maintain her part of the bargain, Cookie volunteered the kids to work as farmhands. They rise every morning to milk the cows, shovel horse manure, bale hay, and tend the crops. "I know how this works," I tell Camille. "If they don't step up, they'll get beaten."

"Yeah," she sighs. "That's what I'm afraid of."

"Well, at least they're in a small town. When we figure out how to fix this, hopefully it will be easy to find them."

She gives me Clyde's phone number, which Jackie shared with her. I pop more quarters in the pay phone. A gruff, bothered male voice answers. "Yeah?"

"Is this Clyde?"

"Yeah?"

"I'm Regina, Cookie's daughter, calling from New York. Can you please put Rosie on the phone?"

After some murmurs and the croak of Cookie's voice objecting in the background, I finally hear Rosie's tender voice: "Gi?"

Tears gush out of my eyes. *"Bambina?"* I ask her. "Are you and Norman okay?"

She stays quiet.

"Is Mom standing right there?"

I hear her debating over how to respond. "Yeah."

"Okay. I'm going to speak quietly, but here's what we'll do. I'm going to ask you some questions. If the answer is yes, you'll pretend to answer me about life on the farm. Like, 'Yes, there are lots of animals here.' And if the answer if no, you'll do the same thing—'No, it hasn't snowed here yet. Silly Regina, it's only October.' You ready?"

"Yes, there are lots of animals here."

I giggle. "Good, you get it!" Through a conversation carried in this kind of code, Rosie makes it clear that she and Norm are attending school regularly, but also that Cookie and Clyde are abusing her. That night I call Ms. Harvey, who says the usual: "There's really nothing we can do."

Over the next week, I continue making these coded calls to Rosie and Norman, and they reveal as much as they can through the feigned conversations. Then I call information and ask for the number to the elementary school in Oakview, Idaho. "May I speak with the guidance counselor please?" I ask.

When he's patched through I tell him about Cookie's history and what's been happening to Rosie. Then Cookie calls me at Addie's to tell me the guidance counselor brought her in for a meeting to check out my story. "And when I asked the kids what the hell was going on, they told me the whole thing," Cookie says. "You three have a code when you call here. You give them the third degree, then you think you have us all figured out. Well guess what," she says with a low growl. "I told the guidance counselor the truth: that you're a juvenile delinquent and alcoholic liar who was committed to a foster home to keep your ass out of jail. And do you think I was *proud* to tell him that Rosie is a promiscuous nine-year-old who made advances toward Clyde? Then when he rejected her, she started making up stories! That's how it went, Regina. It was humiliating to talk about what derelicts my children have turned out to be. Although, knowing the kind of man your father is, I don't know why I'm surprised. And for the record, the marks on her body? *Those* are from the farmwork. You don't get to live and eat for free, in Idaho or Long Island or anywhere else."

Sobbing, I call Ms. Harvey and beg her to speak to Rosie and Norm's guidance counselor in Idaho and tell him that she outright lied to him about the kids and me. "Please, to hear this woman, she's totally insane!"

Ms. Harvey refuses. "Your siblings are in the hands of another state now, Regina. For the last time, I'll tell you: There is nothing we can do."

"Ms. Harvey, you promised me you all would protect my brother and sister if I signed that report telling everything my mother has done." I slam down the phone so hard, I see Pete rise from his recliner as I run down the hall to my room. In trying to help the kids, I've made it worse for them. Without me there to take Cookie's abuse, Rosie bears the brunt of my attempts to save them. I've failed to protect her the way

Cherie and Camille protected me. I want to tell Rosie that the brutality she's enduring is torturing me, too.

IT'S THE FALL of tenth grade when the new county phone book arrives at Addie's. I quickly rip it open and thumb my way to *A*:

Accerbi, Paul & Joan

I sigh with relief: My father's still close; and if the phone book's factual, so are all his relatives. I haven't worked up the courage to contact him, but for now it's enough to know that I could. On November 9, 1981—my fifteenth birthday—I begin a countdown for the thirty-six months I have to reach out to him before I might actually need to ask him for some help.

I hope he'll be proud. I'm getting solid grades in all my classes, but history and English are where I'm earning easy A's. I make sure I tell Mr. Kelly and Mr. Maguire how hard I'm studying, and they both begin to discuss college with me. "I know you're a foster kid," Mr. Kelly says after class one day, "but don't believe what anyone else tells you. There *is* a way out of your situation: It's through continuing your education past high school." Then they both co-opt my guidance counselor to get in on the cause.

I feel torn for Camille's sake. She also wants to go to college, but her senior class guidance counselor told her at the beginning of the year not to bother trying to get into the Fashion Institute of Technology, her dream school. "Concentrate on getting married and having babies," her counselor told her. Unfortunately, that advice only further confused Camille because Ms. Harvey had recently told her that she was so detrimentally affected by how we grew up that she probably would never have a functional family of her own. Through all of my sophomore year, I watch Camille quietly prepare to move out of the Petermans'. The summer before my junior year, she moves out and lives with friends. She's begun dating a handsome, gentle-spirited, blue-eyed boy named Frank, whom she met while out dancing, and she tells me that he's starting to talk about marriage. *See?* I want to tell the social workers and counselors. *All of you were wrong; Camille's going to be fine.* I block out everyone's input except my teachers', knowing my only hopes of ever rescuing Rosie lay in my understanding of how the system works and getting respect from the people who work in it. A thousand times a day I repeat this to myself: *College degree.*

BY THE TIME I turn sixteen during junior year, I've gotten a job at Rickel Home Center a few miles away from Addie and Pete's. Until Sheryl takes a job at the register next to mine, the work is so boring that to make the time pass I talk to the customers in a British accent. Sometimes I walk all the way there, and other times I catch the bus that takes me a third of the way, then I walk the rest. Sometimes when they can, Addie or Pete will drop me off or my friends Erin and Tracey will give me a lift, now that they both have their permits.

Of course, friends with cars present the opportunity for more interaction with boys, because now we're able to go places unsupervised. Addie reminds me to focus on my studies, and I tell her there's no need to be concerned. I've started dating a boy named Eddie . . . but despite the appearances I create for his sake, I have no real interest in bonding with him. First, while he's worried about soccer practice and trying to get me alone to make a move, I'm more concerned about my studies and plotting out my next conversation with Cookie to see how Rosie's really doing. Plus, I know what troubles boys can bring—the same troubles Cookie's always getting herself into. So with Eddie, I let on like I'm invested, while also doing my best to control my tendency to cut and run when he gets too close. There's a much more important man tugging at my heart: Paul Accerbi, who, as of this autumn, no longer appears in the Suffolk County phone book.

For months after I notice his listing missing, I contemplate what to do. Finally, I rip out the page where his name used to be and study it on the annual February Disney World quest. While hidden away in the top bunk of the mobile home, I stare obsessively at the place where his name used to be . . . then something new jumps out at me: There's an Accerbi in Lindenhurst, whose names sound familiar: Frank and Julia. *How is this just now coming to me?* I recall Cherie and Camille talking about an aunt Julie and an uncle Frank and the willow tree we would sit under with them. But with no phone on the camper, I can't call my sisters to verify the memory.

Cherie and Camille used to tell me stories about different places we lived when I was little, and the names they'd given them all. There was the Bubble House and the Happy House and the Glue Factory and the Brady Bunch House. I learned the Bubble House was our first foster home, where we all slept in the same room and our foster parents and their daughter, Susan, would lull us to sleep by turning on a globelike machine that would spin around and show bubbles on the blue walls of our room. The Glue Factory was where we lived the longest as a family in Saint James. But I couldn't remember living in the Happy House, a place were Cherie and Camille seem to remember that we three girls were loved, cared for, and fed beyond anything else we've ever experienced. As we moved from place to place, they would reminisce about the Happy House and the Bubble House—"At the Happy House, the curtains were always open to let the light in," Cherie would say, or "When I hear this song on the radio, I always turn it up because it reminds me of the Bubble House." Since we never could figure out where the Happy House was, we all finally agreed that it must have been born from our own folklore. We settled on the fact that we learned how to keep a home at the Bubble House.

But we'd also agreed that, at one point, there'd been an aunt Julie and an uncle Frank in our lives. There was something that made us believe they weren't our true aunt and uncle, but people we'd met along the way.

As soon as Pete pulls the motor home back into our driveway in Centereach, I run out of the camper to the yellow kitchen phone and call Camille.

"Julia and Frank Accerbi—could they be the same people we called aunt and uncle?"

"Regina, maybe . . . maybe these people *are* related to Paul. But I don't know how we would have known them, and I wouldn't believe whatever crazy story Cookie would come up with if we asked her. It doesn't quite fit together."

But she didn't rule it out . . . and I so badly needed to know if Paul had moved away or, God forbid, died, so I convince myself that they would know. For weeks, I rehearse draft after draft of what to write. On Easter, I select a note at random from a stack of the very best I've written. I address it to Julia and Frank Accerbi and include only my name and house number on the return address line—not the Petermans' names, or their phone number. I don't want any of the Accerbis letting the Petermans know that I've reached out to the man I believe is my biological father.

April 3, 1983

Dear Mr. & Mrs. Accerbi,

My name is Regina Marie Calcaterra. I am 16 years old and believe that Paul Accerbi is my father. I also believe that there is a possibility that you are related to him. If you are, please pass this letter on to him.

Dear Paul,

My name is Regina Marie Calcaterra. I am 16 years old and was born in November of 1966. I believe that you may be my father. I am now living in a foster home because my mother, Camille Calcaterra, was a bad mother, not because I was a bad kid. I divorced her several years ago so I can work toward taking care of myself. I have a B average in school, am on the gymnastic team, and work at Rickel Home Center at nights and on the weekends. I plan on going to community college when I graduate high school.

My mother told me that you were my father many times during my upbringing and she never strayed from her belief. Unfortunately my mother is an alcoholic and drug addict, which caused her to be incapable of caring for my siblings and me, so we spent most of our youth raising ourselves. When I turned fourteen, I asked the court to emancipate me from her so I could make my own decisions about where I should live and what school I should go to. I have been in this foster home for 2½ years beginning from when I was in the 9th grade. I am now in the 11th grade.

I have limited contact with my mother, so I am hoping that I can meet you to see if you could possibly be my father, as my mother is convinced you are. Please write me back at the address below.

Sincerely,
Regina Marie Calcaterra

For weeks I try to get the mail before my foster parents do to see whether there's a letter from any of the Accerbis. On a Sunday night in early May, after I return around ten o'clock from working at Rickel's, I'm preparing for school the next day. Addie knocks on my door. "Come in!"

She has a disturbed look on her face. "Regina, Pete got a weird call tonight around seven o'clock. It was very peculiar—there was this man who called, and when Pete answered the phone, he asked if you were home. When Pete said no, he asked where you were, so Pete said you were at work. When Pete asked him to identify himself he refused, but he asked Pete if he was your foster father."

"Really?" I say innocently. "That's odd." Meanwhile my heart is pounding.

Addie's face grows more puzzled and her words come out slower as she continues. "When Pete said yes, this person wanted to know when you would be home again. So Pete asked him again who he was, but he still refused, and Pete told him that you won't be home until late, so if he wants to speak to you he should call back tomorrow after you're back from school. Do you know who that could have been, and why they're calling here?"

"I think it's my real father, Paul Accerbi."

I wish I could rewind my words . . . but already Addie's taken them in, trying to calculate the facts. "Well then, how did he get our number, or know Pete's name?"

"I don't know," I lie. "Well, actually . . . I may know how." I tell Addie about the letter, how I'd been watching my father's name in the phone book for years, praying that he'll be there for me when I turn eighteen.

But Addie's already lost in tears. "Why did you contact him?" she says. "Aren't you happy here with us? Don't we do enough for you? Do you want to leave us?"

I stand motionless, watching her pour out emotions that I've never seen before—toward me or anyone she knows. "You mean you want me to stay here?" I ask her. And suddenly it's all too much to bear. I begin shaking. "I didn't know that I could hurt you," I tell Addie. "But I need to know who my real father is. I have been curious for years, since I was eleven and he walked into the back of the deli I was working in. He examined me so closely, Addie, and now he actually took the time to find out my phone number and Pete's name. I know it's him calling. I just wanted to let him know that I'm okay. That I'm a good kid."

The next day I struggle to concentrate in school and skip my last two classes to come home early so I can sit by the phone and wait. But every time the phone rings, it's never Paul, and I rush the person off the other end to keep the line open.

When Addie arrives home, she says she spoke to social services. "They said that you're not allowed to meet him alone, and you may not even speak to him on the phone if Pete or I, or Ms. Harvey, are not around. This is a strange man—it's possible he isn't your father at all, it could be someone who likes seeing you at Rickel's or who remembers you from having dated your mother. So they want to avoid you putting yourself in a bad situation with this person without us here to protect you." As she finishes expressing her concern for me, the ring of the phone busts through the tension. She looks at me. "Regina, let me answer that."

The exchange is curt. "Yes, I am Addie Peterman, the foster mother of Regina Marie. And you are . . . ? And you are . . . ? Mr. Accerbi—"

My heart leaps.

"—although you refuse to identify yourself, we know who you are. I'll have you know: Regina told us that she reached out to you." Then she shoos me toward the phone in her bedroom so she can listen in on our conversation from the kitchen phone. "Yes, Mr. Accerbi. I'll get her on the phone now."

I rub my sweaty hands on my Jordaches before I answer the phone. "This is Regina." My heart pounds. My voice wants to shriek in delight.

"Young lady," he says. "You should know what a disruption you have created in my life."

"Pardon me?"

"My wife is sick and has been crying on the couch for days over this. I don't have a strong heart, and your behavior could very well result in a second heart attack. I don't know who you are or why you believe what you believe, or even why you wrote such a letter to my family members. You have created an embarrassing situation for all of us and I am sure that you have also upset your foster parents as well."

Now this is personal—he will not get away with trying to manipulate me this way. "Hey Paul," I dare ask him, "how did you get our phone number or figure out my foster parents' names?"

"It is no concern to you how I found it out," he says. "I just did."

I know I've cornered him. This verbal volleyball is like fighting with Cookie. "Who was here? Was it you?"

He falls silent.

"So I'll assume that you drove by the return address that I left you in the letter, saw the Petermans' names on the mailbox, and looked up their number." I whisper: "Didn't you?" It's in that breath I realize without a doubt that he has to be my father—why else would he be calling me, going to these lengths to find out the names of my foster parents, and our phone number?

He ignores my question and says he wants to meet me.

"Good, I want to meet you, too . . . but there are rules. Either my foster parents or my social worker have to be present."

"I'm not meeting you with others around."

"Look, I don't have a choice. I'm a sixteen-year-old girl living under the roof of foster parents, and I have to obey or else I could end up back on the street. Those are the terms. That's the only way."

"I'll think about it," he says. "And I'll call you tomorrow."

The next day Addie speaks to the social worker who says Paul can meet me at the house in a room separate from the supervision. "Or if he wants to meet outside the home, Pete or I have to be there but we can make it inconspicuous," Addie says.

I skip school as Addie and I plan how we can set up the meeting . . . and record it. If they weren't going to be in the room then they needed to somehow bear witness to the conversation so that if Paul Accerbi changed his story later, it would be my word against his. "Ooh, I've got it!" Addie says. "He can come to the house, in the living room, and we'll put your boom box with a blank cassette tape behind the chair he'll sit in. Then, when he's walking up to the front stoop, we press Record!" Addie's relishing our sleuthing strategy.

"Pete and I will busy ourselves in the garage or outside in the garden! This way, we won't impose, see . . . that will allow you and Paul to speak freely."

Our plan is in place . . . but he never calls the next night.

Or the night after that.

Then, on Thursday night the phone rings. This time, Pete answers and hands the phone to me.

In my ear, Paul reiterates what an "uproar" I've created in his home and how disrespectful it was for me to have done such a thing. Then, after his lecture, he calms down and says, "I've decided I'd like to meet you." When I remind him of the conditions, he raises his voice in anger. "Regina, what I wanted to tell you is that you are probably not my daughter. Your mother was promiscuous; she slept around a lot and was sleeping with many men all the time. She had quite a reputation for being—you know—you know what I mean. You're old enough to understand what I'm saying, right?"

"What, that my mother was a slut?" I ask him. "Yes, Paul. I am well aware of my mother's behavior and so are all my siblings. But when it came to who our fathers are, we were able to tell when she lied and when she told the truth. But when she would say the same story over and over again—the way she did about you, whether she was straight or sober—we knew that to be the truth. When her stories would change, that was the lie. She never changed her story about you, Paul. And she still hasn't."

"Your mother and I had a one-night stand and that was it," Paul said. I note an emphasis in order to satisfy what seems like an audience on his side of the phone.

"A one-night stand. You are saying that you were a one-night stand of my mother, and that based on that, she thinks you're my father. Really, Paul? Well, if you were a one-night stand, then how come she told me that you were in the Korean War, wanted to be a paratrooper, own a fence company, grew up in Lindenhurst, have an ex-wife named Carol and a daughter named Barbara? Frankly, Paul, you're full of shit. If you were just a one-night stand, then you certainly talked a lot for one night!"

The call goes dead.

I slam the yellow phone back on Addie's wall. "*That* man is my father!" I yell at Pete, who's curiously watching me pull out my boom box from its hiding place. "I won't be needing this back here since there will be no Paul Accerbi meeting to record."

He never calls back, and I don't care. He's no better than my mother—I should have figured that out a long time ago. She picked some winners, and he was just like all the rest.

By the summer I've closed off the whole experience; compartmentalized it and detached from it, the way I've learned to do with all the craziness in my life, which always stems back to Cookie. I busy myself working at Rickel's to save money for college . . . then there's finally something to celebrate when Addie and Pete come through with a car for me. "You can buy our Pinto for two hundred seventy-five dollars," Addie says, "if you're willing to put down a seventy-five-dollar deposit." There's more good news when I come to them with the seventy-five bucks: They've decided to waive the two hundred and let me keep the car as an early graduation present.

The fall of my senior year, I'm named cocaptain of the gymnastics team. Under the guidance of Mr. Kelly and Mr. Maguire, I take my college exams and list my two schools of choice. They're convinced that I'll get accepted to the university, insisting that if I do, I have to go. "A bachelor's degree from Stony Brook would serve you better than an associate's from the community college," Mr. Maguire says. It makes sense, but I'm afraid to get my hopes up. Preoccupied with whether I'll have a home during or even after college, I look up a number in the phone book for the only possible family who might be able to help me:

Calcaterra, Michael and Rose

Grandma Rose warms up on the other end of the phone when I tell her I haven't had a relationship with my mother for the last three years. I hear tears overcome her voice when she tells me, "We always wanted to know you kids. Will you let me take you shopping before you graduate? We're so proud of you." Before Easter, she and my grandfather—Grampa Mike—accompany me to JCPenney, where they let me pick out a prom dress and put it on their charge card. As Grandma Rose and the cashier exchange niceties at the cash register, I wonder: Why did you punish me when I was little by cutting me off? How was it acceptable for my siblings and me to bear the burden of Cookie alone? As she hands me the hanging plastic bag with my dress inside, Grandma Rose looks in my eyes . . . and suddenly I understand that this purchase is her amends to me. I realize that in this moment—as I'm about to leave high school and enter the world as an adult—I have a choice: I can distance myself and remain cynical toward her, or I can forgive her in the interest of developing a relationship with someone who's actually my family.

After I graduate in June 1984, Addie knocks on my bedroom door. "Your mother's on the phone," she says.

My face twists in confusion. "Cookie? Called here?"

Addie's expression tells me she's confused, too. "Yes."

I pick up the phone in her bedroom. "Hello?" I hear Addie gently hang up her end of the phone in the kitchen.

"I called to wish you a happy graduation." Cookie's voice is gruff and strained. "I've got something for you."

I hesitate for the punch line. "What?"

"A boot up your ass!"

I chuckle along, slightly stunned that she's contacted me.

"Actually, I have something in mind," I tell her. "I've saved money to take a plane to Idaho for a visit. Would you be willing to have me?" My tone is sweet. If I disarm her, she may let me come out to see the kids. I still think about Rosie constantly, even though it's been four years since we've seen each other in person. I try to convince myself that she knows I did everything I could to save her.

"I guess that'd be okay," Cookie says. "If you agree to leave your attitude in New York."

When I tell Camille I'm going, she's concerned how I'll do when I have to face Cookie. "You haven't seen her since that day in the motel room," Camille says. "Are you nervous?"

"Nah. She knows she has to pick me up from the airport, and I'll make it clear right up front that I'm the boss of that relationship now."

Cookie and Norman stand by as I lift my suitcase into the car. "Get a load of you," Cookie says, looking me over. In the last three years, my hair's grown back thick, and I set it with rollers so it's shiny and full. The bare limbs stemming from my tropical pink shorts and T-shirt are fit and trim, and I wear gold jewelry around my tanned neck and wrists. I've grown into a young woman with features that Addie says intimidate the boys, and right before graduation I found out I was accepted to the local community college. Feeling certain about my future, I stand before Cookie with satisfaction of who I've become. Already it's clear nothing about her has changed.

Rosie, who's obviously afraid to speak in front of Cookie, is blossoming, too. Just a few months shy of twelve years old, my baby sister is almost unrecognizable from the little peanut I knew four years ago. She's peaked much sooner than the rest of us did, already a head taller than fifteen-year-old Norm. Her father, Vito, was a tall, broad man and Rosie's frame is taking after his. As a result, although she's still a preteen, she could easily pass for a sixteen-year-old. Her body is muscular from working on the farm and her face has filled out with sharp cheekbones. Her hair has turned from blond to a shiny, sandy brown. No question, no paternity test needed: Rosie is Vito's daughter.

Rosie and I spend most of the time alone near the water, tubing or lying on the rocks near the river. We talk and talk, and she drops hints that she's embarrassed for me to see the way they live. It's clear she trusts me as her sole confidante when she informs me about the tensions in the house. She joined cheerleading and often sleeps at a friend's house or at the home of one of her teachers to avoid the chaos at Cookie and Clyde's. Thinking of her as a cheerleader makes me sad . . . she's the one who needs cheering on. I keep those thoughts to myself, familiar with the security that comes with having an organized schedule and stable places to go. Cookie's house is cluttered with junk, and the barn cats act like they own the house—it's obvious just from the smells.

At one point, when I want to make a call home, Cookie demands that I leave her twenty bucks to pay for the call. We end up in a yelling match in which she threatens to beat the shit out of me. "Let me set you straight like old times!" she says.

I start laughing. "You can't touch me, remember? I'm not your daughter anymore, you can't push me around." But as the words come out, they sting me because I know who the recipient of her anger is now that I'm no longer there . . . and suddenly I'm overcome with guilt.

I don't make it through a single day during that weeklong visit without hearing Cookie threaten to take me back to the airport. By the end of my stay, I'm counting down the hours until I head back home. When the moment arrives at last, I take my *bambina* in my arms. "No matter what she says, you remember our codes, and always keep my phone number hidden away," I whisper.

"I know it by heart," she says.

I kiss her cheeks and tell her to make sure she checks the mail at her friend's and her teacher's houses, because I'll be sending her money so she can mail me letters, call me, and buy whatever she needs for school.

IN LATE AUGUST 1984, a few weeks before I'm to start classes at the community college, I receive an unexpected phone call from Stony Brook University Admissions informing me that I've been accepted off their wait list. "If you wish to accept our offer," the admissions worker says, "you'll need to attend orientation later this week."

When I hang up the phone, I call Ms. Harvey right away. "She's out," the secretary says.

"Then get me her supervisor, please! Tell him it's Regina Calcaterra."

He picks up. "This is Mr. McManus."

"Mr. McManus, I got into Stony Brook!" I tell him. "Admissions needs a letter to prove I'm a ward of the state so I can apply for a school loan and the Pell grant."

There's silence on the other end of the phone.

"Mr. McManus?"

"Regina," he says, "can't you hear me smiling?"

I laugh. "Really?"

"You did it, Regina!" he exclaimed. "We are all so proud of you. I'll get the letter done so you can pick it up today and bring it to the university before five o'clock. Sound okay?"

"That's perfect," I tell him. "Mr. McManus, can I tell you something?"

"You can tell me anything, Regina."

"Thanks. This is the biggest day of my life."

"So far," he says.

"So far."

But while my work and academics are falling into place, I'm far from living worry-free. Later that summer, just weeks after I've seen her, Rosie's challenges at home seem to escalate, and her communications with me begin to increase. I send letters to her, addressed to her friends' houses or teachers' addresses, that include money for her to use to go out with her friends or buy anything she can get away with that won't raise Cookie's suspicion.

Just when it grows too much for me to manage, Cherie calls to tell me she's thinking of moving out to Idaho to help Rosie. Cherie and her husband, who have been separated for a while, are now divorcing, and his parents had a judge give them custody of her son. "I didn't want to tell you any of this, Gi, because you have enough to worry about. But they took my son from me and I can't fight them anymore," she says. "This is my chance to try and help Rosie."

And not much later, she is gone.

9

Out of Idaho

Fall 1984 to Spring 1986

I'M SEVENTEEN IN the fall of 1984, when I start my freshman year of college at Stony Brook. I quit my job selling ceiling fans and outlets at Rickel's (where, after a year, I was promoted to a sales job with commission) to take a job selling shoes at Thom McAn in the Smith Haven Mall. Status-wise this is a step up; plus, I've joined the university's gymnastics club, and early in the semester my gymnastics coach seems to detect my sense of discipline. He operates a camp every July in Southampton and asks me to come and work for him next summer. As long as I coach every day from nine in the morning to nine at night—"With breaks in between, of course," he says—I'll get to sleep there for free and make a respectable sum of money at the end of July to use for the next semester. Not to mention the fact that I could spend the entire month of July out in the Hamptons . . . and not have to pay.

The spare minutes of free time I have, I spend with Camille, who's now twenty. She married Frank last fall after they'd been dating for a year and knew, without question, that they were born to take care of each other. While a small part of me had feared that marriage would take Camille away from me, it's actually made our relationship even better. Camille inspires me. She doesn't look back; she doesn't get shaken by our past with Cookie . . . and her strength is what reminds me to keep looking forward, too. My sister and I are aware that we're both laying the foundation for our next phase in life—especially Camille, who learns in the spring of 1983 that she'll become a mother in November.

Camille has in fact found refuge from our life at home by beginning her own family. Not only is she the happiest I've ever seen her, but my sister—whom the social workers once documented was too affected by our upbringing to ever have a functional family of her own—is also proving wrong all the naysayers from our past who predicted so pessimistically what our futures would look like. What our social workers said was impossible was now happening for us both.

Camille gives birth to baby Frankie on November 16— exactly one week after my eighteenth birthday. I edge in next to Camille on her hospital bed, and she passes the baby into my arms. From the very first moment I hold him, I feel how determined he is and how sensitive his heart will be for others. I marvel at him: his eyelashes, his cheeks, his face. His hair is dark brown, just like mine and his parents', and it's an instant miracle how much joy and excitement he brings us just by breathing in his trusting, restful sleep. When I look up at Camille, we both have tears in our eyes. It's our silent promise that no child we love will ever experience the pain that we did . . . and that Cookie will never come near this baby.

While Camille enjoys her new son, Cherie is forced to come back to New York to defend her right to keep hers. Once again, Rosie and Norman are left without any of their older sisters nearby to watch over them. While we work to keep our contact with them, I continue to try and create normalcy in my life by wrapping up my freshman year in college and heading out to the Hamptons to work for the summer at gymnastics camp.

This first summer away from the home of a parent figure, combined with the coaching staff's seventy-hour workweek, makes letting loose on the weekends a wild occupational bonus. With my coworkers, I befriend the bouncer at Toby's Tavern, who lets my fellow coaches sneak me in although I'm underage. The agreement? We entertain them with flips and back-handsprings inside the bar. Plus, I'm aware that I'm in the healthiest, fittest shape of my life. My legs, which were once scrawny and bruised are now tanned and muscular. My shoulders and torso, once sunken from malnourishment, are sturdy and strong. By the time Monday rolls around again, my colleagues poke fun at my morning chirpiness . . . and I have no intention of letting them know that this job is the easiest, most lucrative, most fun responsibility I've ever been granted. At the end of July, when Coach hands me my pay envelope, I hold the package in my hand, feeling its thickness and weight. For the first time, it occurs to me that maybe my impossible upbringing sets me apart from the rest. I've cultivated a strong work ethic and faith in my capacity to take care of myself.

THE WEEK OF Thanksgiving 1985 I receive a letter accepting my transfer to the State University of New York at New Paltz, majoring in education with my friend Sheryl from high school. With Frankie now a year old, such a fun and engaging baby, there couldn't be a more conflicted time for me to consider leaving Long Island. *I'll tell Addie closer to the holidays,* I tell myself. *I want my own life.*

In my bedroom at the Petermans' the night before Christmas Eve 1985, I'm deciding where to pack my Baby Jesus figurines when Addie raps on my door frame. "What's all this?"

I glance around my room, where I've begun piling warm clothes into black garbage bags and a shoe box of cassette tapes that I'm alphabetizing—the Cure, the Four Seasons, Genesis, Billy Joel, Diana Ross, and Van Halen. There's no more hiding what I've been putting off. I tell her: "For the spring semester I've decided to transfer upstate to SUNY New Paltz."

After a moment of shock, Addie tugs on her cardigan to gain control of her expression. "I didn't know you'd applied," she says. "When will you be leaving?"

"First week of January. What's that, three weeks?"

"Well," she says, "congratulations. I'm sure with Camille's marriage and the new baby you've gotten the itch to experience adulthood, too. Why are you packing now?"

I shrug. "Just excited, I guess."

Addie nods curtly. I hear wheels turning in her head. "Regina, I have to say this, and I'll only say this once: If you go away, that's it. That's the start of life on your own."

She's affirming my fear; the reason I didn't want to tell her. "What do you mean?"

"If you leave, you will be on your own for good—do you understand? Once you're out, you're out."

"But—even for holidays, and intersession . . . and the summer?"

"Yes, Regina. Let me tell you something: This house is not a hotel. You're constantly in and out, spending the night at Tracey's and Camille's and all the places I know you prefer to be. It's clear I haven't done a very good job establishing this, but you can't just come and go as you please."

"What would you prefer I do, Addie? Live as the bastard daughter with no life? No friends, and no future? Counting down the days until I get pushed out of here once the checks stop coming in? I'd rather take control now."

She clenches her fists, fuming, and her chin begins to quiver. "Either you live here, or you don't; and if you leave, you don't. Is that clear? And I'd prefer if you don't challenge me again."

In a total of twenty seconds, Addie Peterman has just re-inforced the way I've felt since I first set foot on her perfect carpet five years ago—or actually, since I first understood what foster care was. I'm just a Rent-a-Kid. I'm suddenly suspicious that the reason she and any foster parent has given me shelter was to keep the checks coming. Anger boils in me and my words sear my tongue as I tell her what I've feared since I met her. "You've always been in this for the money!" I yell. "It's not for the kids, or because you're some saint! Now that I'm going away, *I* will get the government's subsidy—not you. And you can't stand that, can you? If you were in this for me, if you were really concerned about supporting me, then you would *want me* back at holidays and breaks. This whole stupid act—you're not my family! You're just the people who get paid to act like it. And you know what? I've already gotten rid of one mother. Don't you dare think I won't do it again."

"Regina, you're jumping to conclusions," she says steadily. "We could always discuss some kind of rent arrangement so that you can come back."

In my seasoned insistence to get the last word, I scream in her face, "Don't worry! This is the last place I'd ever come back to!"

During this last half-decade in Addie's home, I've been grateful that she's provided every necessity a young woman needs and some sense of family so I could feel like a normal kid. At moments I was even distracted from my guilt for failing Rosie and Norm. Addie and Pete have filled that emptiness by being the family who greet me when I walk in the door; for being involved in my life for more than the length of a beating or a heated phone call like the negligent fools who are my biological parents. Addie and Pete have been there so much that sometimes my teachers and my friends and their parents have asked why they never adopted me.

Deep down I've always been aware that I'm just like the forty thousand other foster kids in America who age out of care every year to end up homeless, incarcerated, addicted, or dead. Transferring to New Paltz is a stepping-stone toward finally creating some presence in the world, to make a living and something of my life.

Three weeks later, it's really time. Camille and Frank host a special farewell dinner for me at their home. Camille squeezes me tight after I put on my coat to leave. "I heard that living away at college is all fun, all the time. Will you promise me something?"

I pull away to look at her. "What?" I anticipate a motherly request to be careful.

"Forget everything, and for once, just enjoy yourself," she says into my ear. "You deserve it." Frank hands over baby Frankie, who plants an openmouthed kiss on my cheek, and the expression on my brother-in-law's face is enough to convince me how much they believe in me.

Sheryl, who is as eager to leave as I am, pulls into the Petermans' driveway with her music cranked. "Road trip!" she says, and she and Pete load my two suitcases into her trunk.

Addie and I stand silently with our feet pointed toward each other. Suddenly, she tackles me in a hug. "Regina, I don't want you to leave!" she says.

Exhausted by the emotions of the past month and my entire life, I hug back only halfheartedly. "Addie, I have to do this."

"But I'm going to miss you." She pulls back from the hug to look in my eyes. "Regina, there's something I've never told you."

"Addie, this is really not the time for any more shock from another parent—"

"I love you."

My eyes and forehead soften. My gaze takes in both her eyes, looking for evidence of a bluff. As I realize she means it—that she really loves me—I wrap my arms around her and begin to cry. I take in her smell—lemon Pledge and cotton—and listen to the whimper of her cry in my ear. Pete and Sheryl give us the moment . . . and finally I peel away.

When Sheryl shifts her car into reverse and whirs out of the driveway, I try to identify what I'm feeling:

Anxiety?

Fear?

Excitement?

Uncertainty?

And then I find the word: *Freedom.*

Over and over, on the four-hour ride upstate, Sheryl rewinds Bruce Springsteen's "Glory Days."

On the door of my dorm room is a sign that reads *Regina & KiKi.*

"KiKi, huh?" Sheryl says. "This should be good."

She helps me unpack my clothes then insists on taking me out. "Let's hit Pig's for a beer, then we'll get a late-night knish with mustard at the bagel shop near the bars."

"There's a bar called Pig's?"

"Oh, just you wait."

On the way there, we stop by the student union where there's already mail waiting for me in the form of a course schedule. It's packed with classes I'll take for the education major I've declared, plus a course in international politics to fulfill a history requirement. "Brownstein's the professor," I say to Sheryl. "What do you know about him?"

"Mr. Brownstein at eight in the morning? Ouch," she says. "Whatever you do, don't sleep through tomorrow."

Back in the dorm, I meet KiKi's bare torso before I know what her face looks like. A blur of a guy grabs a shirt off my desk chair and races out of the room. "Your boyfriend, I take it?"

KiKi pulls a T-shirt over her black, shiny hair and punches her arms through the sleeves. "He's one of them."

Suddenly, I realize an eight o'clock class might not be my worst nightmare, but my greatest salvation.

Mr. Brownstein is a kindly looking man in his early forties with nondescript glasses, thick, dark hair and a beard to match. "For the past decade I've been studying the Israeli-Palestinian conflict," he says. "I taught at Hebrew University in Jerusalem and have taken multiple research trips to Israel and the territories." He might as well be speaking whatever they speak in Israel, because none of his words make any sense to me. "I don't do roll call," he announces. "Instead, I'll go around the room, and I want each of you to introduce yourself. Then," he continues, "you'll tell us whether you're registered to vote. If you are *not* registered to vote, you will explain *why* this is so. And those of you for whom this is the case will read and debate President Reagan's sixth State of the Union address. Which means, of course, that you'll need to watch the State of the Union when it's delivered on February fourth—*and* read about it the next morning in the *New York Times*."

I look around sheepishly, then raise my hand. "Mr. Brownstein . . . where do we get the *New York Times*?"

"Young lady, are you asking because you're not registered to vote?"

I tap my pen on my desk and look around as though I didn't hear him.

"The school library puts the *New York Times* out every

morning at seven o'clock." The class moans. I'm in over my head with the rest of them.

As the semester picks up pace, I find I have to study as much for Mr. Brownstein's class as I do for all my other classes combined, and I'm still pulling Cs and Ds on his assignments . . . but I keep showing up for class. It's not just to escape KiKi and her revolving door of visitors; it's also that I'm beginning to make a connection between every current event I read about in the *Times* and the topics we talk about in Mr. Brownstein's class.

Mr. Brownstein gives us assignments to report on the genocide in some parts of Africa, where men are being killed and their mothers, wives, sisters, and daughters are raped. I'd seen commercials of the starving kids on TV, but I never really knew why they were suffering, or how deeply. For the first time, I'm able to look differently at my childhood; at some parts, even gratefully.

But the doors that his class is opening in my mind don't offer escape from my past. The week before midterms, Cherie calls my dorm's pay phone every night with updates about Rosie that are so dark, at moments I have to tune her out. I hear phrases—

"—Clyde—"

"—Cookie blames her—"

"—severely depressed—"

"—pills went missing—"

"—only thirteen!"

Mr. Brownstein's not surprised when I pop in during his office hours. "More discussion about our laws and republic?" he says with a smile.

"No. Not really. Mr. Brownstein, I have some things happening in my family." I feel that he's the only professor I can trust to share my background with.

He removes his glasses and gestures toward the open chair across from him. "Regina, please. Sit."

"Look," I tell him. "I prefer not to share all of this with my professors. I'm here to learn, not for sympathy."

"That's fine."

"I don't know if you know why your class matters so much to me, but learning the ins and outs of policy is . . . well, it's how I've been able to survive."

"In your life?" he says.

"Yes." Nervously, I fold my hands. There's no turning back, as hard as I've tried to paint an impression for Mr. Brownstein, the professor I admire most, that my life is neatly tied up in a bow. "Things in my family have always been difficult, and now my little sister is having a really bad time. My mother is . . . well, she's a difficult woman, to put it mildly, and I really don't know what's going to happen next. And there's the midterm next week, and I'm studying really hard—"

"I know you are, Regina."

"But if I don't end up with a good grade on it, I don't want you to think this class isn't a priority to me."

"When I teach history and politics," he says, "I don't teach it for you only to memorize answers to a test that will be forgotten days later. I teach this class so you can learn who you are as an individual—to appreciate what those more learned than you have long valued. I see how hard you're working, Regina, and I see a lot of potential in you. I told the class at the start of the semester that if it's not clear to me that a student has an appreciation for our government and how our nation fits into the world, I'll fail them. But we're not even halfway through the term, and I have a good feeling you'll pass this class."

I leave his office, too exhausted to meet Sheryl and our friends from home for dinner in the cafeteria. When I go to plop my head on my pillow, I discover that KiKi's written a message on ripped-off notebook paper: *Call Camille.*

Rosie's situation was rough enough when Cherie was there and now it's gotten worse. Cherie had told me a few months back that she pulled up to the house for a visit only to find Rosie in the field, collapsed in tears next to a cow. "What's wrong, Roseanne?" Cherie asked her, brushing dirt and hay off her clothes. "Did this cow hurt you?"

"No, Cherie," Rosie said. "*I* hurt *her*. Mom beat me and I was so angry that I came out here and beat up this cow." Cherie talked about how she sobbed in remorse, and I imagined the vulnerable cow's pain and confusion. She cried for her and Rosie, for all they had in common—both innocent and unprotected against totally undeserved, uncontrollable madness.

"God, Camille," I say into the pay phone. "Why does it have to be this week that I'm trying to memorize the names of the leaders of every country in Africa?" There's a silent despair that rests between us on the line as we realize how immersed we've become in our new existences, no longer free to drop everything and travel three thousand miles to check on our baby sister.

I call my social worker, begging her to contact social services in Idaho to help protect Rosie. "We have to get her away from Cookie once and for all," I plead.

"Regina, your sister is a resident in another state. There is nothing we can do here."

"Nothing?"

"The only thing I might be able to suggest would be for social services in Idaho to call me here and verify everything you've just told me."

I contact the phone company in Idaho and locate the number of the child welfare agency that would be responsible for the town of Oakview. When a patient-sounding male social worker picks up the phone, I share the graphic details of what Rosie is being subjected to. "You can verify Cookie's record if you contact Suffolk County social services," I tell him.

"I'll take up the issue directly," he assures me.

That night he calls me at my dorm and tells me he located my mother. I purse my lips in hope he'll deliver the details of Rosie's intake by the foster system there. "Rosie was present when I informed your mother about your call," he says.

"You did *what*?"

"I spoke to Cookie first, then waited for Rosie to return from school. I questioned her in front of Cookie."

"Did you *just* finish Social Work 101? Of course Rosie's only response was to deny it! Do you know what Cookie would do if Rosie told you the truth and you didn't act fast to take her in?"

Later that week he calls my dorm again. "I'm calling to inform you that I'm closing the case, Ms. Calcaterra."

"*Closing the case?* Explain why!"

"Because Rosie denied the abuse, and your mother explained . . . well, I understand you have some emotional issues that might cause you to embellish certain accounts."

"Emotional issues?"

"Your alcoholism," he says. "And your . . . ability to tell outrageous tales that harm others. Ms. Calcaterra, you should know I've informed the local police, the school district, and the child welfare agency that any complaints we receive from New York are coming from an alcoholic, drug-addicted juvenile delinquent. Your mother told me you were permanently removed from your siblings because of your violent outbursts and promiscuous conduct."

Is this really happening? "I'm not any of those things!" I respond. It's obvious that Cookie manipulated this social worker. Any further attempts I could make for Rosie will be hopeless.

I hang up on him and run back to my room, digging into my dwindling laundry coin stash to call Cherie. I fill her in on what just happened with the social worker in Oakview. "You have to go back out there!"

"Hang on!" she says. "Let me think a minute. Just make sure I can get through if I call you tonight."

I prop open my dorm room door and face my desk chair at the hallway, listening for the pay phone to ring. I calculate how effectively I'll be able to keep others on my floor off the phone—it's the middle of March, so most are using their free time having long conversations with girlfriends or boyfriends from home who they have not seen in months. "Didn't you hear about the pending drug search?" I tell one unsuspecting neighbor as she approaches the pay phone, taking a quarter from her pocket. "I heard the R.A.'s going to pull the fire alarm and the police are coming into our rooms to search." She stares at the phone in confusion, then slinks away.

Around midnight, when KiKi brings a group of friends into our room, I slam our door shut behind me and take a spot on the hard couch in the common area near the pay phone. First I lie seething, then tears streak down my temples and into my hair. I think about Mr. Brownstein's lectures on the role of government in our lives, how it needs to be there as a safety net . . . right now I'm the only one who's been saved by any net, while my baby sister navigates a high-wire act with no protection whatsoever; no sisters or social workers there to defend her. Exhausted by my tears, I drift to sleep.

I'm awakened by the sound of the phone.

It's rung four times when I'm finally within arm's reach.

Then, it stops.

I slam my fist against the painted cinder-block wall and press my forehead against the phone. "Dammit!"

Then it rings again.

"Hello?"

"Cherie is flying out to Idaho tomorrow," Camille says.

"And?"

"She's getting Rosie!"

"How?"

"We've got this whole plan. She's flying into Boise and will rent a car, then she'll stake out at Rosie's bus stop. She'll have to talk fast to convince her to get inside, but when she does, she has a hiding spot where they'll put on wigs and change clothes."

"Isn't that a little extreme?"

"It's a small town, Regina. If anybody sees Rosie in a car with Cherie, they'll call Cookie, then Cookie will call the cops, then Cherie will get arrested. Cherie has to play it safe. Then the two of them will rush to the airport in Boise and fly back to New York."

"You feel like this plan is foolproof?"

"As foolproof as it ever will be."

"Okay. I have a test to take tomorrow, then I'll hop on a

bus to Manhattan and catch the train out to you and Frank so we can wait together."

"No, Regina—you have school. You can't screw it up."

"Camille, I screwed up the thing that's most important to me in the world the day I signed that affidavit when I was fourteen! Rosie's life has never been the same, and nothing matters more to me than this." Two of my neighbors groggily stick their necks out of their rooms. "I'll see you tomorrow," I whisper into the receiver. "I'll call you when the train drops me at the Ronkonkoma station."

I ARRIVE AT four thirty and spot Camille's car with the head-lights on. I knock on her car trunk. "Hey, open up!"

She climbs out of the car and pops the trunk with her key.

"Why did you haul a garbage bag of clothes? You need to do laundry this weekend?"

"No. I want to be ready if this takes awhile."

"Regina, what about school?"

"Camille," I tell her. "Please."

Frank's warming himself on the front porch when we arrive at their house. "Cherie just called," he says. "She got Rosie to the airport, piece of cake."

"So we still have hours before Cookie even notices Rosie's gone!" I've calculated the logistics of the escape, considering every possible glitch. This is the best-case scenario; exactly what we prayed for. There's a feeling of relief beginning to rise in me . . . but this is no time to get comfortable.

"They're probably boarding right this second," Frank says. "Cherie said they're scheduled to land at JFK just after nine o'clock. You two have time to eat. Come in and let me make you a sandwich—"

"No," I tell him. He and Camille look at me, alarmed. "I want to go to the airport *now*. If that plane touches down early, I want to be there the second our *bambina* walks off of it."

Frank looks at Camille. "Let me clear out the car so there's room for the four of you. Hey," he says, "why don't you let me drive you?"

"No, sweetie," Camille tells him. "Stay home with Frankie and close to the phone. Cookie could call—she doesn't know you. You're the only one she won't dare to grill."

When Camille and I arrive at the airport at seven thirty, we establish our post at the arrivals area. Camille looks around to make sure we're not being watched or targeted, while I check and recheck the television monitor to make sure their flight is on time.

When they finally deplane, Cherie's carrying only her purse. Both she and Rosie—now with a modest feminine shape and taller than any of us—have their wigs tugged down tight on their heads. Rosie's wig is thick and dramatic, a cartoonish contrast to the tired, blank stare on her face. It's impossible for me to tell if she's numb from the unexpected plane ride or the trauma of what she's been living through with Cookie and Clyde.

The four of us walk fast to short-term parking, finally huddling in the car to embrace Rosie the second we're all inside Camille's backseat. "My *bambina*," I whisper in her ear. The car fires up with the turn of Camille's ignition, and Cherie and I stay hugging Rosie. I imagine the tighter we hold her, the faster she'll heal; but in response, Rosie does nothing. She utters no sound; she makes no expression. "Are you in shock?" I ask her.

She shakes her head. *No.*

"What is it then? You're afraid Cookie's going to come after you?" She sits silently, then nods slowly. *Yes.*

"No," Cherie says. "We're going to do everything we possibly can to keep you here. You'll live with me while Regina's at school, then in the summer she'll come and live with us. We'll have a home together—Regina, Camille, you remember how good it was? Like in the Happy House, and the Bubble House, and the Glue Factory."

"And the Brady Bunch House," Rosie says.

"Yes! You remember the Brady Bunch House! All we need is us," Cherie says. "We've done it before, when we were all much younger. We can do it so much better now."

Camille's house is filled with the aroma of pasta and meatballs. "Grab a plate, ladies," Frank says as we pile into the kitchen. "I'm just about to pull the baked ziti out of the oven." When baby Frankie starts crying from his nursery, Frank whispers in Camille's ear, braces his hand on her shoulder, and smiles. Then he walks quietly down the hall.

When I finally break from staring after him, I notice Rosie's doing the same. "Where's he going?" Rosie asks. Never before have we seen a man so caring and capable.

"He's going to take care of Frankie so we can stay up together."

We lounge on the living room couch and love seat, gently taking note as Rosie begins to drop hints of a smile as I rest with my arm around her and play with her hair. The name *Cookie* never comes up. The word *abuse* is never spoken. The four of us sleep head-to-toe in the living room; and in the morning, Camille starts the coffeepot and sets out a box of gooey glazed donuts while Frank dresses Frankie and steps out to warm up the car. "Rosie, how about we head out to the mall and get you some warm, new clothes?" Camille says.

Rosie's eyes light up. She looks out the window at the car and then back to me. "Can I sit on your lap?"

"Sure, lovebug," I tell her, securing a lock of loose hair the color of sand behind her ear. "You remember the Smith Haven Mall, where we used to hang out when we were working on the farm?"

She smiles. "Yes."

Cherie wiggles in next to Frankie's car seat, and I close my eyes with my cheek against Rosie's back the entire way to the mall.

While Rosie and Cherie browse through the racks, Frank, Camille, and I powwow in the car. "I think we need to wait a few weeks to register her for high school here. We don't want to make it easy for anyone from Idaho to track her down with the help of the school system," Camille says.

"I agree."

"And when we do register her, we don't tell the school that she's a transfer from Idaho. As far as they're concerned, she's just moved to a new part of Long Island."

"I know. We'll work with her on dropping the twang."

"She'll catch on fast," Frank says. "She still talks like a Long Islander. 'My teacha,' she said—did you hear that? She's still got Long Island in her."

The three of us laugh as Frankie coos and clenches his fists from his car seat—he, too, is in on our important scheme. When Rosie and Cherie are back with their bags a half-hour later, the mood goes quiet again. "What'd you get, cutie?" I ask Rosie.

"Some jeans, a coat and sweater . . ." Her voice trails off. Frank calmly pulls out of the parking lot, onto the highway.

At no point during the weekend do we ask Rosie what she experienced. There's just no reason to make her relive it, and her silence has told us enough already.

On the third day, Rosie and I move into Cherie's studio apartment in Bayshore, but just as Rosie begins to feel comfortable with her new home, Camille calls us: She's begun getting calls from Cookie's brother, Nick.

"Shit," Cherie says. "What'd he say?" Rosie and I crowd close to her. She tilts the receiver so we can hear Camille speak.

"Well, the first time, he called and informed me that Rosie was missing and the Idaho authorities think Regina is hiding out with her somewhere in Idaho." Just like always, Cookie's blame points straight to me. "I told him it was impossible since you're at school and in fact you'd been in all your classes taking tests this past week."

"Good."

"But whatever you three do, it's not a good idea to come by my house. Nick's watching, and he's looking to bite. Regina, you should head back to school."

"I will go back when the time is right."

"The time is right *now*." Her firmness stuns me. "If Nick or the cops find out that no one's seen you at class or in your dorm, he'll figure out where you are and then we're all done."

"Then who's going to stay with Rosie while Cherie's working at the deli?" I demand. "This child has been through enough, Camille. I am not leaving her alone and unguarded without one of us here."

"So it's going to be the three of you smooshed together in Cherie's tiny studio apartment?"

"We've lived through way worse . . . or have you finally forgotten?"

"Are you doing this for Rosie, or for yourself?" she says. "Fine, Regina, stay there. Just be safe. Nick will come pounding on Cherie's door, and I'm afraid it won't be pretty."

It's the silent treatment between us for two days until she calls again. "Nick's showing up at my house now, demanding to know where Cherie lives."

I wring my fingers.

"Frank's been answering the door. He keeps telling Nick to leave, that Cherie and I had a fight and aren't talking. 'The last Camille heard, Cherie was still living out of state,' he tells Nick. But I don't know how much longer we'll be able to hold him off."

We now know it's only a matter of seconds before Cherie's ex–in-laws hand her number over to Nick. Every time the phone rings, Rosie and I jump up from wherever we are and huddle on Cherie's bed, as though holding each other will protect us all from the assault of Nick's voice on the answering machine.

First, it's *Cherie, this is your uncle Nick. Call me.*

Then *Cherie, this is your uncle Nick. We think Regina took Rosie. Call me back as soon as possible.*

Then the third message: *Cherie, this is your uncle Nick, I'm coming over and will force my way in to talk to you. Pick up the damn phone right now.*

Rosie and I hide our belongings, throw on our coats and shoes, and I grab my denim satchel. We bolt out of Cherie's place and take off down a back alley.

"Where are we going?"

"To a mall," I tell her. "We need somewhere with a crowd."

From a pay phone I leave a message on Camille's answering machine. "Camille, where *are* you? Listen, I'm taking Rosie to the movies at Sunrise Mall. Nick called Cherie's three times today. We'll be out—don't panic if you can't get ahold of us. Cherie's at work, her boss wouldn't let her talk."

The man at the cinema ticket counter has fat fingers and a slow pace. My eyes dart around the theater's lobby as he paws our change out of his register. "Mister, can you hurry it up a little?" I tell him.

He stares at me.

"We're going to be late for the show."

Finally, we sail past the popcorn concession and straight into the theater, in the far left corner. We sit through two viewings of *Pretty in Pink*, and I'm ready to sit through a third when Rosie stands.

"Sit down!" I hiss. "What are you doing?"

"Let's get out of here."

"We can't— Why?"

"Let's at least see another movie or something."

I glance around. "Well, hurry, so we can walk out with everybody else. Put up your hood and put down your head." We link arms to hustle through the theater's lobby, but the instant we turn the corner into the mall corridor, I see the worst possible thing: Nick comes running at us, accompanied by two mall security guards. As I yank Rosie into a semicircle spin, I spot Cherie a few steps behind them.

Rosie and I race back into the cinema, down the aisle of an empty theater, and out the emergency exit. I push Rosie to scramble under a big metal garbage bin and then shimmy under next to her. "They'll think we're hiding *behind* something—not *under* something," I whisper.

"How do you know?"

"Because I've done this before!"

We lie there. *It will be a miracle if the pounding of my heart doesn't lead Nick right to us.*

Rosie rests her cheek on the cold pavement. "We have no control, Gi," she says.

Her return to using my nickname strikes me; softens me. "That's why we have to *get* control, sweetie. We can't let you go back with her. You'll be fourteen in October, that's only seven months from now. We have to get you emancipated, too."

"Where will I hide?"

"With me up in New Paltz. I can rent a room in an apartment and we can live off campus."

Suddenly Cherie's voice rings from the darkness. *"Regina! Rosie!"*

"Close your eyes," I whisper, near silence. "She's with Nick." It's just like when I was four years old living in the Glue Factory apartment. I ran away, and Susan called out for me. *"Regina! Regina!"* I rose from my hiding place and ran into her arms, then she carried me out of the woods and toward the street, right back to Cookie.

We ignore Cherie's calls. We stay silent and still. Minutes pass. Cars pass. Rosie passes her hand to me, and I lace my fingers through hers.

After quiet falls around us, we shimmy out into the night. We walk through unlit parking lots on Sunrise Highway until I find a phone booth on a dark corner. Camille picks up on the first ring.

"Regina." She's crying. "Where are you two?"

"We're fine. I'd rather not say where we are right now. But we're fine."

"It's too late, Gi. He said that if we don't turn Rosie over to him, he'll call the police and we'll all be arrested for kidnapping. He said he'll use that to have the courts take away Cherie's visitation with her son and she'll never see him again, and the courts will take Frankie away from me, too. Frank and I are just sick, we don't know what to do."

"I'll call my social worker tomorrow. Maybe she can help us."

"Regina, he wants Rosie at his house tonight, or else he is calling the cops on all of us."

"Jesus Christ, he's sick!" I wring my forehead, trying to work out a solution. "Let me talk to Rosie. I'll call you back."

I gently place the phone back in its silver cradle. I can't quite bring myself to look at Rosie. It's 1986, five and a half years after we were separated for the last time and placed into different foster homes. Today she's the same age I was when I made the decision that ruined her life with my unfounded faith in my social worker and the system. If I tell our story, I thought back then, no one in their right mind would ever return any of us to Cookie. As good as the government has been to me, it let Rosie down. Even worse, *I* let Rosie down. How could I promise her that the same county system that deserted her five years ago would suddenly decide to help her? We're poor. We have no connections and even fewer resources, and we've learned not to trust anyone who says *You can trust me*. We've had to put our faith in the people who treat us coldly, who attempt to prey on our vulnerabilities and take advantage of us; but in the end, no one can really save us from our own hard reality. Every single one of us has had to climb out of our childhood and help ourselves. It was true for Cherie and Camille; it's true for me; and now it's true for Rosie.

"There's nothing else I can do," I tell her. Hot tears spring to my eyes.

She glares at me in a way that's both hopeless and accusing. "Call Camille," she says. "Let's get it all over with."

There's a throbbing silence between us as we wait, and wait, for Camille's car to pull up. "I'm freezing," I say. "Are you cold?"

Rosie says nothing. I clamp my arms around her in an effort to stay warm, until I realize it's me who's shivering.

After a lifetime of waiting, Camille's headlights finally cut through the night. Rosie takes a step toward the car. "Wait," I tell her. "Let me see who's with her." I walk out in the open concrete lot, peering into Camille's window.

"Get in," Cherie sighs. "We'll stay at Camille's tonight."

I flag Rosie toward the car, waiting for Cherie and Camille to rip into me. But the only sounds are the hum of the motor; the click-click-clicking of Camille's turn signal in the night. I lean up toward the front seat. "Can somebody turn on the radio?"

Neither Cherie nor Camille budges.

In the morning, Camille finds me dialing the kitchen phone. "Who you calling?"

I hesitate. "The social worker."

She comes to me and braces my shoulders. Looking in my eyes, Camille says, "Gi, honey: We've done all we can. *She has to go back to Idaho.*"

There's a ringtone in my ear.

"Hello?"

"Ms. Harvey, it's me. Regina."

Camille sighs, rubs her temples, and goes to the cupboard to pull out a can of coffee. I tell Ms. Harvey everything—how we tried to rescue Rosie after social services in Idaho triggered Cookie to lash out; how Nick was chasing after us and we need to keep Rosie with us. "Ms. Harvey, can you call the police in Idaho and tell them how social services put Rosie in danger?"

"Regina, you *kidnapped a minor across state lines*. That's against the law, *and* because Rosie's guardian lives in Idaho, no. There's nothing I can do from here."

I shoot a glance to Camille and react the only way I can think: I slam the phone back on the wall and storm outside in my bare feet for air.

The storm door claps shut behind Camille. "None of us likes this, but sweetie, we all have so much at risk—especially Rosie. We have to take her to Nick's."

"The hell we do."

"Gi, we're out of options."

Rosie steps onto the front porch and folds her arms tight across her chest. Cherie steps out behind her.

"We'll tell him that you'll only stay there as long as Cherie and I stay, too," I tell Rosie.

"Fine."

"Then Regina and I will drive you to the airport," Cherie says.

Nick's Dobermans charge the door when we ring the bell, and I steady Rosie in her terrified reaction. Cherie and I grab Rosie's hands and walk into Nick's home, taking in the stained walls and carpet, the smell of mildew combined with wet dog and urine. With his hands that are perpetually filthy from his job in printing, Nick wrangles his dogs from pummeling us, while his docile wife attempts to coax them from his grip. Then he turns his lips down and points his finger in my face. "You," he says. "This is all because of you. You have always thought that you were better than us, you think you're so high and mighty. If I could, I would beat that smugness right off your face, Regina. You need to be brought down a few notches, you snotty bitch, and I could still do that to you."

I glare at Nick and his wife, who's hovering behind him like a wilting weed. "Thank God you weren't able to have any kids—now we know for sure how you would have raised them!" I pause, for effect. Then I say, "Nick."

"I am your uncle, goddammit!" he howls. "*Uncle Nick!* You should respect your elders!" His cragged forehead's broken out in sweat.

"Nick," I tell him calmly, "you have to *earn* respect. It's not just given to you. You never did a thing to help us. You only made it worse by siding with Cookie. You, like her, do not deserve my respect."

"Get the fuck out of my house, you lying whore."

"Nope," I tell him. "If Rosie's here, then I'm here."

Nick stares at me. Then he stares at Cherie. Cherie stares down at the floor, reminding us all she has a custody fight for her child to worry about. "You're staying here tonight," he says. "And tomorrow, the kid goes with me to the airport."

"So do we," I tell him.

Nick wraps his hand into a fist so hard the knuckles crack. "Jennifer, take these sluts to the back room," he says. With her eyes, his wife begs us to save her. She points us down the hall, into the room next to theirs.

"It smells like slime in here," I tell my sisters. Rosie's gaze is fixed in worry on the bed, where scattered about are pictures of hairy, naked women. "I'm not sleeping on that thing."

"You think the floor is much better?" Cherie says.

"Cherie, help me put the sheets on the floor. We'll sleep on top of them with Rosie in the middle. We can cover up with our coats." The next morning, after we leave the sheets in a heap on the floor, we walk out to the driveway where Nick's leaning against his rusted Camaro. "What the fuck took so long to get ready? You three dyking it out in there?"

We march past him, toward Cherie's car.

"What the hell—you two don't actually expect me to believe you're going to drive this kid to the airport."

Cherie opens her car door. "Rosie's riding with us, Nick. If you want to be there to see it, you'll have to follow."

"You cunts—"

I swing around. "Shut the fuck up, Nick, you fucking ignorant, stupid prick!" I walk up to him and get in his face. "She's riding with us, you got it? You Calcaterras are nothing but a bunch of lowlife scumbags!"

"And you're one of us," he says.

I wrap my arms around Rosie's shoulders. "In name only." I use my body to nudge Rosie inside the car, resisting my instinct to tackle Nick and beat him senseless. In the backseat I keep Rosie cloaked, as though trying to protect her now could still do some good.

Even deeper inside the airport with the March chill left outside, I feel Rosie shivering. We escort her all the way to security, where she glances back at Nick and takes off her coat. Her action strikes me as symbolic: In the end, the only thing we were able to do was keep her warm with that coat, and now she's giving it back, knowing what was meant to protect her here will bring her harm when she gets where she's going. The only prayer she has to survive Cookie's reaction will be to pretend this trip to New York never happened.

Cherie and I both reach out and take the coat, which seems to weigh four hundred pounds. This was supposed to be Rosie's forever rescue, and I've failed her yet again.

The crowd of travelers at the gate fills in around us. In response, Cherie's actions seem to pick up with a pace of urgency, but for Rosie I'm calm and gentle as ever. As she hugs Cherie, her limbs move as though they're weighed down with lead, as if any part of her that's lively or able to feel love is dead. I take her cheeks in my hands, staring into her sculpted face, her eyes that show she's seen too much. Everything about her seems older than it is. *"Mia bambina amore,"* I whisper.

Suddenly, she throws her arms around me and buries her face in my hair. For a moment, I can feel her resisting sobs; and then she whispers: *"Je t'aime."*

The other travelers seem somehow empowered by the luggage they're carrying onto the plane, but Rosie approaches the ticket counter with nothing . . . because she came with nothing. Cherie and I grip her coat between us. A loose, sandy curl flips over her shoulder when she looks back and forces a smile.

"I love you, Rosie!" I yell through my tears so loudly that the crowd turns.

Rosie hands her ticket to the agent, who points her to the Jetway.

And then, she's gone.

10

Aging Out

"I FAILED."

Pinching the stem of his glasses between his thumb and forefinger, Mr. Brownstein rubs the bridge of his nose. "Regina, have a seat. You have a lot on your shoulders—"

"Mr. Brownstein, I'll make it up!"

"Don't worry about making it up. It'll work out at the end."

"At the end of the semester, you mean? Or just . . . in general?" I'd recently shared with Mr. Brownstein that I'd grown up in and out of foster care. I want to remind him things don't just "work out" in my life; that my future depends on my grades in ways my classmates' futures don't.

"Regina, I'm here to help. If you'd feel better to share details about what's happening in your family, I want you to know this is a safe place."

I flash back: I'm thirteen again, in the car with the social workers. Rosie and Norm are in the other car, and because I've revealed what's happened to us, I'll never be able to control what happens to my siblings again.

Mr. Brownstein brings me back to earth. "I have utmost faith you're doing your best. Just follow through on the rest of the semester. I told you"—his tone turns fatherly, reassuring—"you'll be *fine*. Right now you have to take good care of yourself and your little sister."

That night, I dial Rosie's number back in Oakview. "Yeah?" Cookie answers. It's the first I've spoken to her in months. Her voice is deeper and more hoarse than ever. *That's what decades of smoking and drinking will do to you,* I want to tell her.

"I need to talk to Rosie."

"Like hell you do."

"Cookie, let me remind you: Everybody knows about you. I told the local authorities and Rosie's school. Remember, one mark on her and there is no denying where it came from."

"Oh, go ahead and ask her how bad it's been. The kid's had it made ever since she got back, I haven't laid a finger on her."

"Put. Rosie. On the phone."

I hear her inhale a cigarette, then exhale. "Hang on."

There's a muffled exchange between them, then the phone cord crackles to signify that Rosie is seeking a more private place to speak. When there's quiet, I whisper: *"Mia bambina amore."*

"Je t'aime," she whispers back.

Through a series of one-word answers, I'm able to discern that things are quiet—Cookie's holding back her anger, at least for now. "In the morning I'll call your social worker and guidance counselor, okay? I want to know that they're keeping tabs on you. Even if they don't believe us, at least we got them to pay attention."

"Okay."

AT THE END of the spring semester I take three hundred dollars out of the envelope from last summer's gymnastics camp for a down payment on an off-campus apartment with Kim and Tami, two girls Sheryl knows from Suffolk County.

I'm living independently for the first time in my life. The older I get, the more I'm convinced: I've suffered for a reason. It's a reason I don't know yet, but for all of my twenty years it's been circling me—a forecast of something mighty. There's no way a person could be born into dysfunction, fighting to survive and helping her family do the same, without some purpose to give it all meaning. On the days that feel dark and endless, I make myself a simple promise: I'll get out of bed in the morning. Then I'll head up the hill to class. If I put one foot in front of the other, day by day, I'll move closer to the light at the end of all this struggle.

At the start of my junior year's fall semester, I take two jobs: one waitressing in an outdated Catskills nightclub; the other fulfilling work study in the campus science lab. On Thursday and Friday nights I share a mirror with my roommates to dress up in my cocktail uniform. Then another opportunity pulls me away from establishing a normal college social life: Before the end of the semester, I'm accepted for an internship in Albany to work for a state senator for the next semester. "She's going to fall for some politician and we'll never see her again!" Tami teases.

In January of my junior year, I move to Albany and attend the orientation meeting for all the interns held by radio host Alan Chartock, the sponsor of the internship. "We'll go around the table," he says, "and I'd like you to tell me why you're here."

My fellow interns cite their reasons as having relatives in law and politics, and a passion for politics or a political ideology or a commitment to advance a specific public policy. Then the circle reaches me. I think of Rosie, of the money I tuck away to send her every month, of how I'll never give up trying to rescue her. Then I share my reason for why I'm pursuing this career. "Politics is the allocation of resources," I tell Professor Chartock. "I want to know who allocates the resources and why some people benefit from them while others suffer."

He eyes me, then announces, "I want to be clear about an inevitability of this program: You ladies will be hit on by members of the Assembly and Senate. If I hear any of my interns are involved in affairs with legislators, you will be removed from the program and will lose the fifteen credits you're on track to earn during this experience."

After the meeting, our cohorts mingle and laugh. Joanne, my new roommate for the semester, is in the program, too. We approach a boy with reddish hair and an unassuming expression. "You didn't take the Senate internship, right?"

"Right. I'm interning as a journalist for the *Legislative Gazette* instead. I'm Ed." He shakes our hands firmly and we're delighted we've just added a new companion to our circle of nerds.

I intern for the state Senate from nine every morning until five in the evening and then waitress four nights a week on Lark Street. Wednesday nights and all day Saturday I coach USGF gymnastics at an Albany gymnastics school. Saturday nights, Joanne, Ed, and I usually meet up for a beer, and Ed pokes fun at how I react when a stranger tries to talk to me. "You're way too intense," he says, laughing. "Lighten up."

I take a sip of my beer. "I didn't come here to mess this up. I'm focused on learning how this all works—*and* I need strong references for a job after I graduate." They both roll their eyes at me and order a round of shots. I allow a small grin before I take mine.

As the internship progresses I observe that the process to alter public policy is like watching a chess game: Sheer strategy and full emotional investment are needed for the most convincing players to win. Recognizing my intensity, State Senator Jack Perry keeps me on past May into July until the legislative session ends to continue on as an aide, and his invitation is further promise that the universe will always find ways to take care of me as long as I'm doing my part: In July I go back to living rent-free in Southampton and coaching gymnastics again.

Heading into the fall of my senior year at New Paltz, I've done my best to plan for the day in November when I turn twenty-one, for the day when I'll no longer be a ward of the state or a foster child and for the day when the Medicaid card that's covered my health care for the last seven years will be void, and the four hundred twenty dollars I receive for rent and expenses each month will just stop showing up in my mailbox.

There's only one choice: to keep working. For the fall semester I move into an off-campus apartment with my high school friend Jeanine, who transferred to New Paltz last year. "Yeesh!" she says. "Waitressing, the science lab, studying . . . do I have to get you a job with me at the Wallkill farm stand in order to actually see you on weekends?"

"I've worked a cash register before," I jibe back. "Get me an application."

Soon we've begun our autumn Saturday routine, peddling warm apple cider and mums then hitting the town hangouts where Jeanine's charm scores us free beers. She introduces me as her geeky sidekick, referring to me as "Miss Constitution" because I can proudly recite all seven articles and twenty-seven amendments to the U.S. Constitution.

Before Thanksgiving break, the debate team coach approaches me as I'm studying in the lounge next to the political science department. "I'd like to speak with you about joining my team of students for the Harvard Model United Nations," he says. "We're one of a handful of schools competing that's not Ivy League, and I need a tough debater on my team."

"Uh . . . sir?" I look around. "Are you sure you're talking to the right person?"

"Regina Calcaterra? Sure I am. I need someone with a strong backbone, somebody bright and assertive. Professor Brownstein recommended you."

Bright and assertive.

I choose global warfare as my debate topic. My peers and I take the train to the United Nations headquarters in Manhattan when our debate coach sends us to meet with the actual

Zimbabwean delegates. We spend winter break preparing for the final debate forum in Boston. We don't place in the rankings, but our whole team cheers when I'm nominated for an award alongside students from Columbia and Harvard.

"Don't lose any sleep over the fact we didn't win," our debate coach tells me on the bus ride home. "I was in the elevator with coaches from the Ivies who were talking about the tough girl from New Paltz. We may not have won, but you helped us make an impact."

In May I receive my BA in Political Science in front of hundreds of my classmates' families. Addie, Pete, and their daughters come for the ceremony, and Pete takes a photo of Addie and me. "Hold up your diploma!" she says. "You've earned this."

Later that week I pack my car and head back to Long Island after Addie extends an offer for me to live rent-free in her basement for two months while I search for a job. Immediately I take her up on it, intending only to buy a little time to make a transition on my own. Unsure of where I'll go after the summer, again I reach out to the only other family connection I have besides my siblings: Cookie's parents, Mike and Rose. "If you ever need a place to stay or just want to spend time with us," Grandma Rose says, "your grandfather and I want you to know that you always have a home here."

"Grandma . . . thanks."

"You're the first family member ever to graduate from college," she continues. "Would you like to join Grampa Mike and me for dinner to celebrate?"

"Of course," I say. "Just tell me when."

The following night, in her kitchen, Grandma Rose takes a break from tending to an oven of pasta and baked clams to open the collar of her quilted pink robe and expose the bruises on her chest. "The cancer in my lungs is getting worse, the doctors say. Between this and my multiple sclerosis, I don't know how much longer I can go on." At dinner, I'm glancing at the bruises that appear on her neckline and Grandma puts down her fork. "Regina," she says, fighting back tears, "our door has always been open to you. We could never understand how your mother turned out the way she did, or why you kids suffered so much with her."

This is my one chance to try and understand. I lean across the table toward my grandmother. "What happened to her when she was young that's made her so angry?"

Grandma Rose shakes her head. She and my grandfather go back to eating.

Weeks later, in early July, Grandma Rose passes away. I tend to Grampa Mike with hot dogs and steaks from the butcher and two jugs of Ernest & Julio Gallo wine, his favorite. Cookie shows up with Norman for the funeral, announcing that the two of them will be staying at Grampa Mike's house to take care of him. Norman carries their bags behind Cookie. "You must be numb with grief," she insists to my grandfather, pushing her way through the door and pouring herself a glass of wine. "Don't mind if I make myself at home." Looking up from lighting a cigarette, she acknowledges me, as though she hadn't seen me sitting there since she walked through the door. "Well, congratulations for graduating," she grunts. "You see, I didn't do such a bad job after all with you kids." I stare at her, dumbfounded.

I try to hold myself back from letting loose on her the way I did on her brother in his driveway the morning we took Rosie to the airport. "Cookie," I tell her—my composure astounds

me even though I am burning inside. "*You did not raise us.*
You left us to raise ourselves—do you understand that? *We*
are responsible for the women we have become. Not you. You
gave birth to us: that was your single wretched contribution
to what we are now. We did the rest, and any help we got
along the way was from strangers—some who were *paid* to
take care of us. Not you."

I anticipate what's coming next: She'll slap my face, or
take me by the hair and slam me to the ground. Instead, she
approaches me slowly. Her eyes soften and so does her voice.
"Regina," she says, "the only reason I hurt you is because
your father hurt me. The other kids' dads didn't hurt me like
yours did . . . he was the worst to me. You see?"

Face-to-face like this, I can smell the alcohol that's seeping
from her pores; the tobacco smoke in the fabric of her clothes.
She steps back—she's contemplating whether I will accept her
explanation. But I know it will never be possible for her to
acknowledge what she did, the same as it will never be possible for me to fully forget it: the years of shielding our bodies
from her blows, hiding our bruises, scavengering for food,
and convincing teachers and authorities that if they gave us a
chance, my siblings and I could be successful.

In a stunned, calm disgust I glare at her . . . and suddenly
I'm recollecting my conversation five years ago with Paul Accerbi. I didn't believe it was a one-night stand. I was the first
to call Cookie out on her life of lies, but the one thing she
never waivered from insisting was that she and Paul had a
relationship. "How did he hurt you?"

She looks at me as if she is trying to determine if I'm asking
this in the spirit of empathy or a demand.

"What did he do to you that caused you so much anger

that you'd take it out on a defenseless child? Huh? Did he beat you like you beat me? Did he use your head to bust holes in walls or doors? Did he, Cookie? Did he tie you up in closets or to radiators or beds? Did he strip you naked in front of others, and beat you with a belt that caused welts around every section of your body? Did he humiliate you or scare you into submission? Did he *rape* you? What did he do to you that would justify what you did to me, or let others do?"

She's smiling, satisfied with my anger. "Oh no," she says. "None of that, Regina. He was a lover—a very kind lover. I was in love with him, and I thought he was in love with me. I thought he'd be with me after he found out about you . . . but instead, he left." She pauses a moment, then lights up another cigarette. "And I got stuck with you."

11

The Happy House

WITHIN DAYS AFTER Cookie flies back to Idaho, my grandfather begins to notice that things around his house have gone missing. There are pots, pans, dishes, silverware, blankets, towels, photo albums, my grandmother's jewelry, and even her nail polishes and makeup that he can't seem to find. I presume he's suffering some kind of grief-induced memory loss.

"Regina, Cookie made multiple early morning trips to the post office to send packages to Rosie because she was home alone," he said.

"Gramps, Rosie moved in with one of her teachers more than a year ago. Cookie doesn't even have guardianship of her anymore." That's when he and I put it together: Cookie pilfered his things while he was grieving.

After Rosie's teacher took over her guardianship, my baby sister was able to begin her healing . . . but Camille and I took quiet note as Rosie made choices to leave her past behind—and that included shutting us out. Rosie never said it, but we sensed she blamed us. No matter how we fought for her well-being, nothing we did could ever be enough when Cookie was the opponent. As much as it destroyed us to see Rosie cut off communication with us, we understood. We'd failed her. We'd grown up always one bad decision away from home-lessness and poverty. We'd tried to raise each other when we were just kids ourselves, sharing everything we had . . . which was never very much. Rosie needed us to save her, and we tried, but we couldn't, because when you live on the fringes of society with no resources, you have no voice and your complaints are easily ignored. So for now our relationship is wrought with an undercurrent of resentment and frustration. For Cherie, Camille, and me, adjusting to the world meant growing farther away from the pain we experienced as kids. For Rosie to do the same, she had to grow far away from us and closer to the people in her community who were finally able to protect her.

ONE BY ONE, my friends begin to transition into work: Some take jobs at banks on Wall Street or at Manhattan advertising agencies or in federal law enforcement. Jeanine and her boy-friend, George, as well as Sheryl and her beau, Thomas, are hinting at their pending engagements. I take a job at Bruno's, an Italian restaurant, working all shifts. Every day during my breaks, I scan the classifieds for a job I feel passionately about.

Unfortunately, the only openings at places even remotely

dealing with public policy are for typists. Of all the courses I took in high school and college, not one was for typing. No matter how I calculate it, there's no possible way I can learn how to type eighty words per minute—with a stopwatch and no mistakes—all by myself. Still, I take the train to the interviews in Manhattan, a place that's romancing me more with every ninety-minute ride on the Long Island Rail Road.

After a few failed interviews, I figure out a way to pass the typing test: Because I'm allowed to practice on the same script and the same typewriter I'll be using for the test, I take my time to type the script with no mistakes . . . then I place it under my typewriter. Then I roll in a blank sheet of paper, and after the timekeeper starts her watch and leaves the room, I switch out the practice paper with the perfect script. Finally, I get a second interview for a typist position at the New York Junior League, a prestigious organization for young women that works on nonprofit causes. It's *perfect*.

I show up for the interview in a dark suit and white blouse with dark, low shoes—conservative and easy to foot around Manhattan. I enter the fine-carpeted cherry lobby, ready to dazzle my future boss with information on the statewide policy issues I worked on during my internship at the Senate and my solid letters of recommendation. But when they ask me to take a typing test under the watch of a timekeeper, I know how this will end.

I type a total of thirty-two words in one minute, with twelve mistakes. Then I thank them, grab my bag, and bow my head to quickly leave.

In August I'm called to interview for a position as an advocate for the Eastern Paralyzed Veterans Association. They are located in Jackson Heights, Queens, in the shining new offices that have been converted from the old Bulova watch factory. I take the Long Island Rail Road to the Woodside station, where a shuttle equipped for wheelchairs picks me up and drops me off in front of the EPVA's office.

Smelling the fresh construction, the prospect of entering this bright building morning after morning adds excitement to my steps heading toward the EPVA's lobby. There I'm greeted by my potential bosses—all quadriplegic or paraplegic men in wheelchairs who were disabled during their service in the Vietnam and Korean wars. During the interview they tell me they need to fill an entry-level position with someone who can advocate on their behalf on the local and state levels. "We need someone who won't have a problem making trips to Albany and traveling across Long Island on our behalf," one explains. "You'll need to go to the capital at least once a month." They then go on to tell me that most of their funding comes from a greeting card manufacturing plant they partially own in New Hampshire and that, as a nonprofit, they don't have the opportunity to pay decent salaries.

I nod. I knew I could continue waitressing in the evenings and on weekends to supplement my income. "This is perfect," I tell them. "I have contacts up there, and I'm familiar with the time and perseverance it takes to get something passed. Plus, I have my own car."

The gentlemen glance at each other with raised eyebrows and promise to review my résumé, my letters of recommendation, and my references. The next day, they call me, offering me the title of an associate advocate for seventeen thousand dollars a year, with benefits. I have no concept for what seventeen thousand will get me, and I don't really care. The only important thing is, I've got a job.

I'm fully aware that this is another step toward mainstreaming—doing what my peers are doing, regardless of how different my background has been from theirs. After a few months of commuting ninety minutes each way from the Petermans' to my office, I move into the dark, barred-window basement apartment of a Tudor home in Forest Hills, Queens, with my college friend Reyne. "This place is a firetrap. You couldn't get a room upstairs?" Cherie says when she comes to visit. I know it's not fancy, but it's all I can afford, and the location is convenient for the travel my job demands.

The disabled veterans group sends me to Washington and all around New York State. I advocate publicly and passionately for the passage of the Americans with Disabilities Act, a civil rights act whose purpose is to remove barriers, societal and structural, for people with disabilities. What inspires me most about this act is that, in its true spirit, it provides opportunities for those who have been held back from mainstreaming and living independently. Every time the phrase *self-sufficiency* is bantered about in lectures or legislative sessions, my commitment grows stronger with the realization that my fight for others to maintain their dignity is exactly the same fight I've known all my life.

While lobbying for the veterans in Albany, I meet Alan Hevesi, the Assembly chair of the committee for People with Disabilities, who, as I learn through friendly banter, happens to also live in Queens. Alan is a professor at Queens College and appears genuinely concerned about the development of young public servants. In 1989, when he decides to run for the position of comptroller, the chief fiscal officer of the city, I volunteer for his campaign. Every night for weeks, I stick stamps on envelopes and hand out literature at subway stations during rush hours.

Alan loses the race, but to prepare for his next run, a small group of us band together to organize the RFK Democratic Club, a new political clubhouse, to attract volunteers. I'm designated the founding chairperson . . . and when Bobby Kennedy Jr. joins us at the club's dedication to his father, I begin to see the payoff of being part of a campaign that is categorized as a long shot.

In April 1991, after two and a half years working for the Eastern Paralyzed Veterans Association, New Jersey Transit recruits me to assist in developing their statewide plan to make their public rail and bus systems accessible to people with disabilities. I spend my time on buses and trains from Queens to Newark, studying how to write a plan to the federal government on behalf of a state agency . . . and it grows clear that, as my career flourishes, I'm going to need a significant understanding of the law.

Every morning, on the walk from Newark's Penn Station to my office a few blocks away, I glance over at the construction site for Seton Hall University's new law school building. Day by day, for months, I see the shadow of a building rising slowly behind the train station. When it grows possible to observe its form—all white, steel and glass—I stop by their admissions office and pick up a brochure explaining their unique program called Legal Education Opportunity (LEO). The LEO program is affectionately known as an "affirmative action boot camp," the admissions officer tells me, and it runs all summer to prepare its students for the *possibility* that they'll be accepted into Seton Hall's law school. The brochure explains that, unlike other institutions that require both a competitive LSAT and GPA, Seton Hall's LEO program considers students with either one or the other. The catch is that applicants need a strong personal story explaining why they couldn't excel in both requirements.

It's only for half a second that I waffle, wondering if being twenty-five makes me too old to begin four years of evening law school when most law students my age are already applying for first-year associate jobs. Still . . . the thought of holding a law degree feels like it could be in reach, if I just had an opportunity to prove myself. After writing a personal essay explaining my less-than-stellar GPA, I kiss the envelope for luck and submit my application.

In spring of 1992 I'm accepted. Affirmative action boot camp begins in June.

At the LEO orientation, the law school dean explains to all seventy-six of us that, while it's unlikely any other law school would have accepted us, Seton Hall sees something in our stories that shows promise. "But this program is going to take an extraordinary commitment from you," he says. "I need to make it clear that for us to accept you is a risk—law school rankings are based upon many things, including how many students pass the bar examination the first time, and by definition, you're here because you failed in one of the two indicators that result in high first-time bar passage rates." He explains that only students who achieve at least a B in the affirmative action boot camp will be admitted into law school . . . and in August of 1992, I learn I made the cut.

I stay full-time at New Jersey Transit and pace myself for a twelve-credit load every semester, grabbing a coffee and a sandwich for dinner from the law school deli before my six o'clock class four nights a week. When class gets out at nine thirty I take the train from Newark to Manhattan's Penn Station, then the subway and the bus back to Queens. By midnight I'm in bed, knowing the next day will look the same. Some nights, as I'm drifting to sleep, I'm jolted awake by the thought of Rosie. Nothing else has ever compared to the depth of emptiness my heart holds for her. Sure, I've mainstreamed professionally and socially . . . but emotionally I've never healed. I've stifled the reality of the emotional scars that I've spent all of my young adulthood ignoring.

The more I learn about policy and the law, the more excited I become to immerse myself in the world of politics. After the half-decade I've dedicated to advocating for the rights of the physically challenged, I'm ready for a change. In 1993, the same year Rudy Giuliani runs for New York City mayor, Alan runs for city comptroller . . . and this time, with the support of the field operation that we cultivated over the past few years, he wins.

Alan places me on his transition and inauguration teams. The first few months into his new administration in downtown Manhattan, I work with fierce intensity while juggling law school in Newark. "You're one of the only people I know who never takes no for an answer," Alan tells me as he designates me as his director of Intergovernmental Relations, charged with passing his state and city legislative agenda. As far as title and responsibility go, they're as thrilling as they are daunting for me—a twenty-eight-year-old law student managing a staff and charged with implementing a New York City–wide elected official's legislative agenda. We successfully secure the passage of ten state laws.

MY PROFESSIONAL SUCCESS gives me the courage to reach out once again to Paul Accerbi . . . something I haven't tried since I was sixteen, twelve years ago. If I can overcome strong and powerful opposition in state politics, maybe I can convince Paul that I'm a decent young woman who just wants to know who her father is. But this time, rather than writing from my foster home, I take a business card and attach a note extolling my academic and work credentials. I mail it to Julia and Frank Accerbi. *Please kindly pass this along to Paul, wherever he may live*, I write.

One week later, Paul calls me at the office. "If you have lived without a father for twenty-eight years, I see no reason why you would need one now," he says.

"I feel my age is irrelevant, Paul," I tell him. "I am someone's child, and believe I am *your* child. I want to respect your space, and I'm just hoping that you could take a DNA test so I know for sure if you're my dad. I want nothing from you, really—just to know." I take a breath. "After the test, I promise: I will leave you alone." I give him no clue that I'm holding back tears, fearing to tell him the truth: I really do want to get to know him . . . but if I share that, his reaction would only be worse.

"Oh, first you're pressuring me for answers and now you're demanding my DNA? I am not taking a DNA test!" His voice crashes through the receiver like thunder. "My life and my decisions are none of your business. Every time you come around you create problems for me! Do you hear me? Never, *ever* contact Julia or me again." He hangs up.

Immediately I dial Camille.

"What did you expect?"

"I don't know. I know what I wanted, but I expected him to be *open* to a DNA test. He can see that I am a well-adjusted person—I want *nothing* from him, except to know the truth."

"Gi, he has run from the truth his entire life. He's right, you survived twenty-eight years without him, and you *don't* need him now. Let it be. You've got so much to be proud of and even more to look forward to. Stop looking back. It's over. It's all over. You need to move on."

Burying rejection is something that's become one of my strengths . . . and with that I vow never to consider contacting him again.

WHILE WORKING FOR the comptroller, I'm constantly interfacing with the most important leaders in New York City, including Mayor Rudy Giuliani and his staff. I look forward to these interactions, not just because they force me to step up and perform at my highest ability . . . but also because the mayor has a young, handsome, stoic-looking aide who's caught my eye. Like me, Todd Ciaravino takes his work very seriously. The catch? We're on opposite sides of the political aisle—me, a Democrat who works for a Democrat; and Todd, a Republican who works for a Republican—and our bosses are always pitted against each other in a political war. I watch Todd from afar, taking note that when we do get to chat, he remains aloof and mysterious—he doesn't see me as the asskicking young hotshot I like to think I am. That summer, I spend my weekends with friends in Newport, Rhode Island,

and Fire Island—a barrier island that protects Long Island from the Atlantic Ocean. I also plan a trip to Utah to visit Rosie in her new home state after she graduates from Idaho State University.

I arrive with my arms full of gifts and ready for hugs, but from the beginning, our interactions are cool and mechanical. This is characteristic of the handful of visits we've had since Cherie, Camille, and I put her on that plane back to Idaho a decade ago, so I arrived bracing for it . . . but that doesn't make it any easier. I'd exhausted myself with hope, imagining this trip to Utah would be a breakthrough.

Admittedly, part of the ill feeling she's harboring I brought on myself: During law school and especially after I graduated in May of 1996, my work has been my clearest priority. It's the one place where I've been successful. When I found out I passed the New York State bar examination, I was finally satisfied and able to put all of my energies into advancing my career. In addition to getting laws passed, Alan's put me in charge of organizing citywide task forces—one of them being a mission to identify leading representatives in the many cultural communities around New York City. When Alan asks me to, I also set up the Immigrant Task Force. "But I've never worked on immigration before," I tell him.

"There's a lot you'd never tried before you got here, but you always find ways to figure it out."

Then, in 1997, when a neighbor of Alan's in Forest Hills calls him, he and his assistant Jack wave their hands fervently for me to come into Alan's office and he sets his phone on speaker. "Go ahead, Gerry," he says, mouthing to me: *Listen.*

"I'm getting on a call with the White House at three o'clock," the woman says. "We're going over immigration issues, and I need someone who can really help me zero in on the leaders of the different ethnic communities in New York."

"I have the perfect person for you," Alan says. "I'm going to send over Regina Calcaterra."

I fold my arms. *What are you getting me into?*

"'Gerry?'" I ask both of them. "Who was that?"

"*That* was Geraldine Ferraro," Alan says.

I sink down in his visitor's chair. "You want me to help *Geraldine Ferraro?*"

Geraldine Ferraro: the former congresswoman and vice presidential candidate. I call Camille, who tells her kids to holler *Good luck!* in the background. Then I think of calling Rosie to tell her, but am worried she'll think I'm as absorbed as ever in my work.

Alan tells me that the call at three o'clock Geraldine has is with President Clinton's New Americans committee. "She's a big supporter of mine, Regina. All you have to do is fax her a memo, then go down there and walk her through it. Give her all the data she requested. Anything extra you know about these ethnic leaders, include it. We have two hours. I'll put you in a cab so you can meet her at her office to go over the list."

"Meet her?" I feel sweat break out of the pores in my scalp. "Alan, I can easily do that over the phone."

Alan looks at me sternly. "Regina, *get in a cab* and go over to meet her. This opportunity will never come again."

Spring flowers blossom on the trees along the route our taxi takes from our office across from City Hall straight up toward SoHo, to Lafayette Street. Geraldine Ferraro's office sits on the top floor of a quaint redbrick building with a black awning over her son's restaurant, Cascabel. As her no-nonsense secretary eyes me from her desk, I begin outwardly perspiring. The harder I focus on controlling my rising nervousness, the harder it exits my pores. I breathe inconspicuously, deeply in and out, and begin counting to calm myself, watching Geraldine through the glass window into her office. Inside the sunny, warm-toned room she moves about assuredly and with grace, her voice rising only once on the phone.

It hits me: meeting Geraldine Ferraro is like meeting Amelia Earhart.

Geraldine is a woman who's blazed trails in the face of the barriers women in politics—and in society—have faced, paying no mind to the thousands of critics who wanted her to fail. She persevered, believing that fighting and being defeated would be better than not fighting at all; but here she is, right in front of me, wearing a soft peach-toned turtleneck scented with something close to Chanel, pearl earrings, and a smile spread across her perfectly proportioned face. "Regina," she says. "Please. Come in."

Finally able to focus on our work, I've ceased my sweating episode. After a few minutes of going over the list together, Geraldine leans forward over her desk and asks me: "Regina, would you mind staying and participating in my call?"

"Your call . . . with the White House?"

"Yes. I'm just thinking—you seem much more comfortable discussing the individuals on this list than I am."

I try to think of some reason I need to run back to the office, then I remember Alan's words: *This opportunity will never come again.*

She directs me away from her desk to the couch in her sitting area, taking a seat across the coffee table in a sturdy armchair. She never strays from the balance between warmth and strength, which is evident when she gently suggests, "You should really do the talking." Early in the call she introduces me to the White House staff and I follow her lead, finally at ease, picking up the tone of her can-do stoicism. I'm in awe as the folks in Washington defer to her, because it's understood to everyone in her presence that even without a hint of condescension, Geraldine Ferraro knows more than you do. For the twenty minutes I'm questioned on the roles of the black, South Asian Indian, and Middle Eastern leaders in New York, Gerry offers assuring nods—at one point, even a wink.

After the call, she rests her arms on the chair she's sitting in across from me. "Regina," she ponders, "I think I could use your help on something."

I perk up, pretending I'm not completely spent.

"I'm working on a book about my mother. She was the daughter of an Italian immigrant who made a lot of sacrifices to provide my brother and me a chance to mainstream as Americans."

Mainstream?! I want to tell her. *I'd say you've done more than mainstreamed!* Instead, I politely lean forward with my hands in my lap. "Yes, Ms. Ferraro?"

"Please," she says. "Call me Gerry." Gerry speaks about her mother, Antonetta—dropping phrases like *widow after my father's death* and *worked as a bead maker in the South Bronx* . . . but in my head I'm watching a movie reel of Gerry's many extraordinary achievements: She built a strong family with her husband, John; she rose to become Queens Assistant District Attorney heading up the Sex Crimes Unit. She became a U.S. congresswoman, and in 1984 became the first woman to be nominated as a vice presidential candidate for a major party. I tune back in when she says, "This is where I need you, Regina: I plan to dedicate the last chapter to present-day female immigrants by highlighting the sacrifices they're making to give their children a chance at opportunities that wouldn't be available outside of America. You're so well-versed speaking about present-day immigration. Can you help?"

I nod slowly, in disbelief that *Geraldine Ferraro is asking me to assist her in a book*—any book!—not to mention, it's about her mother. I float out of her office and, too dazed to hail a cab, I walk the near-mile back to City Hall in my heels. Surely, by the time I arrive there, she'll have called and said, "Never mind, Regina! I've found a bright young scholar to take this on; someone with a sane mother and a normal upbringing!"

When Alan meets me at the office door, indeed he says Gerry has called. "Nice work," he tells me. "Sounds like you made quite an impression."

Instantly the work is a comfort, the familiar feeling of being busy giving me a sense of structure and security. When I graduated law school a year ago, I had more free time on my hands than I've ever had in my life—the first time I've just had one full-time job without waitressing, attending law school, or working on political campaigns on the side. For the next six weeks I spend my nights up to my elbows in the immigration research, feeling soothed by the work, and finally producing a summary and outline based on my vision for Gerry's last chapter. I return to her office and hand over my file, which she accepts with a kind smile.

Then, a week later, she calls. "Regina, do you mind coming down to my office again?"

My stomach sinks. My heart pounds. I slide from flats into

the heels under my desk and hail a cab, directing him to La-fayette Street.

"I've decided that since this book is to be about my mother, that it should begin and end with my mother." Gerry's tone and face are kind, but matter-of-fact. "I'm no longer going to use the content you provided."

I nod, trying to swallow the lump of tears building up in my throat. I knew that, eventually, this is how it would end. "Look, Gerry, I'm just grateful for the chance to have worked with you."

"Well, not so fast," she says. "I still need your help. I'm writing a story about an Italian immigrant, but I'm also find-ing that I need to tell the story against the backdrop of the Italian immigration movement and the progression of Italians into American society. That piece, I don't have. I need your experience on immigration."

"Gerry, see . . . the problem is that I am only familiar with current immigration patterns—not stories from the past. Plus, even though, yes, I am Italian"—in my work I always need to finesse this next point—"I'm not fully aware of my heritage. I'm afraid I just can't be useful at this point."

Her face grows firmer, subtly frustrated at my resistance. "Yes, Regina, actually you can. It's going to take some re-search on your part, but I'm confident you're up to it. In fact, I'm so confident that I would like to pay you for your research," she says.

"Oh, Gerry." It comes out halfhearted, almost a plea to be cut loose. What if I let her down? "Please," I tell her. "Your confidence in me and the opportunity to work on something so deeply personal to you is payment enough."

That night before I go home, I stop at the New York Public Library. I scan the microfiche and take out every book I can find on Ellis Island and Italian immigrants in New York, including *The Madonna of 115th Street* and *Beyond the Melting Pot*.

My contribution to Gerry's memoir, *Framing a Life*, puts solid punctuation on this era of my work for the city. I've far exceeded my own expectations . . . and it's time to move on. With Alan kicking around the idea of running for mayor in the 2001 election, I'm hesitant to stay with him the four years until then. It's a danger to be out of law school five years without ever having practiced. My law degree is my single most worthy credential, and also my safety net—even if other opportunities aren't available, there are always jobs in law . . .

. . . but only if I start using it.

While eagerly waiting for the release of Gerry's book, I begin to look for a job where I can actually use my law degree and also make a higher income. I know this means leaving New York City politics. I'm thirty years old, living with roommates in my third Manhattan apartment. I've spent my whole life sharing cramped, compromised spaces that don't feel like mine; and most of all, I need to begin making enough money to stop deferring payment on my law school loans. The public sector could never pay me enough for rent, living expenses, and a hundred and fifty thousand dollars of law school loan debt.

When I can force myself not to get wistful for a connection with Rosie, even my family situation has grown well adjusted and normal. Camille and Frank now have Frankie, Maria,

and Michael, and Cherie and her new husband have Johnathan and Matthew—all of whom I couldn't love any more
if they were my own. I spend my holidays with them and
they join me in the city for Christmas or to watch the Macy's
Thanksgiving Day Parade. On weekends, I carve out time
to see friends, movies, and Broadway shows. Nicer days are
spent in Central Park, running or Rollerblading. Sundays
are my favorite: I drink coffee in bed and read several papers
from cover to cover.

One Sunday morning close to the holidays in 1997, I'm
in bed reading the paper when the phone rings. Expecting
to hear Camille's voice on the other end, I pick it up. "Hey."

"Regina, I have some mail here for you."

"Addie?" She usually only calls on holidays and birthdays . . . but her voice sounds curious, or startled; somehow
strained, trying to hold back.

"Okay, well just send it to me. It's probably junk."

"I don't think it's junk . . . in fact, I think you may want
me to open it now. It's from a Julia Accerbi—it looks like a
Christmas card."

"Well, open it!" I tell her. "What are we waiting for?"
I hear the envelope rip open, then Addie begins laughing.
"Regina, you won't believe this: Her Christmas card is from
the Eastern Paralyzed Veterans Association."

"Are you kidding?" I laugh. The EPVA's main source of
revenue was through selling greeting cards. "She probably
paid part of my salary while I was there!"

"Now that's irony," Addie says, giggling. "Okay, she
writes—are you ready?"

"Yes!"

" 'To Regina,' then the printed message reads, 'With the

old wish that is ever new—Merry Christmas and a Happy New Year, too!'"

"Anything else?"

"Yes—my goodness. She signed 'Love, Aunt Julia.'"

"Aunt Julia? Addie . . . are you sure?"

"Sure I'm sure. I'll pop it in the mail to you today, you can look at it yourself."

Both when I was sixteen and twenty-eight, I wrote to Paul at Julia and Frank's house, and neither time did I get a response from them, only from Paul. So why now, after never having contact with me, is she suddenly showing interest? Maybe something happened to Paul that she wants me to know about. Or maybe she just wants me to know the truth. Aunt Julia. How do I suddenly have an aunt Julia?

"Regina," Addie interrupts, "are you there? What are you going to do?"

"I don't know. Will you just send it to me? I'll call you in a few weeks for Christmas."

Everything about the card is both intriguing and odd, but there are two points that stand out in particular: First, it was sent to Addie's home—my old foster home—where I haven't resided for close to a decade. Anyone with a shred of knowledge about my life would know that. Second, how did she not mention her husband, my supposed uncle? I dial Camille, the only other person on earth who could know what this means to me.

"What do you think this is about?" I ask her.

"I have no idea," she says thoughtfully. "Do you think Paul *died*? Or maybe this woman is sick and she wants to tell you something before she gets worse. Whatever it means . . . tread carefully, sweetie. I know you're excited, but this could take you to a place that you've already moved past. You could end up really hurting."

It's too late: I'm totally sucked in. "It's not like *I* went and opened the door, Camille. She did. There's something going on that I need to know. How about this: I'll write her back, rather than call her."

"Don't mention Paul until she does—let her bring him up. And don't question why she signed the card 'Aunt.'"

"But why?"

"Because you may scare her away. Just let her know how well you're doing and give her your new address and phone number."

"Oh, come on, Camille. Why don't I just call her, instead?"

"Because, Gi, when you're not getting truthful answers, you can be a little . . . abrasive."

"Ha!" She knows me too well. "I like to think of it as assertive . . . but you're right."

"Just write her first. Take it slow."

"Okay."

By the time Julia's card arrives several days later, matching Addie's description to the dotting of her *i*'s, I've already worked on several drafts of a letter to her, which I'm planning to fold inside a Christmas card. Although there's so much I want to know, I keep my message simple: My work's going well, I've adapted to be happy, normal, and successful. I know better than to ask the big questions: why she signed it *Aunt*, why she sent it to my foster home, why her husband's name wasn't listed in the card, and why she's writing me now.

A month later, I receive a letter back from Julia, this time sent to my Manhattan address:

January 1998

Dear Regina,

Received your card and was so glad to hear from you. I often think of you and your sisters. Regina, any time you want to come to visit me, you know you can. I knew that you had to get my card because it did not come back.

I'm so glad you made something of yourself. I'm so happy for you. I don't know if I told you that your uncle Frank died. It's been pretty hard for me since he's gone. I do wish you and your sisters would come to see me. Let me know ahead of time and I would make a meal for you all.

How are your sisters doing? Did any of them get married? Regina, I'm so happy for you. I know life was not easy for any of you girls. There's so much we could talk about. Lots of luck in your job. I hear from Pauly every so often. He's still in Florida.

Please come see me. I've been having a little trouble with my heart. When you reach a certain age everything falls apart. Good luck again and please get in touch with me. Take care.

Love,
Aunt Julia

I reread the letter several times, too experienced in disappointment to hope I'm seeing it all correctly. She referred so casually to Paul; she explained why Frank's name wasn't on the card . . . but how does she know my sisters? Why is she so plainly signing the card *Aunt Julia* and referring to her husband as *Uncle Frank*? The letter's postmarked from Long Island . . . why is she *just now* getting in touch with me when, minus my three years at college upstate, the farthest I've ever lived from her is ninety minutes away in Manhattan?

I call Camille and read the letter out loud. "So, come on! What do you think?"

She pauses, then cautiously puts this forth: "Maybe we stayed with her when we were kids."

"Camille, I have zero recollection of staying with this woman. *Julia*: Does that sound even vaguely familiar to you?"

"Gi, maybe this is the place I remember that had the willow tree and all the kids."

"When?"

"When you were *really* little."

"Maybe Cookie and Paul were just deadbeats, and so Julia and Frank took us in—"

"Gi, it's possible that this Accerbi is no relation to Paul."

"But she mentioned Paul . . . and why is she calling herself my aunt?"

"We probably just called them aunt and uncle, and that's how she's signing her letters. Plenty of our foster parents did that. That is the only logical explanation—Gi, please don't get your hopes up."

I pause. "She wrote her number in the card. I'm going to call her and go out there."

"How will you get there?" Camille asked.

"I'll rent a car in Manhattan and drive." Ninety minutes is nothing after waiting thirty-one years for answers. "Then I'll come to see you afterward and fill you in on what happened. Unless, of course," I prod gently, "you want to join me?"

Camille sighs, considering what to do for my sake, but already I know her decision. She has no desire to revisit our past and has worked hard to create a new existence with Frank and their kids. Once in awhile I can get her to join me on my melancholy drives to Saint James Elementary School, Cordwood Beach, or the Saint James General Store. I try to remember how we frolicked at these places, how they provided our only space to be carefree kids, but Camille remembers what an older sister would: the turbulence, the abuse, the starving, and the heartache. We were a hapless group of savvy street-smart kids trying to build a home out of nothing; and just because I may get some answers about my past doesn't make Camille excited to go there, too. "You go," she finally says. "With three kids, I have enough going on. She wrote to you— go see her. Then come here afterward."

"Okay. Love you, sweetie."

"Love you, too, bug." She pauses. "Regina?"

"Yeah?"

"Remember what I said: Please be careful."

12

❧

A Child at Any Age

Winter 1998 to 2003

SITTING IN THE parked rental car, I turn up the heat and rest back to absorb the details of the panorama in front of me. The weeping willow in the front yard is the first thing that catches me; its huge, sad branches swaying in the early February chill. My eyes wander to the chain-linked fence encasing the property when a memory comes rushing at me: I'm tiny, standing on the inside of the fence, giggling madly as a boy much bigger stretches his fingers through the metal triangles and tries to tickle my belly.

Shifting my gaze to the garden, I fix on a statue of the Virgin Mary sheltered by a ceramic clamshell. Vibrant flowers bursting in pink, orange, and yellow surround her—a contrast to the brown lawn and bushes that are dry and barren from the winter. I take in the breadth of the house; how ordinary it is: yellow shingles and weathered wooden shutters with nailed-in plastic cutout images of horses and buggies. I notice the cracked cement of the driveway; the neglected trees and bushes that are years overdue for trimming.

I exit the car and cross the street slowly, ignoring my nervousness in order to open the chain-linked gate and walk the broken path to the front door. This close to the flower beds, I see that the clusters of silky color are artificial bouquets stuck upright in the frosted soil. I step toward the front door—protected by an exterior storm door framed with Police Youth League and Jesus and Mary decals. Jesus' face is plastered on stickers representing every phase of his life, and as I move to open the storm door, the inner door suddenly opens. A woman shrunken by age appears. She's wearing a flowered knee-length day dress, slippers, and a tightly sprayed white bouffant. "Regina?" she asks.

"Yes. Hello, Julia."

She opens the door and moves to me on the porch. I stay still while, with wide eyes, she examines me—first my hair, then my face and my clothes . . . then finally my hand as she takes it in hers. Suddenly, her small frame opens, her arms stretching in an invitation for me to walk into them for a hug. I freeze: it's almost too much to take in. By the look on her face, it'll be devastating for her if I refuse, so I fix my arms around her in a political hug—a guarded non-embrace. For a moment we remain this way—Julia, breathing me in; and me, telling myself it's safe to soften to her affection. Finally, she moves away but keeps a gentle hold on the sleeve of my coat. "Go on, dear," she says. "Please, make yourself at home."

Passing through the front door to the living room, I look in at the worn carpeted steps leading to the second floor. It's as if I'm outside of myself, watching a movie of this moment: I recognize all of this place. I know what lies up those stairs—three bedrooms and a yellow bathroom. My eyes move toward the dining area with its oval table and the plastic-covered chair they used to sit me in, propped up on phone books and pillows so I could reach the table. If I walk through the dining room, I'll find the kitchen, with a yellow and brown linoleum floor, a small stove tucked in the corner, and the large window above the sink where I used to bathe. I'll also find the door to the fenced backyard whose knob was always too high for me to reach, and the interior stairs that lead down to a carpeted basement with two small couches that I remember well: That's where my sisters and I used to sleep at night.

Julia escorts me into the kitchen: still yellow and brown. "I baked you crumb cake," she says. "Would you like a slice? Some baked ziti?"

"I'd love some crumb cake, please," I tell her. This moment is surreal; awkward, yet so familiar.

"You look like him, you know."

I pause for a beat. Would she refer to my father so plainly?

"You look like Pauly. When your grandmother held you, she told Pauly that you looked just like him when he was a baby. I think you still do! Those Accerbi features. He's your father, you know. You said the crumb cake, right?"

Is this really happening? "When did Paul's mother hold me?"

"When you were here—you and your sisters lived here when you were little."

I knew it. This is the Happy House, and it was our home. I think of asking Julia whether I can use the phone to call

Camille, but I don't even want to take a breath that could risk derailing our conversation.

"I've been thinking about where to begin, so I guess I'll start at the beginning: with them dating." She sets the cake in front of me and I edge it to the side, more enticed by the revelations that are lingering than the cakey cinnamon scent rising from the plate. "Cookie and Pauly dated," Julia says. "God, I remember my first impression of Cookie: her striking dark eyes, white skin like milk, and those two adorable little girls. Pauly dated a lot of girls after he and Carol divorced, but he wouldn't bring them all around here," she says. "But sure enough, he brought your mom a few times. Pauly has another daughter, you know, from his marriage to Carol. So you have another sister, and two nieces—I think they still live in Alaska."

"How did we end up here?"

She stays silent a moment, then reaches out for my hand. "Frank—that was my husband, Paul's older brother. He died ten years ago. See, Frank already had three kids from his first marriage but his wife died giving birth to the third, God rest her soul. Then we had three more, and Frank worked full-time to support us all. But, you know, for a family of eight, we needed more income. So I watched other people's kids while they worked. Parents brought their children to me either by references or they'd find me in the Pennysaver ads."

I look at her hand, still on mine. With carefully chosen words, Julia explains she hadn't seen Cookie for over a year and a half after she and Paul stopped dating. "So I was . . . surprised, we'll say, when she responded to one of my ads asking for day care for her three girls. The first morning, she shows up with little Cherie and Camille by her side, and she hands me this sweet baby girl—you had just turned a year old. And she says to me, 'I'll be back after work.' So after about ten days of bringing you girls, Cookie appears on my stoop . . . and I'm just staring at this suitcase she's carrying. 'It just has some of the girls' toys,' she says. 'It'll keep them occupied during the day.' That Cookie, I'll never forget it: She smiled and told me, 'Have a great day!' Then as she's waltzing toward her car, she calls over her shoulder, 'Oh, by the way, Regina is Pauly's baby!'

"With you in my arms, I'm standing on the porch calling out to her: 'Cookie, wait!' But she ignores me and just pulls out of the driveway. I remember wondering how she could be so detached from these kids, you know? These three beautiful little girls. After she left, I went inside and opened the suitcase, and what did I find? Not toys. Oh, no. I found clothes . . . and cockroaches."

I look away. "She's disgusting."

"I slammed the case closed and put it out at the curb. Then for the next eight hours I fumed, ready to lay into her when she returned that evening. But even by the time Frank got home, you girls were still here. She never returned. I told Frank, 'You call Pauly and your mother,' and immediately they both came over. As soon as Paul walked in, he saw your two sisters and said, 'What the hell are these girls doing here?' Then he looked to his mother, who was holding you in her arms. She said, 'Paul, this child is your baby.' Pauly turns to me and says, 'Get rid of these kids!' Then he turned around and left the house."

So all the years as a child, when I wondered whether my father existed, he knew I existed. "But you didn't get rid of us?"

"No. We ignored Paul—the whole family did. There was a right thing to do, to take responsibility for you . . . and he refused to do it. And, so, soon the weeks turned into months and the months turned into a year, and nobody knew where Cookie went. We finally turned to Suffolk County social services and asked them to just give us food stamps to cover the costs of our food. And instead of helping us, what does social services do? They demand we turn you girls over to the county for placement in an orphanage or foster home." She rubs her temples, then places one hand, resting on her wrist, on the table. "Frank resisted. He told them he was not going to turn over his niece and her two sisters to complete strangers so you all could end up in an orphanage. All we needed was food stamps, no money. The county refused." She leans back in her chair, resigned. "That's when it all became a big mess."

Julia explains that she and Frank hurried out of the social services' office, and the social workers asked when they were bringing us back. "Frank hollered over his shoulder, 'Never!' I thought he'd have a heart attack. A couple of days later, three social workers and the police showed up on our doorstep and demanded we turn you over. Frank clutched you so tight that it took two social workers to tear one arm at a time off of you, while the third took you from him.

"Your Uncle Frank never saw you again after that," Julia says. "He was devastated. He always wondered what happened to you and your sisters, and finally he came to accept that he was never going to see you again. Then—out of the blue—you wrote him in 1983. When we got your letter, he opened it, thinking it was for him, then he realized you wanted him to hand it off to Pauly. He called Pauly and read it to him. 'You son of a bitch,' Frank says, 'you get over here and talk about this. I am your brother. Let me help you do the right thing.' When Pauly arrived, Frank told him that he knew full well that you were his daughter, that he had to take responsibility for you and get you out of that foster home."

"So what did Paul do?"

"Pauly? Not a thing, honey. Such a shame. My Frank . . . a decade he's been gone and I just could not bring myself to go through his papers. Finally, before last Christmas, I knew it was time to go through them. That's when I found the envelope. Pauly took that letter"—my stomach flips in excitement to hear Paul had cared to keep that much—"but your uncle Frank held on to the envelope all this time. He refused to throw it out. So when I found it, I knew he held on to it so that one day he could contact you . . . let you know the truth. I guess you could say it was for him that I reached out to you. Frank always wanted to right this somehow." She looks at me softly, almost apologetically. "I was worried. It's been sixteen years since you wrote that letter. I didn't know if I'd ever be able to find you, but when the letter didn't come back, I knew you must have gotten it."

Julia goes on to tell me that she'll answer any questions I have under one condition: No one in the Accerbi family can know who I really am. "I'll tell them you and your sisters were some of the kids I used to watch back in the sixties." She leans forward. "Regina, please understand: If the Accerbis ever find out what I've done by getting in touch with you, they'll disown me. We're a close family, you know? Just promise me you'll keep all this to yourself."

I nod and scoot my plate of crumb cake toward me. "I promise."

Julia rises from the table and walks out of the kitchen, holding on to the same banister that I used to hold when I was a toddler. When the bathroom door shuts behind her, I wander around the kitchen, then drift into the dining room, over to the head of the table where I remember perching myself to look out at the backyard, where I remember Julia throwing birthday parties for her kids with streamers, balloons, and piñatas. On the dining room table is a personal phone book with each entry carefully handwritten. I look closer at the open page, *A*: *Accerbi*. Then scroll down the page until I see it:

Paul & Joan.

From the side pocket of my handbag I pull out my address book and pen and write quickly, checking their phone number closely. When the floor creaks behind me, I turn to see Julia standing there. "I see you found what you came for."

"I did." I smile. "Thank you."

"I'm not feeling well," Julia says. "For years I haven't been well. My body gets bloated and it gets difficult to sit or even to breathe. I need to rest," she says. "But I want you to come back and see me soon, please—bring your sisters with you, Regina. I'd love to see them again."

I meet her at the foot of the stairs and kiss her cheek. "Thank you, Julia." Just as I push out of the front door, two middle-aged women open the gate and head toward the house. I shoot Julia a look and she steps in to introduce me. "Regina, these are my daughters: Yvonne and Darlene. Girls, you might remember Regina. She was one of the girls I used to watch. You remember her sisters, Cherie and Camille?"

"Me Too!" Yvonne says. "We called Camille 'Me Too' because every time Cherie asked for something, Camille would say, 'Me too'!"

I smile, remembering the old moniker my sisters used to use. "Yes," I tell them. "Camille was Me Too. It's nice to see you both."

I put the keys in the ignition and let out a deep exhale, giving myself a minute to take it all in. This was the Happy House. It really exists, more than one of the last pieces of a broken, puzzled childhood: also the home of my family. I have relatives. It crosses my mind to drive around once more and stare at the house, but instead I head straight to Camille's.

"Camille, I remembered everything," I tell her. "The linoleum in the kitchen, the Mary statue outside." As I relay the details to Camille, together we reach our conclusion: It was after being taken from the Happy House that we ended up at the home of the Giannis'—the Bubble House. That's when we were finally taken to the Glue Factory and I encountered Cookie for the first time.

Christmas Mama.

"So what are you going to do with Paul's information? Anything?" Camille says.

I'm busy collecting my thoughts. This man—now, almost certainly, my father—rejected me twice, and I refuse to let him do it again. I need time to develop a rational strategy: Either I will inform him that I know that he is my father, or compel him to take a DNA test. Either route requires extremely thoughtful processing. "I'm at peace, surprisingly. For now, this is enough."

"Well, good, sweetie."

Besides, for Julia's sake, I need to tread cautiously.

On my drive back to Manhattan, something else clicks: the screen door with the Jesus stickers and the Mary statue on the front lawn; the ceramic Jesus heads hanging on the wall not too far from the ceramic plate of Jesus and the bronze cross of Jesus. Something about all of the Jesus images weighs on me as I try to recall why they seem so familiar. Instead of taking my car back to the rental agency, I drive straight to my apartment, find a parking spot, and run up the five flights to my apartment. "Camille," I huff into the phone in excitement, "Julia had images of Jesus all over her house, from before you even open the front door. When did I begin to carry the Baby Jesus figurines everywhere?"

"When you were a toddler," she says, laughing. "Now we know where they came from."

A few weeks later, in late February 1998, Camille receives a phone call from Norman in Idaho. "Mom's been diagnosed with cancer," he tells her. "They told her it can't be cured."

I have hope that in Cookie's suffering she accepts responsibility for all the pain she inflicted on us and will finally ask forgiveness rather than point fingers. Still, I know there's no way I can actually forgive her . . . not for what she did to me, but for what she did to Rosie.

CHERIE AND CAMILLE pay for Cookie to fly in from Idaho, hoping finally this woman will try and redeem herself before her death. "Good luck. I'm not sticking around for this," I tell Camille, opting instead to join the Irish guy I've been dating and his family for the holidays in Dublin.

On January 1, 1999, I call Camille's house to wish her a Happy New Year. In response, she tells me that Cookie refuses to acknowledge any wrongdoing during our childhoods.

"Nothing's changed, Regina, but we knew better than to hold our breaths for an apology. You'll be back in New York the day before Cookie's scheduled to go back to Idaho. Don't you think saying good-bye could give you some closure?"

Apparently Cookie told my sisters that everything we believe happened to us was in our imaginations. "I did a fine job raising you girls!" she said. "Look how well you turned out."

Disregarding her denial and my loathing of her, I indulge Camille by seeing our mother one last time. My siblings and their kids crowd around me and my sister's dining room table as I share pictures from my Ireland trip. Cookie sits in the living room, watching television by herself.

"Gi," Camille says, "it's getting late. Should Cherie and I get you to the rail station?"

"Sure." I close my album slowly and kiss each of the kids good-bye. After I put on my coat, I turn and whisper to Camille: "Just a minute." In the living room, I leave a wide space between myself and the recliner where Cookie's sitting, knowing that distance from her is the only thing that has kept me both physically and emotionally safe. Wearing a blue flannel shirt, black stretch pants, and a scowl, she slowly meets my eyes. The TV's reflection flashes off the lenses of her huge, shaded eyeglasses. "Good-bye," I tell her. It comes out cold and flat. When she responds with silence, I nod. This is all I'll get. Cherie opens the front door, and Camille and I exit with her.

When the three of us get to the train station, we all break down in tears. It's a cry of anger for our mother's failure to take responsibility, for the unfairness of having had no say in choosing who brought us into this world . . . and for our relief knowing that soon she'll be gone, for good.

IN THE SPRING of 1999, I receive a call from Camille at work. "Gi, I have some wild news for you. It's something that you'd think could never happen to Frank and me."

"You . . . won the lottery?"

"No! Think of the thing that wasn't supposed to happen."

"You're pregnant?"

"Yes! We're having another baby!" I feel her beaming on the other end of the phone. In 1996, Frank was diagnosed with a cancer that the doctors said would affect their ability to have any more children. Camille stayed with me in Manhattan while her mother-in-law took the kids so that Frank could receive treatments at Sloan-Kettering.

"But after the cancer, the doctors told you it wouldn't be possible to have more babies."

"Well, God thought differently," Camille says. "We're expecting Baby Number Four in October."

As Camille's belly blossoms, so does my relationship with Julia. I receive handwritten notes from her at least monthly, and anytime I travel from Manhattan to Long Island, I make a point to see her. We're both discreet in keeping our relationship from her daughters and her extended family, but Julia's genuine interest in my life has prompted her to become reacquainted with Camille. On holidays and birthdays, she sends letters and cards to both her and Cherie.

In October 1999, Camille delivers Danielle Grace. The birth of a baby girl is a good excuse for all of us to celebrate, made even sweeter thanks to the fact that of the seven children in the family, five are boys: Frankie and Michael, who belong to Frank and Camille; and Cherie's three sons, Anthony, Matthew, and Johnathan. Finally, Camille's daughter, Maria, will have another little girl to grow up with.

With every new life that enters our family, more and more joy abounds. Silently, there's a satisfaction inside me that Cookie can never be part of it: We don't know how long she has, but it's clear she will not outlive this decade. In November, a month after Danielle's birth, I find myself with an irresistible urge to write Cookie a lengthy letter. *Don't ever deceive yourself into believing that you should be credited for our achievements,* I tell her. *Despite the odds and your attempted influences, we've prevailed. Many women can give birth, but that doesn't make them a mom. To us, you're just Cookie.*

Norm reports back that he began to read the letter to her but she told him to stop after the first paragraph. He also informs us she's made a last-minute switch from being Mormon to American Indian because she believes it will be better for her after death.

Thanksgiving passes and Norman shares reports of Cookie's imminent demise. "I have only one wish," I tell Camille. "I pray she will not pass on December sixteenth."

Camille looks at me curiously.

"December sixteenth is Julia's birthday."

By now, Julia and I have grown extremely close and I don't want her special day of the year to be spoiled or overshadowed by my mother's death. But of course, in the early morning hours of December 16, shortly after one A.M. in Idaho and four A.M. in New York, my phone rings.

"She's gone," Camille tells me.

We sit on the phone in silence, letting it all sink in. The

chapter of our lives that we've waited so long to close is now over.

I take the day off from work and Camille picks me up at the rail station. Without discussing our plan, she pulls onto the highway and we both know where we're headed. We drive out to Saint James General Store—past Wicks farm stand, where we used to steal apples, and King Kullen, where we used to sneak our meals out of the store beneath our clothes. We drive past the Glue Factory apartment, now a Sal's Auto Mechanics, where we spent the longest time consecutively as a family. We head to Saint James Elementary School, where we wander the back grounds . . . and we finally end up at Cordwood Beach—the place we used to play for hours, writing our names in the sand, hunting the rocks for clams, and picking fistfuls of onion grass for our dinners.

Arm in arm, my sister and I walk the beach, saying nothing. Under the gray December sky, we look out at the Long Island Sound to where the floating dock once was anchored; to the broken stone house that we used to climb on.

"She did one thing right," Camille says.

"What?"

"She gave us each other."

The lives Cookie gave us were only etched in sand; able to be erased and written all over again . . . better, with meaning. We've all made our stories into what we wanted for ourselves.

Standing side by side on the cold beach, there's just one thought keeping Camille and me from feeling total completion: Rosie. She doesn't want us to be a part of her life or to know her family.

Rosie got married and gave birth to a son, but by the time we knew about any of it, all the momentous events had passed. Occasionally, she mails Camille and me photographs, in all of which she's clearly a loving, doting mother . . . but on the rare occasion the photos are accompanied by a letter, the communication is all very matter-of-fact. *Everyone here is fine,* she says. *Hope you're great.* She wants us to be aware that she's adjusted well as an adult, but she doesn't want us to be present for it.

In December 1999, a colleague tells me he's venturing into Times Square to ring in the new millennium. "You used to work for the City, right?" he asks. "What'll be the best way to navigate the streets?"

I call someone whom I heard now works as the special assistant to the NYC police commissioner: Todd Ciaravino, the handsome, stoic aide to Giuliani whom I knew from my years at the comptroller's office. After sharing the layout of the security route, Todd remembers my burgeoning golf hobby and says it might be nice to hit the driving range at Chelsea Piers when the weather warms up a little.

Todd is sensitive to my guardedness—unlike other guys I've been attracted to, he's consistent, mild-mannered, and kind . . . not at all overbearing or arrogant. Instead of what so many former partners and people from my childhood promised—*You can trust me*—Todd *shows* me he deserves my trust. He looks out for me, and coming from the same field, he doesn't give me a hard time about how busy my work keeps me. By late spring, we've entered potentially-serious-romance territory when Todd begins traveling with the Bush-Cheney presidential campaign. At the same time, I'm transitioning from my position on Wall Street back to working with the public sector and, as a hobby, I begin to appear on Fox News, supporting the Democratic presidential ticket. By August, our courtship, pleasant and passionate as it is, ends . . . not due to our differing views on politics, but because of how committed we both are to our careers.

It's another intense undertaking that distracts me from my split from Todd: It's now two and a half years since I first visited Julia in February 1998, and the more I see pictures of Paul and his brothers, the more convinced I am that he is my biological father. For years I've been emotionally prepared to learn the truth, but now I'm also in a financial position to pursue paternity litigation if he chooses not to amicably resolve my request for DNA.

I SPEND EARLY August researching Paul's address online to find that he now lives in the U.S. border town of Blaine in Washington State. In addition to determining where he lives, I also study Washington's paternity statutes and map out what my next steps will be if he rejects my request for a paternity test. I advise Julia that I plan to contact Paul.

"Given what I've done by forming a relationship with you," Julia says, "please let me make the connection."

When a couple weeks go by, I estimate he's ignoring me . . . or researching potential legal steps. In late August I receive a phone call. "You should know that you are causing my wife and me deep anxiety," he says. "I'm experiencing heart problems, and your so-called curiosity could be making it worse." This familiar response from him confirms to me: yes, he's got a lawyer. The first argument the defense would make in a case like this is to advise the opposition at the outset that they're inflicting emotional distress. "What is it you want?"

I respond that my intentions are pure, that I only want to know if he's my father. "I don't want any support," I assure him.

Then he reveals what he's really worried about. "If I admit that I'm your father, it will be a long and painful process for us all if the State of New York tries to sue me for back child support."

"Paul, you won't have to pay New York State back the money it cost them to keep me in foster care," I explain flatly. "Even if New York does that now, they certainly didn't have such a law in place when I was in foster care as a child. Also, just to appease any concern you have about why I'm contacting you: I do fine on my own. I don't need any money. I just want to know if you're my father." I also want him to know that I know that he's my father—to face the fact that he left me to be brutalized as a child simply because I'd come from him. Of course, as a teenager, I'd hoped to track down my father so that I could actually have a relationship with him, and in my twenties, I wanted to show him how well I'd turned out . . . but now, I just want him to acknowledge his failure to take responsibility.

"I have to go, Regina," he says. "Now's not a good time."

The next day he calls me twice at work, but I'm with clients both times. Then he calls a third time, and again I'm unavailable. He leaves me his fax but not his phone number, so I have no way to call him back and actually carry on a conversation. When I want to speak to him I have to fax him or wait for him to call me, so my correspondence is in writing but his is all verbal . . . another strategic move by him and his lawyer to keep the upper hand.

Then I finally get a fax back, not from him, but from a Wayne Teller, Paul's lawyer. I fight to steady the paper in my shaking hands as I read that Paul no longer wants me to contact him and his decision is final. Then to ensure that I never contact him again, his attorney ended the letter by stating if I fail to comply with his request and contact Paul again that I will be admonished for violating Rule 4.2 of the Rules of Professional Conduct.

Camille is angrier than I am. "What on earth does Rule 4.2 even mean?"

"Rule 4.2 restricts an attorney from ever contacting someone who is represented by counsel. Even though I could be his daughter, I'm also an attorney. He's threatening to bring charges of professional misconduct against me if I ever directly contact him again."

"So he's used your achievement against you," she says. "How unfair, Gi. No good would have come from meeting him anyway." We both know she's just trying to comfort me. "What are you going to do now?"

"I have to try to find a qualified paternity lawyer in the State of Washington who's willing to take my case . . . and it won't be easy. An adult has never successfully sued another adult for paternity before, only minor children have been permitted to sue for DNA. So whoever takes my case must not only be qualified to fight this battle, but also has to really believe in my case."

"I believe in your case," Camille says.

The simplicity of her statement arrests me. In this moment, it's clear: My sister is the only person who has always stood by me, no matter how extreme the scenario. "You do?"

"Yes. You, me, Cherie . . . all we've ever wanted is to know who we are. Who we came from. At least Vito and Norman stuck around long enough to see their kids born, but we three have never even seen pictures of our fathers. I know you and I came from two different men, but I want to know the truth for you as much as you do. If Cookie couldn't help us figure out where we fit in this world, then we have to find out for ourselves."

She's put it perfectly. From where I get my strength to where I get my eyes, all I want is to know. But searching for the right attorney and convincing him or her to take my case will take some time. In the meantime, Paul will think that this letter has ended our connection forever . . . but I'm not finished.

I start by contacting members of the American Academy of Matrimonial Lawyers in Washington. I leave messages for dozens of them, but only receive a call back from the secretary of one. Her message is clear: Never before in Washington State has an adult sued someone they thought to be their father for paternity. "However, there is one lawyer that may consider a case like this. His name is Ralph Moldauer. He used to represent kids suing their fathers for paternity, but he now represents a professional sports team on the defense side."

I laugh. "A professional sports team?"

"Well, sure," she says. "Every professional sports team usually has at least one paternity lawyer on speed dial." I chuckle at the perfect sense this makes. "Let me get you Ralph's number."

By early January 2001, Ralph agrees to take my case, not because he needs another client, but because he feels the proof I have regarding the probability of Paul being my father is so strong and my story so unique that I have a shot at success . . . although over and over he cautions me that this has never been done before in any of the fifty states. "I'm willing to represent you," Ralph says, "but for your sake, let's not get our hopes up." I understand Ralph's need to manage my expectations, but it's increasingly clear he's as invested in this case as I am. I also sense that there are two possible reasons he's so intent to bring it to the court: He thinks my case would be an opportunity to create precedent for other adult children, or out of humanity he wants to go after Paul for what he failed to do when I was a child.

In late January 2001, Ralph writes Paul's lawyer, requesting that we avoid litigation and that Paul merely takes a DNA test. In response, Paul's lawyer says that both Mr. and Mrs. Accerbi find my attempts to contact Paul quite upsetting physically and emotionally and that I have no legal grounds to bring suit; and if I do, that I can expect an "aggressive counterclaim for abuse of action, invasion of privacy, and intentional infliction of emotional distress." As I've presumed all along, from that first phone call back in August, Paul's been planning to countersue me if I bring a claim for paternity—this is why he keeps playing the "physical and emotional stress" card.

"It's a measly swab test!" I tell Ralph. "Just a second." I rise from my desk to close my office door so as not to disturb my coworkers. Taking the phone again I tell him: "There's nothing invasive or physically stressful about this!"

"Regina, I spoke to his counsel," Ralph advises me. "Paul is ready to fight hard if you proceed with a paternity claim. Our problem is that this is a case of first impression. You have absolutely no other case in the U.S. to rely upon, so if you sue him for DNA, he will argue that you are using the courts to harass him. Trust me, this is exactly how it will go. Do you follow?"

"Yes. Keep going."

"The good news is, it's likely his counterargument will be dismissed since you have proof that you tried to resolve this outside of the courts. I can't promise that he won't be successful and demand that you pay his attorney fees and additional damages for intentional infliction of emotional distress. And consider, on top of this you only have affidavits of your sisters and foster mother that reiterate what your deceased mother has told you. If Cookie were still alive, at least she could provide an affidavit claiming that he was the father . . . but she's dead."

Dammit. I never thought I'd have any reason to wish that my mother were still here.

"So your failure to obtain an affidavit from someone who can confidently state that your parents had a sexual relationship around the time you were conceived is problematic."

He goes on to explain what I already know: Paternity tests are DNA tests. The taking of someone's DNA, regardless if it's by a blood test or a simple mouth swab, is protected by the Fourth Amendment's protections against unreasonable search and seizure and the right to privacy . . . However, an exception to the U.S. Constitution's Fourth Amendment is made if there is a compelling government interest for the courts to rule otherwise. The courts will make exceptions if a crime has been committed or a child is in need of support, so that if there is a father, he's to be held responsible for the costs of raising that child.

"Regina, you're an adult in your thirties and it's going to be hard for us to demonstrate that getting Paul's DNA is necessary to your well-being," Ralph says. "But the one argument we have going for us is that the Washington State paternity law does not define what a child is."

"Ralph—that's brilliant."

"Well, we'll see. But it seems to me that whether you're five or thirty-five, you are still someone's child. It appears that the legislature left the door open for an adult child to bring a paternity suit." He pauses, then says, "The only piece that's missing is an affidavit from someone alleging that there was a relationship between your mother and Paul Accerbi at the time of your conception. Regina, if there's any way you can secure that, we'll be on better footing."

For the past six months, since Paul and I first spoke in August, Julia finally let everyone know who I actually am. Since I've met with various members of the family over the past three years, I sense that they view me as a self-sufficient, independent, decent young woman who simply wants to know the truth about who she is. When they invited me to their most recent family holiday dinner, the Accerbis seemed to completely understand that I'm not seeking financial support of any kind. And as I told them about my past contact with Paul, they understood that I tried to avoid litigation and making my plea part of the public record.

Now that my pursuit has taken on a life of its own, I drive to Long Island on a Sunday afternoon to make my request: "Julia, my lawyer says we need to submit an affidavit written by someone who was witness to Paul's relationship with Cookie. Is that going to stir conflict between you and the Accerbis?"

She wrings her hands gently in her lap. "No honey, in fact, I think they'll be supportive. Regina?"

"Yes?"

"You know you're welcome to call me Aunt Julia . . . don't you?"

"When we've finally gotten the truth, I promise that you

will be my aunt Julia. Right now I don't want to do anything that could jinx this case."

"Okay, honey," she says. "That's fair enough." She sends me home with a week's worth of home-cooked dinners in tightly sealed Tupperware and stacked in a grocery bag.

The next day, I call Ralph. "I'm planning to fly out to Seattle and meet you," I tell him. "Now that we've got Julia on board, this case is looking more promising. It's outcome will impact my life forever so I need for you to be able to put a face on the plaintiff you're representing."

It's February 28, 2001, when I land at the Seattle airport. I take my carry-on luggage and head straight to the front of the airport. On my way to the taxi line I stop to view a map of the city to get a sense of the direction the taxi driver should take . . . and suddenly, as I'm studying the route, I feel unsteady. My body sways, and I try to grasp onto the nearest column—am I so overwhelmed that I'm about to pass out? But as I lunge for support, I see the whole building shaking and people running outside with their luggage. "Bomb! Bomb!" they cry, and I join the crowd that's running out the door.

I stand there, watching the airport's security staff climb up poles to see the damage around the airport. "It was an earthquake," one announces, and the chaos quiets down to a murmur.

Two hours later I finally climb in a cab and head to the city of Seattle. We ride in silence past remnants of the earthquake, clocking in at 6.8 on the Richter scale. The driver turns up the radio, where a reporter states this was a victimless quake. "The city built its infrastructure to withstand an earthquake of this magnitude," we hear, and with a sense of relief, I reflect on the irony: it's a shaky day all around. There will be aftershocks. And I trust that no matter how it works out, when it's over I'll still be standing. I'm just content that I've gotten this far.

The next morning Ralph and his assistants greet me in their boardroom to discuss our legal strategy.

"Regina, there is more at risk in bringing your case than just how it will turn out for you," Ralph says. "Since this will be a precedent in Washington State and a case of first impression for other states, if the courts determine that a child is not a child at any age, but a child is anyone under age eighteen, you have closed the door for any other adult children to bring a successful paternity suit."

I rest my elbows on the table and take a moment to think. "I understand, Ralph. But this law has not been tested before because the burden of proof is high. But with all of our affidavits—Julia's, my sisters', my last foster mother's, and mine—combined with the fact that Paul never denied having a sexual relationship with my mother, we are well prepared to prove that I am his child and compel a DNA test." While we both are comfortable with the facts, I understand that he may actually have an additional concern; his credibility as a highly reputable paternity lawyer will be tested. "I'm confident that you would not be taking my case if you didn't think that we had a fighting chance to convince the court that I am his child. A child should be a child at any age when it comes to knowing who their father is."

Ralph calls me. "Your case was filed with a judge in Whatcom County where Paul resides. The court hearing is scheduled for early summer." Once I receive the briefing papers that Paul filed with the court in June, I'm eager to read what his defense to the action will be. With his pleadings in hand, I quickly skip through the section titled "Background," which is usually the defendant's view of the facts. I go straight to Paul's defense.

Through his attorney, Paul argues that since I am an adult, my asking for a DNA test is a violation of his constitutional right to privacy and freedom against unreasonable search and seizure. He goes on to argue that, as a result, I should reimburse him for his court costs and attorney fees for even bringing this case against him. His argument is exactly what I expected.

Carefully I begin to read the pleading word for word:

> The petitioner is a 34 year old female . . . licensed attorney . . . who resides and practices in New York . . . The respondent is a 66 year old retiree residing in Whatcom County, Washington, is married and resides with his wife of 34 years . . . suffered a heart attack in 1986 . . . and is under the care of a cardiologist . . .

I chuckle at the inclusion of his heart ailments. He's prepared to file a counterclaim against me for intentional infliction of emotional distress by bringing this suit. When we first made contact, Ralph explained that Paul's emphasizing how this case could affect his health would flop because the DNA is taken with a simple swab test—nothing invasive or extraordinarily stress inducing. Then I read the first three lines again, then again, and again . . . I'm thirty-four years old, and he's been married for thirty-four years.

He married his wife while my mother was pregnant with me.

That's it.

While I was an infant, Cookie left me with Frank and Julia

so Paul would be forced to face what he did. That was Cookie's revenge; her twisted way of informing him that they'd parented a child together.

The brutal episodes I suffered as a child at the hands of an emotionally unstable woman were caused by the heartbreak my father put her through.

On June 7, Ralph calls me with news. "The Whatcom County Court judge ruled in your favor and ordered that Paul submit to a paternity DNA test."

Not surprisingly, four days later Paul appeals.

The oral argument before the Whatcom County Superior Court judge is scheduled for August 3, 2001. At this point I cannot afford to fly out to Seattle for the hearing as I'm saving my funds for the starter co-op I'm about to purchase in Manhattan. I also need to set aside more money for additional litigation costs: Whoever loses this appeal will seek to get it overturned on a higher court level.

Ralph calls me after the hearing and tells me he's not very optimistic that this judge will rule in our favor. "The judge implied that he doesn't want to rule on whether a child is a minor or a child is a child at any age in cases of paternity," Ralph says. "He understands that such a ruling would have substantial legal reverberations. He said this is something better decided by a higher court." A few weeks later the judge dismisses my case.

I have two more options: an appeal to the Court of Appeals of the State of Washington; then, if we lose there, onto the Washington State Supreme Court. Ralph warns me about proceeding and the impact this will have on others . . . and of course on my bank account. "But, Regina, I've got to tell you, I have confidence in your facts. We still have a chance here, but it will take a year until the hearing is scheduled and the court issues a determination."

"Good," I tell him. "I want to appeal." I just need to know.

I remember a verse I once spotted that Julia had highlighted in her Bible: *The truth will set you free.* I've never been able to forget those words. Even when it hurts, it's more empowering to know the truth than to stay blind to it. Once I know the truth—and once Paul knows the truth—I'll be finished. In my life I've found that you can't let something go until it's really over and it's never really over until you learn the truth.

The morning of September 11, 2001, I'm serving as an election monitor in Queens for my old boss, who's campaigning for mayor, when the poll workers alert me that a plane has crashed into one of the towers of the World Trade Center. A few minutes later, the second tower is hit.

That afternoon, with all the bridges and tunnels that lead into Manhattan closed, I can't return home. I drive east toward Camille's, where I watch news coverage of the attack and begin to grieve for those who perished and the impact all this will have on our country. A few days later, Ralph calls from Seattle. "I just wanted to hear that you're safe," he says. "I've been trying to get through for days."

I wait for him to mention that maybe Paul's lawyer reached out to him to check on me. "No word from Wayne Teller?"

Ralph lets me down easy. "No."

I nod, as though he can hear my deflation through the phone. Paul Accerbi hasn't even checked to make sure I'm still alive. I take a deep breath, reminding myself of my strength: I'm doing this for me—to know for certain that he's my father.

In the Spring of 2002, in our written appeal, Ralph argues that the trial court erred in dismissing my action and that the statute as adopted by the State of Washington back in the mid–1970s does not restrict paternity suits to minor children only.

Then, of course, Paul reiterates his defense: He should be awarded Fourth Amendment protections of freedom from unreasonable search and seizure. The oral argument before the three-judge panel was held in May 2002, but Ralph warns me it could be another six months before the court makes its decision.

In late October I receive a fax from Ralph. It's the cover page of the decision from the Washington State Court of Appeals in Seattle. On the cover sheet are two key words: *Reversed* and *Remanded*.

Holding my breath, I flip to the next page where the decision is written by Judge Grosse, with the two other judges, Applewick and Baker, concurring, making the decision unanimous:

> Under the Uniform Parentage Act establishing
> a father-child relationship does not depend on the
> minority of the child. A child has a constitutionally
> protected interest in an accurate determination
> of paternity. The statute and [this] case preserve
> the right of child of any age, who alleges sufficient
> underlying facts, to seek a determination of the
> existence of a paternal relationship. . . . The inclusion
> of the phrase "at any time" shows the intent of the
> Legislature. In adopting the Uniform Parentage Act,
> the Legislature balanced the interest of the child

against those of a putative parent. While Accerbi's
right to privacy is an interest affected by an order
compelling DNA or blood test, that right is not
absolute. The State may reasonably regulate this right
if it has a compelling interest. The privacy invasion of a
DNA test is minor. Even if it is determined that Accerbi
is the father of Calcaterra, there are admittedly no
child support issues, and he can disinherit Calcaterra
if he so chooses. Accerbi's psychological well-being
does not outweigh the interests of a child.

I'm thrilled it was a unanimous decision, but I reserve any urge to celebrate. The fact is, this isn't over. I know Paul's next move.

Six days later, his attorney confirms my prediction when he files his appeal to the Supreme Court of the State of Washington. Ralph tells me his counsel was merely repeating their earlier arguments. He also tells me that the Supreme Court rulings in Washington allow the prevailing party to recover court costs.

"Ralph, you mean if I win in the state Supreme Court, Paul will have to reimburse me the nine thousand dollars it cost me to bring this case just so he could take a twenty-five-dollar DNA test?"

"Not quite," he says. "The court cost is the actual filing cost that accompanied your appeal. In this instance, it would just be $414.71. If you lose, you have to pay that to Paul; and if he loses, he has to pay that to you."

I laugh.

Seven months after Paul's appeal in June 2003, the Washington State Supreme Court rules in my favor. They keep the appellate court decision in tact that compelled him to take a DNA test and issue an order that Paul reimburse me for $414.71. Again, I don't celebrate—he could still appeal to the Federal courts . . . and he still needs to take the DNA test.

He chooses not to appeal. Through July and August 2003, Paul resists paying the $414.71 as ordered by the court. I agree to compromise: Rather than seek another judgment against him, I agree that if the DNA test comes back negative he won't have to pay me . . . but if it comes back positive, I expect a check for the full amount. Through his attorney, he complains that although I won the court case, he shouldn't be forced to pay the twenty-five-dollar DNA test fee. "Regina is the one seeking Paul's DNA," Wayne Teller emphasizes. So in another effort to move the DNA testing forward, I agree to his request.

A few weeks later, in September 2003, I receive a letter from Genelex, the lab that compared our DNA. I race up to my apartment and rip open the envelope. The letter reads:

> *Paul Accerbi is not excluded as the biological father of Regina M. Calcaterra. 99.64% probability of paternity.*

I collapse into a chair at my kitchen table and cry— jubilant, elated tears.

Paul Accerbi is my father.

My father is Paul Accerbi.

I lived through three and a half decades of anxiety about the abuse I received from my mother, why she hurt me over and over and over . . . why she tried to break me. Now I finally know: It really is because I was Paul's daughter.

In this instant the parts of me she damaged can finally begin to heal with this single word of certainty about my life. Paul Accerbi knows that I am his child, and he knows I know that he abandoned me. He can never deny that again. It's over.

It's over.

Before I call Ralph, there's a more pressing phone call to make. I dial the Happy House.

"Aunt Julia?"

I hear her voice tremble. "Yes?"

"I just got the test results. Paul is my father . . . and, more important, you are my aunt."

When I arrive at her house to celebrate that night, the phone rings. "It's Paul's brother, Sonny," Julia says. "He wants to talk to you."

I cradle the phone against my ear. "Regina, it's your uncle!" he says. "When can you come visit so I can share the family's heritage with you?" The inflections in his voice sound just like Paul's. I make plans to drive to Sonny's just ten minutes from Julia's house when I leave that evening.

"What now?" Julia asks me. "Will you go see Pauly?"

"Right now, no. We're both too heated from the litigation battle to want to see each other. He still has to sign a document so the court can officially record that he's my father. Then I can amend my birth certificate." I'm finally going to put Paul Accerbi's name in the box that's been empty my entire life.

Christmas week I receive a check from Paul's lawyer—
$389.71

$414.71, minus the $25 cost for the DNA test.

13

⚬

Beacons of Light

FOR CHRISTMAS 2004 I treat myself to what I've wanted my whole life when a small package arrives in my mailbox. The return address reads:

> **State of New York**
> **Department of Health, Vital Records Section**

When I step inside my kitchen and hang my coat and bag over a chair, I gently open the envelope.

It's my birth certificate.

My *complete* birth certificate.

The first time I'd ever needed to retrieve my birth records from the Islip town hall was in high school when I applied for my first job, at Rickel's. Viewing my birth certificate as a teenager, the mere few "vital statistics" it displayed did nothing to surprise me . . . in fact, it would have struck me harder if all the details *had* been filled in. What I saw then was my residence at birth—Lindenhurst, which my meeting Julia revealed is the very same town where the entire Accerbi family resides. The certificate listed in which hospital I was born, the presiding medical doctor, the date and time of my birth; and of course, next to the space for *Mother* it listed:

CAMILLE DIANE CALCATERRA

But the line next to *Father* had been blank. At age thirty-eight, for the first time ever, the facts of my existence are all here. Next to the line reading *Father* is typed in bold, perfect letters:

PAUL ACCERBI

Paul fought long and hard to hide our connection . . . but in the end, he signed the court's judgment, stating his awareness that we are father and child.

The next day I take both birth certificates to the framing shop in my neighborhood and choose a bold, red matting. "I'd like this birth certificate to go here," I explain to the gentleman behind the counter, placing the original in the top box, "and this one to go"—I put the new one on the bottom—"right here." When the frame is finished, I call Camille. "Now I just need to find the right spot to hang it," I tell her.

"I know where," she says. "Here."

"At your house? The whole point is to keep it just for me. Besides, you have a house full of kids. Your walls are covered enough."

"Not at my house, Gi," she says. "I mean here, in Suffolk

County. Why don't you just do it? Make the move, come back home for good."

Where is this coming from? I spent my childhood trying to get out of Suffolk County. Why would Camille believe I'd want to move back? Given how intent she always was to break away from our past, I never would have expected that she'd be the one to find her happiness on Long Island. Of course, the people with whom I share the deepest connections all live there, but it is still the place where all the hurt in my life took place. The smallest stimulus—a certain bar, an old gas station—triggers memories of Cookie; her torment, her smell, her constant reminders that nobody wanted me. So many of the towns were locations where I came and went swiftly, pushed into a random family's house then swept out again before it ever had the chance to feel like mine.

My three other siblings have also not returned. Rosie's been in Utah since she graduated from college and Norman and Cherie live near each other in Pennsylvania. Of all the places I've thought of settling, Suffolk County may be the last spot on earth I ever imagined myself calling home.

But Camille is persistent. "Maria asked me yesterday: 'Mom, what's the longest Aunt Gi has ever lived anywhere?'"

"But Camille, Long Island is not exactly—"

"Long Island is home. I have the same bad memories you do, Gi. But the kids are growing—they want you around at their games, their plays . . . you're our family. When we didn't have anything else, we had each other."

Through all the turns and transitions my existence has taken . . . Camille, Frank, and their kids have been the only constant in my life. Even so, constant shifting has remained more comforting to me than consistency . . . which is why, when I run into Todd Ciaravino one afternoon in August 2006, I'm confronted with yet another situation that calls me to stretch out of my comfort zone. I'm between meetings, exiting a shoe store in the Time Warner Center in Manhattan's Columbus Circle. Just then, Todd walks by and meets my eyes. We take each other in for a moment before we break into smiles, both polished in suits. "What are you doing here?" I ask him.

"I had a meeting upstairs." We exchange a few niceties, and then cell phone numbers, and by the following month we're back together as an item.

Embracing what Camille has been encouraging me to do, I agree to *look* at properties in Suffolk County, taking plenty of time to explore the North Fork of Long Island. It's much more low-key than the Hamptons, which sits just across the Peconic Bay, but with its rolling farmlands, peach orchards, and picturesque vineyards, I'm increasingly convinced the North Fork is a place I could see myself planting permanent roots.

Todd's with me in the fall of 2006 when I view a small cottage on the North Fork with a backyard view of a creek off the bay. The shoreline and blue sky remind me of the beach landscape in Saint James where my siblings and I frolicked as kids . . . and I know it's meant to be mine when it dawns on me how aptly its little hamlet is named: New Suffolk.

The realtor tells me the house has been on the market for years, and admittedly it's not hard to see why: As soon as we pull up it's clear the whole structure needs a lot of TLC; and from the fireplace mantel to the bathtub the décor is an unappetizing shade of pink . . . but I turn to Todd. "This is it," I tell him. "The bones are all here." I watch him examine the framework and grasp onto my vision. "Can you imagine what I could do with this place?"

In January 2007, I close on the house and move in with my two cocker spaniels. Todd spends the weekdays at his place in Brooklyn and drives out on the weekends to work on the rehabilitation and helps me overhaul the landscaping, even installing a fence for my dogs.

On warm weather weekends, Camille drives over with her two youngest girls, Danielle and Christina, and we all walk with beach chairs and towels to the shore. As the girls ride their boogie boards and bury each other in the sand, I mention my latest idea to Camille. "I've been thinking . . ."

"Yeah?"

"What if we throw a party here for Norman's fortieth? He could take the bus from Pennsylvania and I'll pick him up in the city. I'll try to get in touch with Rosie—"

"Gi, let's take things one at a time. Sure, see if Norm's up for it." The next day we team up on the phone and talk him into taking a week's vacation and spend it with us near the beach, just like old times.

We've tried to bring our family together . . . slowly . . . but Rosie's made it clear that she's determined to stay independent from us. According to the annual phone conversations we have, I know she's still married, now with three children whom I've never met. My perpetual, raw wound is not being able to witness my baby sister as a warm, tender mother.

In 2008 I set up a Facebook page and begin hunting through social media sites so I can keep up with Rosie's life from afar. I read comments she's written about her children's schooling and have seen a picture that I knew had to be her daughter Alexis: She's the *exact* image of little Rosie.

In January 2009, I'm stunned to receive a message on Facebook. Rosie says she feels isolated being so far away from all of us. She says she's realized that as her older siblings, we really did our best to protect her, and she wants her children to know us. "Can we try to work on us?" she writes. She's finally ready to bring her siblings back into her world.

I read Rosie's message to Camille over the phone. "Camille, I want to fly her out here. It's been more than fourteen years since she's been to New York, and that last visit was really strained."

I hear Camille thinking it over. "Let's see if she wants to talk."

I send Rosie a private message and tell her to give me a call.

"Gi, I miss you guys," she says, choking up with tears. "I know that I've kept my distance, but I don't like that you're not in my life. I want to be a part of our family again."

Crying, I respond: "We want you with us too, sweetie. We always have."

We talk once a week for the next month, then we plan for her to fly out for a long weekend in late March. I park my car at JFK and walk into the baggage claim. She's grown even taller since I last saw her, and she stands out among the women around her. When she turns to me, her face lights up so that even her eyes smile. Then I can see she's welling with tears, and I wrap my arms around her.

I wheel her suitcase to my car and when we're both in and buckled, I take her hand and don't let go. As I'm driving, I keep looking at her to make sure she's really there. She smiles at me, still with moist eyes: *I'm here.*

I set her up in my guest room. On the nightstand is a vase with dried hydrangea, cut from one of my plantings the previous summer. Camille comes out to my house to spend the night, and on my couches the three of us cozy up and talk throughout the night.

This is when Rosie reveals that she's never known about my difficult history with Cookie, or that Cherie and Camille suffered, too—she thought she was the only one whom our mother tortured and despised. Rosie doesn't remember seeing me beaten the time before we were all separated, or ever. "Those memories didn't stay with you, did they?" I asked.

She shook her head, trying to place some recollection. "No."

"Good."

We give the past only a part of our weekend, and the rest we spend catching up on each other's lives, when Cherie and Norman join us. I share with them that I'm thinking about throwing my hat in the ring for the November 2010 election for state Senate. "The incumbent's been in office for more than thirty years . . . I'm sensing that the people here want a change. I know it's a long shot," I tell them, "but everything I've done up to now has been a long shot, too."

I BEGIN MY campaign early and run hard, knocking on residents' doors to chat with them about what issues in the district they're most concerned about. I stop only to enjoy a week in August when Rosie; her husband, Bobby; and their three kids arrive to spend a week at my house. For the first time, Rosie's daughter and two sons meet their aunts, uncles, and cousins.

Seeing *mia bambina* as a wife and mom is positively magical. Our entire family goes for long walks along the water, and my neighbors pause from gardening and lean forward in their Adirondack chairs to take in the sight of us. "You got a permit for that parade?" they shout. When I count, there are a dozen of us walking down the road, chatting arm in arm and laughing.

I run a campaign that covers almost half the terrain in a very large county until supporters of my opponent challenge my eligibility to run. They assert that I'm not fit to run because I spent time living in Pennsylvania where my law firm was located and I testify that indeed it was an insignificantly small period where I represented the State of New York as a plaintiff in a global corporate fraud case and spent much of my time working and living in New York anyhow. I've spent nearly all of my life living in New York State, and my return to Suffolk County has cemented it: This is home.

After I'm removed from the ballot in August 2010, I tell Todd I need some time to decompress and regain my privacy. For a few days, I shut myself in and lie on my floor asking: *How did I get here? Why did I fight so hard for this? There are so many battles in my life that are so much more worthy of my energy.*

When Todd suggests we get away for a vacation. I realize there's only one place to consider: Utah, to see Rosie. Todd books two tickets for Labor Day weekend, and because it's off-season, we stay in a large hotel suite in Park City where Rosie and Bobby bring Daniel, Brody, and Lexi to go swimming, and we all wrap ourselves in luxurious white robes to watch silly movies and order a dozen things from the room service menu. I tell Rosie how I've been watching Lexi in wonder, recognizing the exact mannerisms she's inherited from the little girl her mother used to be.

On the flight home it hits me how I have more than I ever expected I'd be blessed with: a legal career with a noteworthy law firm that makes it possible for me to make a difference in the world, the whole truth about my biological background, and an unconditional partner who's always along for the ride, who loves my independence, who supports my every adventure and drives me to go even further.

And now I have Rosie.

A year later, in 2011, I'm eager to embrace politics again when I'm introduced to Steve Bellone, the Democratic candidate for Suffolk County Executive. After Steve is elected, he asks me to join his administration as the chief deputy executive.

I voice my hesitation, telling Steve, "If I accept this position, I'll need to resign as a board member for You Gotta Believe—an organization that actually gets older foster kids adopted so they can avoid homelessness or worse. They have a contract with the county and that could be a conflict."

Steve assures me my job helping him run Suffolk County will even better position me to impact the lives of foster kids. "With the county's resources, you can help lots of homeless kids," he says. "And you'll still be supporting me in the day-to-day operations of the county."

I start my new job as the chief deputy executive of Suffolk County on January 1, 2012. Eleven days into the new position, at the end of a senior staff meeting, one of my colleagues asks whether I read this morning's Long Island *Newsday*. "Regina, you've got to read this," she says. On the front page is a profile of Samantha Garvey, a seventeen-year-old student at Brentwood High School on the southern shore of Suffolk County. Samantha has been selected as a semifinalist in the Intel Science Talent Search—she's one of three hundred students up for the most prestigious high school science award in the United States. The challenge is that she lives in a homeless shelter with her family.

When her family was forced from their home, their pit bull, Pulga, was put in an animal shelter. According to the story, the Garvey family is as worried about Pulga's being euthanized as they are about how they'll find a home.

I go back to my desk and call the shelter where Pulga has been placed. I tell them confidently, "I'd like to give you my credit card to get the dog into a boarding home where it's certain she won't be put down, please." She can stay in the boarding facility until we address the family's housing needs.

By one o'clock that afternoon, a dedicated team of county employees indentifies the only vacant house the county owns and they put a plan in place for Samantha and her family to move into it within two weeks. When Steve announces that Samantha will have a home again, families, businesses, and contractors in the community contribute their energy, furniture, and labor. The county workers who work with Steve and me help us with renovations and setting the house up for the Garveys' move-in, and my ten-year-old niece Christina accompanies me on a shopping trip to decorate the home.

I save all the news clippings that feature Samantha's family . . . and Pulga. Christina and I pick out frames for the news clippings, a pup-inspired welcome mat, dog bowls, and a leash for Pulga. We hang the leash on a hook near the entryway and, remembering how as a child I'd push it out of my mind anytime I wished for family photos on our walls, Christina and I place the frames with the news clippings through-out the house. That afternoon, when Steve gives Samantha and her family the keys to their new home, in just one short month I see the rewards of my career and the power of government and community.

I work from January through the fall focusing primarily on Suffolk County's budget, but one morning in September, I'm pulled away from work after I read texts sent from Camille's second daughter.

Danielle Grace
7:13 a.m.
Aunt Gina, Mom had a stroke! She's in an ambulance on the way to the hospital. Please call!
7:35 a.m.
Aunt Gina, where are you? Please call!

I call her older sister, Maria.

"Aunt Gi, Mom had a massive stroke. She was paralyzed when the paramedics took her away. We're driving behind her ambulance to the hospital. Please hurry."

I leave home and drive the forty minutes to Stony Brook University Hospital, where Maria meets me in the doorway of the waiting room. "She's just had a second stroke," she says . . . and by the time Cherie arrives moments later, she's experienced two more. Our forty-eight-year-old sister—a mother of five—has just experienced four strokes. "You're a very lucky baby," her doctor tells her. "No one this young has the strokes that you have and regains all their cognition and function the way you have." Surrounded by Frank, their five kids, and Cherie and me, Camille's body takes a few days to recover from paralysis. Just before the following weekend, she's released and sent home.

As a birthday gift, I buy her fresh exercise clothes, sneakers, and a heart monitor so she can begin to strengthen her heart, which was weakened by the strokes.

A FEW WEEKS later, I take an afternoon off from work to honor the only other passion that has ever pulled me away from my career: my family, which is growing again. No longer a baby, but still full of unconditional love, Camille's son Frankie is getting married. Cherie, Rosie, Norman, and I are there to celebrate his marriage and support Camille, who is now well enough to walk her eldest son down the aisle . . . *and* to dance at the wedding. From the dance floor she catches my eyes and waves me to join her as the DJ cues up a special request: "Ain't No Mountain High Enough."

Rosie, Cherie, and Norman follow me out and the five of us huddle in tight and sing to one another with all our hearts.

Epilogue

IN LATE OCTOBER, the National Weather Service forecasts a "Superstorm"—a hurricane they're referring to as Sandy. For the first time ever, the NWS sends a representative out to Long Island to prepare us county leaders and our first responders for how serious this storm will be. "Death and devastation," they tell us repeatedly. "Your residents have got to take this storm seriously. The devastation won't be because of the wind or the rains, but because of the storm surge. The topography of Long Island and most likely all of greater New York City will be changed forever."

"Do not let any of the kids leave your house," I tell Camille. "There will be power outages and fallen trees and worse—in fact you all need to sleep in a part of the house that's far away from trees."

The thousands of homes along Long Island's coastline are

extremely vulnerable . . . including mine. I lock it up and say a prayer, spending the next few nights at the county's emergency management unit in Yaphank. The center is filled with the U.S. Coast Guard, New York Army National Guard, social services, police, fire chiefs, Red Cross, and swarms of other emergency response units. With them I stay up through the night as they work to protect as many Suffolk County residents as possible. We also figure out ways to keep communication lines open to the people who are in flood zones and refused to evacuate before it was too late.

It's a night of heavyheartedness that I'm certain will stay with me forever—we're witness to the flooding that causes complete neighborhoods to be destroyed. It's a harsh reality check as I hope that these citizens' homes will be the worst thing that they lose.

In the light of day, I join the team of emergency responders and leaders whose job it is to find emergency shelter, food, and supplies for the hundreds in the county who are suddenly homeless or without power. Now I'm working to put the lights back on for the very same community that, decades ago, did the best it could to keep mine from dimming.

The National Weather Service's dire warnings to our emergency responders were not overstated. Sandy stretched almost two thousand miles as it traveled up the Atlantic coastline. Adding to the depth of the storm was a disastrously timed high tide in a full moon cycle, resulting in tremendous storm surges. Sandy brought parts of the Northeast to a standstill and resulted in extensive flooding in Manhattan and the shorelines of both New York and New Jersey. And sadly, as predicted, Sandy brought many untimely deaths and utter devastation to some of our communities.

At one point during the storm, electric service was lost to several million customers in New York alone. The loss of power crippled hospitals, fuel ports, fuel terminals and gas stations, mass transportation, and telecommunications. The impact this had on the region led New York's Governor Cuomo to issue an executive order creating what is referred to as the Moreland Commission on Utility Storm Preparation and Response that was charged with investigating the emergency preparedness and storm response of utilities within the state, with recommendations for stricter oversight of utilities and to assist in determining how best to restructure the Long Island Power Authority to provide safer transmission and distribution to its customers going forward—in emergencies and fair weather. On November 13, 2012, he appointed a panel of esteemed commissioners to preside over this investigation . . . and on November 20, Governor Cuomo appointed me as the Commission's executive director.

As I write this epilogue, I am a few weeks into the Commission's vital tasks. My sister Camille is still working to build up her strength from multiple consecutive strokes, and her doctors still have not concluded what caused them on that cloudy September day. It was while Camille's entire family was huddled around her hospital bed that I suggested we change the topic and try, as a family, to select a title for this story. Considering the main events I'd detailed in the manuscript, we reflected on our countless homes—fragile, temporary sand castles that we were forced to create in the most resourceful ways, only for them to be knocked down by the rising tides and uncontrollable elements around us. Thus, we decided together that my book should be titled *Etched in Sand*.

I am also writing this on December 16, a day which I acknowledge is the anniversary of Cookie's death—but I much prefer to remember it as Aunt Julia's birthday. This is the first year since 1999 that I have not called nor visited Julia for her birthday: She passed in April 2012, one day before the passing of my uncle Sonny.

That simple, beautiful message that Rosie wrote almost three years ago has closed that gaping hole in my heart that was ripped open on that dark November day in 1980 when I revealed to the social worker that indeed we were being abused. Further healing came when Cherie moved from Pennsylvania back to Suffolk County this past spring. Her fiftieth birthday celebration this past September brought all five of us together again in one place . . . for the second time in thirty-two years.

Despite the challenging seas we had to navigate and the limited beacons of light that were available to guide us on our journey, we all landed safely. We pushed ourselves up through the riptides. Through our journey, my siblings blessed me with plenty of nieces and nephews, who through *Etched in Sand* will be learning our story for the very first time. We created a whole generation of children that will never suffer intense poverty, homelessness, or abuse. Together, we stopped the cycle.

Through his strength of character, stoicism, and love of family (and my pets), Todd has guided me and for the first time in my life provided me the consistency and stability that I actually welcome.

Today, I have my own happy home.

However, every year in the United States, forty thousand children in foster care will age out of the system and have nowhere to go and no one to help them. It is still a generally accepted policy to deem older foster children unadoptable. So rather than working toward finding older foster children forever homes, they are provided brief instruction on how to live independently and are sent out to find their own way at the age of eighteen or twenty-one. When a young adult ages out with limited resources and no safety net, they risk becoming homeless and the cycle starts again. With the opportunity to benefit from the unconditional love of a forever home, a foster child can eventually pay it forward. In my commitment to this belief, I rejoined the board of You Gotta Believe to ensure that more foster children will also one day have their own happy home. If there's one thing I want every foster child to know, it's that.

We all have to believe.

Acknowledgments

My JOURNEY WAS substantially smoother and sometimes purely adventurous because of my loving sister Camille, who although our paths are quite different, never stopped walking beside me as I carved out mine. Her trust in me telling our story through my perspective was vital to this book being written. My oldest sister Cherie was apprehensive at first, but after reading an early draft quickly came around to supporting the book and went further by encouraging me to share the tough aspects of her story. She is now delightfully relieved that we can finally embrace our history rather than fear its disclosure, and for her confidence I am truly thankful. Much appreciation goes to my brother Norman for supporting the book, despite his quest for peaceful solitude. Boundless love and adoration to Rosie, who has her own story to tell, which I'll encourage her to do as she did with mine, but, of course, only when she is ready.

I am forever grateful to my companion, Todd Ciaravino, who, regardless of how unconventional my endeavors, is always along for the ride. He wholeheartedly encouraged me to write my story when it was just a seedling, and he helped me bring it to full bloom, as did his very endearing family. Also, I owe much to my confidante and closest friend, Melanie McEvoy, whose glitter makes all those around her sparkle. She shares my life with me on the North Fork—it would not be home without her nearby. You both ground me.

A significant chapter of my story would have been missing had it not been for my aunt Julia—her courage and steadfast commitment to the truth set me free. She never stopped looking out for me and I know that she still is.

There are those who prevail in their lives using instinct—understanding the pitfalls yet willing to stray from the familiar. To bring my story forward three women did just that—Lisa Sharkey, Amy Bendell, and Krissy Gasbarre. This book would not have come to fruition without Lisa Sharkey of HarperCollins. Lisa had the courage to take my story on and follow her instinct—she never wavered from her faith in me or my story. Amy Bendell, my editor, was my other early enthusiast. Her intuition and sensibilities shepherded this story throughout. She knew what we should tell more of, when less was more, and never failed to remind me of its beauty. Then there is my talented cowriter, Krissy Gasbarre. Krissy guided my story by gently unlocking memories and gave me confidence in deciding which ones should be memorialized. She diligently scrutinized my writings with precision, magically improving them with flawless ease while ensuring that my voice prevailed throughout. I also have considerable gratitude to all those at HarperCollins Publishers for willingly taking on a first-time author.

Many, many thanks to Ed Moltzen, whose thoughtful contributions are reflected throughout the book and to those who reviewed and improved the full manuscript: Dina Nelson, Bobbie and Jerome Ciaravino, Terry and Bill Gasbarre, Jennifer Culp-O'Brien, Bobbi Passalacqua, Lauren Grant, and Nancy and Tom Gleason.

There are others who collectively impacted my life that deserve acknowledgment: my foster parents who diligently worked toward providing me structure and consistency, specifically the Petermans, and all of my dear friends along the way who did not judge me based upon my circumstances and embraced me for me, and some of whose families went further by ensuring that I was fed and properly clothed: Kim and Celinda Garcia, Sheryl Williams, Tracey McMaster, Tracy Ressa, Erin DeMeo, Jeanine Illario, Cynthia Tait, Tammy Fisher, Kim Forsa, Veronica Sullivan, Monica Murray, and Beth Seltzer, and Reyne Macadaeg.

Much appreciation to Jo LoCicero, who fifteen years ago told me to start writing, and Patty Cooper and Katherine Barna for their early encouragement and guidance.

My story could have gone dark had it not been for the educators that illuminated my light even though they only had a moment in time to keep it burning before I moved on. Those educators who stood out and truly touched me include Kevin Ferry and Bob Maguire, Centereach High School; Lewis Brownstein, Nancy Kassop, and Gerald Benjamin, SUNY New Paltz; John Farmer, Seton Hall Law School; Ms. Van Dover, Saint James Elementary; and Ms. Muse, Branch Brook Elementary. The same sentiment is extended for the public library systems.

This page would not be complete if I did not express sincere gratitude to the charities and county and state government that provided us desperately needed services and the dedicated public servants whose attention kept us moving forward. We are now thriving and as a result have created a generation of independent, compassionate children, who are already giving back through church and charity.

About the Author

REGINA M. CALCATERRA, ESQUIRE, serves for Governor Andrew Cuomo as the executive director of the New York State Moreland Commission on Utility Storm Preparation and Response. Regina's state appointment rose from her position as chief deputy to Suffolk County Executive Steve Bellone, where she assisted him in managing the day-to-day operations of the county and managed the county's response and immediate recovery to Superstorm Sandy. The majority of Regina's private sector experience was as a partner to Barrack, Rodos & Bacine, an internationally recognized securities litigation firm, where she represented defrauded public and labor pension funds by recouping billions of dollars from those who committed corporate fraud on Wall Street. Combined, she has twenty-five years in public- and private-sector experience, including serving as an adjunct professor of political science at CUNY Baruch College. For over a decade Regina served as a frequent commentator of policy and politics on nationwide television and also contributed op-eds on national and local issues. She proudly serves as a board member to You Gotta Believe, an organization that works toward finding older foster children forever homes. She is a graduate of the State University of New York, New Paltz, and Seton Hall University School of Law, and is admitted to practice law in the State of New York, Commonwealth of Pennsylvania, and the Eastern and Southern U.S. District Courts.

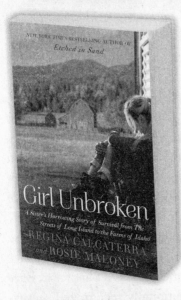
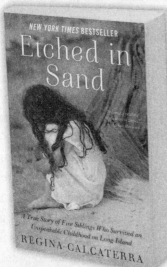